GENERAL PRINCIPLES OF EU

GENERAL PRINCIPLES
OF EU CIVIL LAW

Norbert REICH

intersentia

Cambridge – Antwerp – Portland

Intersentia Publishing Ltd.
Trinity House | Cambridge Business Park | Cowley Road
Cambridge | CB4 0WZ | United Kingdom
Tel.: +44 1223 393 753 | Email: mail@intersentia.co.uk

Distribution for the UK:
NBN International
Airport Business Centre, 10 Thornbury Road
Plymouth, PL6 7 PP
United Kingdom
Tel.: +44 1752 202 301 | Fax: +44 1752 202 331
Email: orders@nbninternational.com

Distribution for the USA and Canada:
International Specialized Book Services
920 NE 58th Ave. Suite 300
Portland, OR 97213
USA
Tel.: +1 800 944 6190 (toll free)
Email: info@isbs.com

Distribution for Austria:
Neuer Wissenschaftlicher Verlag
Argentinierstraße 42/6
1040 Wien
Austria
Tel.: +43 1 535 61 03 24
Email: office@nwv.at

Distribution for other countries:
Intersentia Publishing nv
Groenstraat 31
2640 Mortsel
Belgium
Tel.: +32 3 680 15 50
Email: mail@intersentia.be

General Principles of EU Civil Law
Norbert Reich

© 2014 Intersentia
Cambridge – Antwerp – Portland
www.intersentia.com | www.intersentia.co.uk

Artwork on cover: La Ville n° 2, Delaunay Robert (1885-1941) © Paris, Musée national d'Art moderne – Centre Georges Pompidou, MNAM-CCI, Dist. RMN-Grand Palais / Philippe Migea

ISBN 978-1-78068-176-4
D/2014/7849/11
NUR 820

British Library Cataloguing in Publication Data. A catalogue record for this book is available from the British Library.

PREFACE

This book takes up a continuing, controversial and to some extent rather confusing debate in EU law – in both academia and in ECJ (the Court of Justice of the EU as it will be abbreviated in the following) case law – on the discovery, shaping and perhaps defence of general principles which may unite its rather heterogeneous involvement in private law, or, as I prefer to call it, civil law relations. The study is not meant to "open" the route to some type of codification, consolidation or restatement of EU civil law, but more modestly to explain its present status, thus making any "optional instruments" nugatory. The debate on EU law principles is much more advanced in EU constitutional and administrative law. EU civil law seems to be lagging behind, but will certainly gather steam the more EU law takes an interest in – some call it "invades" – "horizontal" relations between private persons, and shapes remedies, both substantive and procedural, of its own.

The seven principles, explained in the introduction and treated in detail in the seven following chapters, have an impact on substantive, procedural and methodological matters which have traditionally belonged to the law of Member States but which have seen a shift in competence and legitimacy towards the EU – a shift welcomed by many, but also feared by others. This study does not take a stand in this debate, but simply analyses the remarkable competence "creep" promoted and to some extent provoked by the abundant case law of the ECJ which forms the basis for the "bottom-up" approach used in this study.

The study covers many areas of EU civil law, such as free movement and competition issues, employment relations, consumer law, non-discrimination issues, services in the general economic interest, EU attempts to create a Common European Sales Law (CESL), as well related procedural matters within the scope of EU law. Last but not least, reference to fundamental rights is made continuously, namely to those enshrined in the EU Charter of Fundamental Rights, but also to those in the European Convention of Human Rights (ECHR) and earlier case law of the ECJ. A caveat should be added: the study never tries to exhaustively discuss any of the areas referred to. It takes them rather as examples of the horizontal approach to finding general principles in EU civil law. Several areas of EU civil law had to be completely left out of this book, in particular conflict of laws, company law and intellectual property law.

As basis for this study I used many of my prior publications, which are mentioned in the bibliography preceding every chapter. Chapter 1 on "the

Principle of 'Framed Autonomy'" is based on section 17 of the second edition of my *Understanding EU Law* of 2005, to be updated by Annette Nordhausen Scholes, Manchester University, in the third edition of the joint publication *Understanding EU Internal Market Law* (forthcoming).

The development of this book further owes thanks to four places where parts had been prepared, presented and debated. First, the European University Institute, Florence, under the guidance of Hans Micklitz who initiated several conferences and publications on various aspects of the topic. I was able to use my contribution to the book edited by Hans Micklitz with R. Brownsword et al. (eds.), *The Foundations of European Private Law*, 2011, pp. 185–220 on "Balancing in Private Law and the Imperatives of the Public Interest" for Chapter 5 of this book. The Law Faculty of Oxford, with Dorota Leczykiewicz and Stephen Weatherill, was responsible for organising a stimulating workshop published as *The Involvement of EU Law in Private Law Relationship*, 2012, where I gave a paper on "The Impact of Non-discrimination Principle on Private Autonomy" (at pp. 253–278), which has an updated sequel in Chapter 3 of this book. The Stockholm University EU Law Institute headed by Ulf Bernitz hosted a conference on "General Principles of EU Law and Private Law" in the beginning of 2013 where I presented a paper on "The Principle of Effectiveness and in EU Private Law" to be published with the proceedings of this conference; this is the basis for a more extensive discussion in Chapter 4. Groningen University, with Laurence Gormley, Aurelia Ciacchi and Bart Krans, gave me the chance to spend time for research and debate as a visiting professor in spring 2013, where I was able to present the introduction to this book for critical assessment. I owe many thanks to the debates in these institutions which encouraged me to put my somewhat inchoate ideas together in a comprehensive work on "General Principles of EU Civil Law". Of course, I have sole responsibility for any remaining mistakes, misconceptions and misunderstandings.

Hamburg, summer 2013

CONTENTS

Preface v
Table of ECJ cases: alphabetical xi
Table of ECJ cases: chronological xvii
Table of EU legislation xxiii
List of abbreviations xxvii

Introduction. What are General Principles of EU Civil Law? 1

1. An ongoing debate: "principles" vs. "rules" 2
2. Some preliminary suggestions 6
3. The express recognition of general principles by the Charter 8
4. What do we mean by EU civil law: *acquis communautaire* vs.
   acquis commun 11
5. The competence dilemma of EU civil law 14
6. Why seven principles? 16

Chapter 1. The Principle of "Framed" Autonomy 17

1. Freedoms framed by law 18
2. Fundamental freedoms, autonomy and public interest restrictions 21
3. Freedom of contract as fundamental yet limited right and principle 28
4. Competition law and autonomy 30
5. Conclusion: framing of autonomy under welfarism aspects – going
   beyond the traditional approach? 34

Chapter 2. The Principle of Protection of the Weaker Party 37

1. Elements of protection of the weaker party 38
2. Minimum standards of working hours and paid annual leave 41
3. EU consumer law: information vs. protection 47
4. Conclusion: generalising the protection of weaker parties and its limits . . . 56

Chapter 3. The Principle of Non-Discrimination 59

1. "Spill-over" effects of non-discrimination on civil law? 60
2. Non-discrimination in employment law relations: overview 64

3. Citizenship: extending the scope of the principle of
   non-discrimination by primary law 72
4. Extension of the non-discrimination principle to business-consumer
   relations by EU secondary law. 74
5. A controversy: unisex tariffs in insurance and conflicts with private
   autonomy 76
6. Non-discrimination in access to and treatment in services of general
   economic interest and in network services: framed autonomy 81
7. Equal treatment beyond non-discrimination? 84
8. Conclusion: the varied impact of the non-discrimination principle
   on civil law relations 87

Chapter 4. The Principle of Effectiveness 89

1. Article 47 of the Charter and Article 19 TEU: anything new? 90
2. The "eliminatory" function of the effectiveness principle. 91
3. Effectiveness as a "hermeneutical" principle 95
4. Effectiveness as a "remedial" principle: "upgrading" national remedies . . . 97
5. Some examples applying the effectiveness test in EU civil law 99
6. Primary Union law: rules on competition. 112
7. Compensation for violations of directly applicable provisions of
   primary Union law 117
8. The importance of Article 47 of the Charter and Article 19(1) TEU
   for EU civil law revisited. 120
9. Conclusion: how effective is the effectiveness principle? 129

Chapter 5. The Principle of Balancing 131

1. Introduction: a dialogue on balancing in EU civil law 132
2. Balancing in unfair term jurisprudence: transparency, "core terms"
   and the unfairness test 134
3. Balancing to avoid "over-protection" 141
4. Role of Balancing in social conflicts: fundamental rights vs.
   fundamental freedoms? 146
5. Conclusion 153

Chapter 6. The Principle of Proportionality 155
1. Importance of the principle of proportionality for EU civil law:
   some general remarks 157
2. The Draft Common Frame of Reference 162
3. The "feasibility study" and draft Common European Sales Law. 169
4. Open method of coordination, convergence and improved law-
   making in reflexive contract governance in the EU. 180

5. The "positive proportionality" principle in EU civil legislation:
    two examples 182
6. Conclusions on the principle of proportionality as an instrument
    of legal control and support of EU measures 187

**Chapter 7. An Emerging Principle of Good Faith and of a Prohibition
of Abuse of Rights?** 189

1. Some misunderstandings about good faith in contract law: elements
    of a duty of loyal cooperation in contracting 190
2. Good faith in commercial law settings 193
3. Directive 93/13 on unfair terms 195
4. Absence of good faith obligations for the bank in B2C financial
    services 202
5. "Co-responsibility" as an indirect good faith-obligation: some
    examples 203
6. Elements of good faith in recent soft law initiatives. 206
7. Relevance of Article 54 of the Charter to an EU concept of abuse
    of rights? 208
8. Conclusion: good faith on the move? 211

Summary. Seven Theses and a Conclusion 213

Index. 215

TABLE OF ECJ CASES:
ALPHABETICAL

ABSL v Bosman (C-415/93) [1995] ECR I-4921. . . . . 1.7, 3.3,4.28
AGM-COSMET (C-470/03) [2007] ECR I-2749 . . . . 3.8
Aklagaren v H.A. Fransson (C-617/10) [2013] ECR I-(26.03.2013) 3.2
Albany Int. BV v Stichting Bedrijfspensioenfonds Textielindustrie (C-67/96)
    [1999] ECR I-5751 . . . . 1.18
Albore (C-423/98) [2000] ECR I-5965 . . . . 1.6
Aldona Malgorzata Jany et al v Staatssecretaris van Justitie (C-268/99)
    [2001] ECR-8615 . . . . 4.28
Alsthom Atlantique v Compagnie de construction mécanique Sulzer SA
    (C-339/89) [1991] ECR I-107 . . . . 1.4
Andrew Owusu v NB Jackson et al (C-281/02) [2005] ECR I-1383. . . . . 5.12
Annelore Hamilton v Volksbank Filder (C-412/06) [2008] ECR I-2383 . . . . 0.3, 5.9, 6.11
Anton Cas v PSA Antwerp (C-202/11) [2013] ECR I-(16.04.2013) 1.10
AOK-Bundesverband v Ichthyol-Gesellschaft Cordes et al (C-264/01 etc.)
    [2004] ECR I-2493. . . . . 4.28
Arblade (C-369 + 376/96) [1999] ECR I-8453 . . . . 6.13
Arcelor Atlantique and Lorraine et al (C-127/07) [2008] ECR I-9835. . . . . 3.1
Asociatia ACCEPT v CNPCD (C-81/12) [2–13] ECR I-(25.04.2013) 3.8
Association de médiation sociale v CGT (C-176/12) (opinion of AG Cruz Villalón
    of 18.07.2013) 0.3
Ass. Belge Test-Achats et al (C-236/09) [2011] ECR I-773 . . . . **3.15**, 6.19
Asturcom v Christina Rodrigues Nogueria (C-40/08) [2009] ECR I-9579 . . . . 4.15
Audiolux (C-101/08) [2010] ECR I-9823. . . . . 0.3, 3.22

Banco Español de Credito v Camino (C-618/10) [2012] ECR I-(14.06.2012) 4.18
Bayr. Hypotheken und Wechselbank v Dietzinger (C-45/96) [1998] ECR I-1199. . . . . . . 2.9
BECTU v Secretary of State for Trade and Industry (C-173/99) [2001] ECR I-4881 . . . . . 2.1
Belov v CHEZ (C-394/11) [2013] ECR I-(31.01.2013) (opinion of AG Kokott of
    20.09.2012) 3.13
Benincasa (C-269/95) [1997] ECR I-3767. . . . . 2.9
Berliner Kindl Brauerei v A. Siepert (C-208/98) [2000] ECR I-1741 . . . . 2.9
Bond van Adverteerders v The Netherlands State (352/88) [1988] ECR I-2085 . . . . 1.5
Brasserie du Pêcheur v Germany and R v Secretary of State for Transport,
    ex parte Factortame Ltd (C-46 and C-48/93) [1996] ECR I-1029 . . . . 4.24
Brennet v Paletta (C-206/94) [1996] ECR I-2357 . . . . 5.11
BRT v SV SABAM (127/73) [1974] ECR 314. . . . . 4.24

Caixa Bank France v Ministère de Finances (C-442/02) [2004] ECR I-8961 . . . . 1.11

Caja de Ahorros y Monte de Piedad de Madrid v Asocación de Usuarios de servicios bancarios (Ausbanc) (C-484/08) [2010] ECR I-4785. . . . . 5.8

Carmen Media (C-46/08) [2010] ECR I-8149 . . . . 1.5, **6.1**

Car Trim v Key Safety (C-381/08) [2010] ECR I-1255 . . . . 6.15

Casati (203/80) [1981] ECR 2595. . . . . 1.6

Centrum voor gelijkheid van kansen en voor racismebestrijding (CGKR) v Firma Feryn NV (C-54/07) [2008] ECR I-5187 . . . . 3.4, 4.36

CIA Security International SA v Signalson SA and Securitel SPRL (C-194/94) [1996] ECR I-2201 . . . . 0.8

CIVS v Receveur des Douanes de Roubaix (C-533/10) [2012] ECR I-(14.06.2012). 4.5

CMC Motorradcenter v P.B. (C-93/92) [1993] ECR I-5009 . . . . 1.4

Codorniú Sa v Council (C-309/89) [1994] ECR I-1853. . . . . 3.1

Comet (45/76) [1976] ECR 2043. . . . . 4.1, 4.3

Commission v Anic (C-49/92P) [1999] I-4125. . . . . 4.27

Commission v Belgium (C-478/98) [2000] ECR I-7587 . . . . 1.6

Commission v France (C-381/93) [1994] ECR I-5145. . . . . 5.14

Commission v Italy (C-518/06) [2009] ECR I-3491. . . . . 1.10

Commission v Italy (C-565/08) [2011] ECR I-2101 . . . . 1.10

Commission v Netherlands (C-144/99) [2001] I-3541 . . . . 4.10

Coote v Granada Hospitality (C-185/97) [1998] ECR I-5199. . . . . 4.13

Courage Ltd v Crehan (C-453/99) [2001] ECR I-6297 . . . . 4.5, **4.25, 7.12**

Crailsheimer Volksbank (C-229/04) [2005] ECR I-9294 . . . . 4.21

Danske-Slagterier (C-445/06) [2009] ECR I-2119 . . . . .4.5, 7.11

DEB Deutsche Energiehandels- und Beratungsgesellschaft mbH v Bundesrepublik Deutschland (C-279/09) [2010] ECR I-13849. . . . . 3.2, 4.30

Dekker v Stichting Vormingscentrum voor Jong Volwassenen (VJV-Centrum) Plus (177/88) [1990] ECR I-3941 . . . . 4.13

Delimitis v Henninger-Bräu (C-234/89) [1991] ECR I-935 . . . . 1.15

Dellas (C-14/04) [2005] ECR I-10253 . . . . 2.3

Deutscher Handballbund eV v Maros Kolpak (C-438/00) [2003] ECR I-4135. . . . . 4.28

di Pinto (C-361/89) [1991] ECR I-1189 . . . . 2.9

D. McDonagh v Ryanair (C-12/11) [2013] ECR I-(31.01.2013) 2.1, 5.10

Dominguez v CICOA (C-282/10) [2012] ECR I-(24.01.2012) 2.1, 2.4

Draempaehl v Urania (C-180/95) [1997] ECR I-2195. . . . . 4.13

Driancourt v M. Cognet (355/85) [1986] ECR 3231 . . . . 1.8

Dynamik Medien Vertriebs GmbH v Avides Media AG (C-244/06) [2008] ECR I-505. . . . . 5.18

EARL de Kerlast v Union régionale de coopératives agricoles (Unicopa) and Coopérative du Trieux (C-15/95) [1997] ECR I-1961 . . . . 3.1

Eco Swiss China Time v Benetton International NV (C-126/97) [1999] ECR I-3055 . . .4.23

E.M.M. Claro v Centro Movil Milenium (C-168/05) [2006] ECR I-10421 . . . . 4.15

EP v Council (C-436/03) [2006] ECR I-3733 . . . . 6.13

EP v Council (C-540/03) [2006] ECR I-5769 . . . . 2.4, 3.1

Eric Libert et al v Gouvernement flamand (Joined Cases C-197 + C-203/11)
  [2013] ECR I-(05.05.2013) 1.6
Eugen Schmidberger v Austria (C-112/00) [2003] ECR I-5659 . . . . 5.14
Europese Gemeenschap v Otis et al (C-199/11) [2012] ECR I-(06.11.2012) 4.26

Fachverband der Buch- und Medienwirtschaft v LIBRO Handelsgesellschaft
  (C-531/07) [2009] ECR I-3717 . . . . 1.4
Football Association Premier League Ltd v QC Leisure et al (C-403 + 429/08)
  [2011] ECR I-9086 . . . . 1.11
Francovich et al v Italy (C-6 + 9/90) [1991] ECR I-5357. . . . . 4.24
Frederico Cipolla et al v Rosaria Fazari, née Portolese et al (C-94 + 202/04)
  [2006] ECR I-1142 . . . . 1.10
Freiburger Kommunalbauten v Hofstetter (C-237/02) [2004] ECR I-3403 . . . . 7.4
Friz (C-215/08) [2010] ECR I-2749 . . . . 0.3, 5.9, 6.11

Garcia Avello (C-148/02) [2003] ECR I-11613 . . . . 3.11
Gebhard v Consiglio dell'Ordine degli Advocati e procuratori di Milano
  (C-55/94) [1995] ECR I-4165 . . . . .1.9, 6.1
Gebrüder Weber + Putz v Wittmer + Medianess El. (C-65 + 89/09)
  [2011] ECR I-5257 . . . . 2.5, **4.18**, 6.17, 7.10
Genil et al v Bankinter et al (C-604/11) [2013] ECR I-(30.05.2013) 7.10
G. Defrenne v SABENA (43/75) [1976] ECR 455 . . . . 3.4
Germany v Parliament and Council (C-376/98) [2000] ECR I-8419 . . . . .0.11, 6.4
Groener v Minister for education and City of Dublin Vocational Committee
  (379/87) [1989] ECR 3967 . . . . 3.3
Grunkin and Paul (C-353/06) [2008] ECR I-7639 . . . . 3.11
Günaydin v Freistaat Bayern (C-36/96) [1997] ECR I-5143 . . . . 5.11
Günter Fuß v Stadt Halle (C-243/09) [2010] ECR I-9849 . . . . 2.3
Gysbrechts (C-205/07) [2008] ECR I-9947 . . . . 1.9, 5.8, 7.19

Hartlauer Handelsgesellschaft v Wiener Landesregierung et al (C-169/07)
  [2009] ECR I-1721 . . . . 5.4
Heininger v Bayr. Hypo und Vereinsbank (C-481/99) [2001] ECR I-9945 . . . .**4.20**
H.J. Banks & Co. Ltd v British Coal Corporation (C-128/92) [1994] ECR I-1209 . . . . . . 4.25
Hoffmann-La Roche v Commission (85/76) [1979] ECR 461 . . . . 1.17
Honyvem Informazioni Commerciali v Marieella de Zoti (C-465/04)
  [2006] ECR I-2879 . . . . 7.3

IATA and ELFAA v Department for Transport (C-344/04) [2006] ECR I-403 . . . . 6.4
Idealservice (C-541 + 542/99) [2001] ECR I-9049 . . . . 2.9
Ingmar GB Ltd v Eaton Leonard Technologies Inc. (C-381/9)8 [2000] ECR I-9305. . . . . . 7.3
International Transport Workers Federation (ITW) and Finnish Seamans
  Union (FSU) v Viking Line (C-438/05) [2007] ECR I-10779 . . . . .3.3, 4.28, 5.12

J.C.J. Wouters et al v Algemene Raad von de Nederlandse Ordre van Advocaaten
  (C-309/99) [2002] ECR I-1577 . . . . 3.3, 4.28

Johann Gruber v Bay Wa AG (C-464/01) [2005] ECR I-439 .... 2.9
Jürgen Römer v Freie und Hansestadt Hamburg (C-147/08) [2011] ECR I-359 .... 3.8

Kadi et al v Council of the EU (C-402 + 415/05P) [2008] ECR I-6351 .... 4.30
Katharina Rinke v Ärztekammer Hamburg (C-25/02) [2003] ECR I-8349 .... 3.4
Kefalas et al v Greece (C-367/96) [1998] ECR I-2843 .... 5.11
KHS v Winfrid Schulte (C-214/10) [2011] ECR I-(22.11.2011). 2.4
Kiel v Jaeger (C-151/02) [2003] ECR I-8389 .... 2.1, **2.3**

Ladbrokes Betting & Gaming Ltd et al v Stichting de Nationale Sportstotalisator
    (C-238/08) [2010] ECR I-4757 .... 6.4
Land Nordrhein-Westfalen v Beata-Pokrzeptowicz-Meyer (C-162/00)
    [2002] ECR I-1049 .... 4.28
Laserdisken (C-479/04) [2006] ECR I-8089. .... 1.6
Laval & partneri v Bygnadds (C-341/05) [2007] ECR I-11767 .... 3.3, **4.28**, **5.12**
Levez v Harlow Pools (C-326/96) [1998] I-7835. .... 4.5
Lisa Jacqueline Grant v South-West Trains (C-249/96) [1998] ECR I-621 .... 3.6
Luisi and Carbone v Ministero del Tesoro (326 + 286/83) [1984] ECR 377 .... 1.6

Mohamed Aziz v Catalunyacaixa (C-415/11) [2013] ECR I-(14.04.2013). 4.5, 4.15
Mangold v Helm (C-144/04) [2005] ECR I-9981 .... 0.3, **3.6**, 4.14
Maria Chiara Spotti v Freistaat Bayern (C-272/92) [1993] ECR I-5185 .... 3.3
Markus Stoß (C-316/07) [2010] ECR I-8099 .... 1.5
Marshall (II) v Southampton Health Authority (C-271/91) [1993] ECR I-4367 ....4.13, 7.11
Masdar v Commission (C-47/07P) [2008] ECR I-9761 .... 0.8
Mietz v Intership Yachting (C-99/06) [1999] ECR I-2277 .... 2.9
Mono Car Styling (C-12/08) [2009] ECR I-6653 .... 4.30

Nelson et al v Lufthansa et al (C-528 + 619/10) [2012] ECR I-(24.10.2012) 0.6, 4.8
Nemzeti Fogyaszróvédelni Hatóság v Invitel (C-472/10) [2012] ECR
    I-(26.04.2012) **4.15**, 4.30, 7.5

Océano Grupo ed. v Quintero et al (C-240–244/98) [2000] ECR I-4941. .... 4.15
*Omega Spielhallen- und Automatenaufstellungs-GmbH v Oberbürgermeisterin
    der Bundesstadt Bonn* (C-36/02) [2004] ECR I-9609. .... 5.14
Öst. Gewerkschaftsbund, Gewerkschaft öffentlicher Dienst/ Republik Österreich
    (C-195/98) [2000] ECR I-10497 .... 4.30

Palacios de la Villa (C-411/05) [2007] ECR I-8531 .... 3.6
Pannon v Erzsébet Sustikné Győrfi (C-243/08) [2009] ECR I-4713 .... 4.15, 5.5
Pavel Pavlov et al v Stichting Pensioenfonds Medische Specialisten
    (C-180–185/98) [2000] ECR I-6451 .... 1.18
Pereničová and Perenič v SOS financ (C-453/10) [2012] ECR I-(15.03.2012) ..4.30, 6.16, 7.5
Pfeiffer et al v DRK (C-397–403/01) [2004] ECR I-8835 .... **2.3**
Pia Messner v Firma Stefan Krüger (C-489/07) [2009] ECR I-7315. ......0.3, 5.9, 6.11, 7.10

*Pilar Allué and Carmel Mary Coonan et al v Universitá degli studi di Venezia and
Università degli studi di Parma* (C-259, 331 + 332/91) [1993] ECR I-4309 . . . . 3.3
Poseidon Chartering NV v Marianne Zeeship et al (C-3/04) [2006] ECR I-2505 . . . . 7.3
Productores de Música de España (Promusicae) v Telefónica de España SAU
(C-275/06) [2008] ECR I-271 . . . . 1.6, 3.1., **5.1**

Quelle v Bundesverband der Verbraucherzentralen (C-404/06)
[2008] ECR I-2685 . . . . 5.8, 6.17

Raccanelli (C-94/07) [2008] ECR I-5939 . . . . 3.3, 4.28
REWE Central Finanz (33/76) [1976] ECR 1989 . . . . 4.1, 4.3
Robinson-Steele et al v Retail Services et al (C-131 and C-257/04)
[2006] ECR I-2531 . . . . 2.4
Roman Angonese v Casa di Risparmio di Bolzano (C-281/98) [2000] I-4139 . . . 1.7, 3.3, 4.28
Rosalba Alassini et al v Telecom Italia (C-317/08) [2010] ECR I-2214 . . . . 4.5, 6.21
R. Prigge et al v Lufthansa (C-447/09) [2011] ECR I-(13.09.2011) 3.6
*R v Secretary of State for the Home Department, ex parte Wieslaw and
Elzbieta Gloszczuk* (C-63/99) [2001] ECR I-6369 . . . . 4.28
*R v Secretary of State for the Home Department, ex parte Eleanora Ivanova
Kondova* (C-235/99) [2001] ECR I-6427 . . . . 4.28
*R v Secretary of State for the Home Department, ex parte Julius Barkoci
and Marcel Malik* (C-257/99) [2001] ECR I-6557 . . . . 4.28
*R v Secretary of State for Health, ex parte British American Tobacco
(Investments) Ltd et al* (C-491/01) [2002] ECR I-11453 . . . . **6.4**
RWE Vertrieb v Verbraucherzentrale NRW (C -92/11)
[2013] ECR I-(21.03.2013) 5.8, **7.4**
Ruckdeschel (117/76 + 16/77) [1977] ECR 1753 . . . . 3.1

San Georgio (199/82) [1983] ECR 3595 . . . . 4.1
S. Bulicke v DBS (C-249/09) [2010] ECR I-7003 . . . . 4.5
Schulte (C-350/03) [2005] ECR I-9215 . . . . 4.21
Schulze-Hoff et al v DRB (C-350 + 520/06) [2009] ECR I-179 . . . . 2.4
S. Coleman v Attridge Law et al (C-303/06) [2008] ECR I-5603 . . . . 3.9
Seda Kücükdevici v Swedex (C-555/07) [2010] ECR I-365 . . . . 0.7, 3.6, **4.14**
Shearson Lehmann Hutton v TVB Treuhandgesellschaft (C-89/91)
[1993] ECR I-139 . . . . 2.9
Sky Österreich v Österreichischer Rundfunk (C-283/11)
[2013] ECR I-(22.01.2013) 1.13, 3.21, 5.1
Simap (C-303/98) [2000] ECR I-7963 . . . . 2.3
Simone Leitner v TUI Deutschland (C-168/00) [2002] ECR I-2631 . . . . 4.12, 7.13
Société de Vente de Ciments et Bétons v Kerpen & Kerpen (319/82)
[1983] ECR 417 . . . . 1.15
Société Technique Minière v Maschinenbau Ulm (56/65) [1966] ECR 235 . . . . 1.15
*Société thermale d'Eugénie-les-Bains v Ministère de l'Économie, des Finances
et de l'Industrie* (C-277/05) [2007] ECR I-6428 . . . . 1.2
Sonja Chacón Navas v Eurest Colectividades (C-13/05) [2006] ECR I-6467 . . . . 3.9

Steen v Deutsche Bundespost (C-332/90) [1992] ECR I-341 . . . . 1.8
Sturgeon et al (C-402/07 and C-432/07) [2009] ECR I-10923 . . . . 0.6

The Society for the Protection of Unborn Children v Grogan (C-159/90)
 [1991] ECR I-4685 . . . . 1.5
TV10 v Commissariaat v.d. Media (C-23/93) [1994] ECR I-4795 . . . . 5.11

Unibet v Justiekanslern (C-432/05) [2007] ECR I-2271 . . . . 4.30
Unilever Italia v Central Food (C-443/98) [2000] ECR I-7535 . . . . 0.8
Union Syndicale Solidaires Isère (C-428/09) [2010] ECR I-9961 . . . . 2.2
UK v Council (C-84/94) [1996] ECR I-5755. . . . . 0.11, 2.2

Van Binsbergen v Besteuur von de Bedrijfsverening voor de Metaalnijverheid
 (33/74) [1974] ECR 1299 . . . . 5.11
Van Schijndel and Van Veen v Stichting Pensioenfonds (C-430–432/93)
 [1995] ECR I-4705 . . . . 4.15
VB Penzügji Lizing v Schneider (C-137/08) [2010] ECR I-10847 . . . . .2.5, 4.15, 6.11, 7.5
Vicenzo Manfredi et al v Lloyd Adriatico Asssicurazioni SpA et al
 (C-295–298/04) [2006] ECR I-6619 . . . . 4.5, **4.25**
Vodafone (C-58/08) [2010] ECR I-4999 . . . . 6.3
Volvo (C-203/09) [2010] ECR I-10721 . . . . 7.3
Von Colson and Kamann v Land Nordrhein-Westfalen (14/83) [1984] ECR 1891 . . . . . . 4.12
VZ HH v O2 (C-19/03) [2004] ECR I-8183. . . . . 1.2

Wachauf v Bundesamt für Ernährung (5/88) [1989] ECR I-2609. 3.2
Walt Wilhelm et al v Bundeskartellamt (14/68) [1969] ECR 1 . . . . 1.8

TABLE OF ECJ CASES:
CHRONOLOGICAL

56/65 *Société Technique Minière v Maschinenbau Ulm* [1966] ECR 235 . . . . 1.15

14/68 *Walt Wilhelm and others v Bundeskartellamt* [1969] ECR 1 . . . . 1.8

127/73 *BRT v SV SABAM* [1974] ECR 314 . . . . 4.24

33/74 *Van Binsbergen v Besteuur von de Bedrijfsverening voor de Metaalnijverheid*
    [1974] ECR 1299. . . . . 5.11

43/75 *G. Defrenne v SABENA* [1976] ECR 455 . . . . 3.4

33/76 *REWE Central Finanz* [1976] ECR 1989 . . . . 4.1, 4.3

45/76 *Comet* [1976] ECR 2043 . . . . 4.1, 4.3

85/76 *Hoffmann-La Roche v Commission* [1979] ECR 461 . . . . 1.17

117/76 + 16/77 *Ruckdeschel* [1977] ECR 1753 . . . . 3.1

203/80 *Casati* [1981] ECR 2595 . . . . 1.6

199/82 *San Georgio* [1983] ECR 3595 . . . . 4.1

319/82 *Société de Vente de Ciments et Bétons v Kerpen & Kerpen* [1983] ECR 417. . . . . 1.15

14/83 *Von Colson and Kamann v Land Nordrhein-Westfalen* [1984] ECR 1891 . . . . 4.12

326 + 286/83 *Luisi and Carbone v Ministero del Tesoro* [1984] ECR 377 . . . . 1.6

355/85 *Driancourt v M. Cognet* [1986] ECR 3231. . . . . 1.8

379/87 *Groener v Minister for Education and City of Dublin Vocational*
    Committee [1989] ECR 3967 . . . . 3.3

5/88 *Wachauf v Bundesamt für Ernährung* [1989] ECR I-2609 . . . . 3.2

177/88 *Dekker v Stichting Vormingscentrum voor Jong Volwassenen*
    (VJV-Centrum) Plus [1990] ECR I-3941 . . . . 4.13

352/88 *Bond van Adverteerders v The Netherlands State* [1988] ECR I-2085. . . . . 1.5

C-234/89 *Delimitis v Henninger-Bräu* [1991] ECR I-935. . . . . 1.15

C-309/89 *Codorniú SA v Council* [1994] ECR I-1853. . . . . 3.1

C-361/89 *di Pinto* [1991] ECR I-1189. . . . . 2.9

C-339/89 *Alsthom Atlantique v Compagnie de construction mécanique Sulzer SA*
    [1991] ECR I-107 . . . . 1.4

C-6 + 9/90 *Francovich et al v Italy* [1991] ECR I-5357 . . . . 4.24

C-159/90 *The Society for the Protection of Unborn Children v Grogan* [1991] ECR
    I-4685 . . . . 1.5

C-332/90 *Steen v Deutsche Bundespost* [1992] ECR I-341. . . . . 1.8

C-89/91 *Shearson Lehmann Hutton v TVB Treuhandgesellschaft* [1993] ECR I-139 . . . . 2.9

C-259, 331 + 332/91 *Pilar Allué and Carmel Mary Coonan et al v Universitá degli*
    studi di Venezia and Università degli studi di Parma [1993] ECR I-4309 . . . . 3.3

C-271/91 *Marshall (II) v Southampton Health Authority* [1993] ECR I-4367 . . . . .4.13, 7.11

C-49/92P *Commission v Anic* [1999] ECR I-4125. . . . . 4.27

C-93/92 *CMC Motorradcenter v P.B.* [1993] ECR I-5009 . . . . 1.4

C-128/92 *H.J. Banks & Co. Ltd v British Coal Corporation* [1994] ECR I-1209 . . . . 4.25
C-272/92 *Maria Chiara Spotti v Freistaat Bayern* [1993] ECR I-5185 . . . . 3.3
C-23/93 *TV10 v Commissariaat v.d. Media* [1994] ECR I-4795 . . . . 5.11
C-46 + 48/93 *Brasserie du Pêcheur v Germany and R v Secretary of State for*
   Transport, ex parte Factortame Ltd [1996] ECR I-1029 . . . . 4.24, 7.11
C-381/93 *Commission v France* [1994] ECR I-5145 . . . . 5.14
C-415/93 *ABSL v Bosman* [1995] ECR I-4921 . . . . 1.7, 3.3,4.28
C-430–432/93 *Van Schijndel and Van Veen v Stichting Pensioenfonds*
   [1995] ECR I-4705 . . . . 4.15
C-55/94 *Gebhard v Consiglio dell'Ordine degli Advocati e procuratori di*
   Milano [1995] ECR I-4165 . . . . .1.9, 6.1
C-84/94 *UK v Council* [1996] ECR I-5755 . . . . 0.11, 2.2
C-194/94 *CIA Security International SA v Signalson SA and Securitel SPRL*
   [1996] ECR I-2201 . . . . 0.8
C-206/94 *Brennet v Paletta* [1996] ECR I-2357 . . . . 5.11
C-15/95 *EARL de Kerlast v Union régionale de coopératives agricoles (Unicopa)*
   and Coopérative du Trieux [1997] ECR I-1961 . . . . 3.1
C-180/95 *Draempaehl v Urania* [1997] ECR I-2195 . . . . 4.13
C-269/95 *Benincasa* [1997] ECR I-3767 . . . . 2.9
C-36/96 *Günaydin v Freistaat Bayern* [1997] ECR I-5143 . . . . 5.11
C-45/96 *Bayr. Hypotheken und Wechselbank v Dietzinger* [1998] ECR I-1199 . . . . 2.9
C-67/96 *Albany Int. BV v Stichting Bedrijfspensioenfonds Textielindustrie*
   [1999] ECR I-5751 . . . . 1.18
C-249/96 *Lisa Jacqueline Grant v South-West Trains* [1998] ECR I-621 . . . . 3.6
C-326/96 *Levez v Harlow Pools* [1998] ECR I-7835 . . . . 4.5
C-367/96 *Kefalas et al v Greece* [1998] ECR I-2843 . . . . 5.11
C-369 + 376/96 *Arblade* [1999] ECR I-8453 . . . . 6.13
C-126/97 *Eco Swiss China Time v Benetton International NV* [1999] ECR I-3055 . . . . . 4.23
C-185/97 *Coote v Granada Hospitality* [1998] ECR I-5199 . . . . 4.13
C-180–185/98 *Pavel Pavlov et al v Stichting Pensioenfonds Medische Specialisten*
   [2000] ECR I-6451 . . . . 1.18
C-195/98 *Öst. Gewerkschaftsbund, Gewerkschaft öffentlicher Dienst v Republik*
   Österreich [2000] ECR I-10497 . . . . 4.30
C-208/98 *Berliner Kindl Brauerei v A. Siepert* [2000] ECR I-1741 . . . . 2.9
C-240–244/98 *Océano Grupo ed. et al v Quintero et al* [2000] ECR I-4941 . . . . **4.15**, 7.5
C-281/98 *Roman Angonese v Casa di Risparmio di Bolzano* [2000]
   ECR I-4139 . . . . 1.7, 3.3, 4.28
C-303/98 *Simap* [2000] ECR I-7963 . . . .**2.3**
C-376/98 *Germany v Parliament and Council* [2000] ECR I-8419 . . . . .0.11, 6.4
C-381/98 *Ingmar GB Ltd v Eaton Leonard Technologies Inc.* [2000] ECR I-9305 . . . . 7.3
C-423/98 *Albore* [2000] ECR I-5965 . . . . .1.6
C-443/98 *Unilever Italia v Central Foods* [2000] ECR I-7535 . . . . 0.8
C-478/98 *Commission v Belgium* [2000] ECR I-7587 . . . . .1.6
C-63/99 *R v Secretary of State for the Home Department, ex parte Wieslaw*
   and Elzbieta Gloszczuk [2001] I-6369 . . . . .4.28
C-144/99 *Commission v Netherlands* [2001] I-3541 . . . . 4.10

C-173/99 *BECTU v Secretary of State for Trade and Industry* [2001] ECR I-4881 ...... 2.1

C-235/99 *R v Secretary of State for the Home Department, ex parte Eleanora Ivanova Kondova* [2001] ECR I-6427 .... 4.28

C-257/99 *R v Secretary of State for the Home Department, ex parte Julius Barkoci and Marcel Malik* [2001] ECR I-6557 .... 4.28

C-268/99 *Aldona Malgorzata Jany et al v Staatssecretaris van Justitie* [2001] ECR I-8615 .... 4.28

C-309/99 *J.C.J. Wouters et al v Algemene Raad von de Nederlandse Ordre van Advocaaten* [2002] ECR I-1577 .... 3.3, 4.28

C-453/99 *Courage Ltd v Crehan* [2001] ECR I-6297 .... 4.5, **4.25**, **7.12**

C-481/99 *Heininger v Bayr. Hypo und Vereinsbank* [2001] ECR I-9945 .... **4.20**

C-541 + 542/99 *Idealservice* [2001] ECR I-9049 .... 2.9

C-112/00 *Eugen Schmidberger v Austria* [2003] ECR I-5659 .... 5.14

C-162/00 *Land Nordrhein-Westfalen v Beata-Pokrzeptowicz-Meyer* [2002] ECR I-1049 .... 4.28

C-168/00 *Simone Leitner v TUI Deutschland* [2002] ECR I-2631 ....4.12, 7.13

C-438/00 *Deutscher Handballbund eV v Maros Kolpak* [2003] ECR I-4135 .... 4.28

C-264/01 etc. *AOK-Bundesverband v Ichthyol-Gesellschaft Cordes et al* [2004] ECR I-2493 .... 4.28

C-464/01 *Johann Gruber v Bay Wa AG* [2005] ECR I-439 .... 2.9

C-397–403/01 *Pfeiffer et al v DRK* [2004] ECR I-8835 .... **2.3**

C-491/01 *R v Secretary of State for Health, ex parte British American Tobacco (Investments) Ltd et al* [2002] ECR I-11453 .... **6.4**

C-25/02 *Katharina Rinke v Ärztekammer Hamburg* [2003] ECR I-8349 .... 3.4

C-36/02 *Omega Spielhallen- und Automatenaufstellungs-GmbH v Oberbürgermeisterin der Bundesstadt Bonn* [2004] ECR I-9609 .... 5.14

C-148/02 *Garcia Avello* [2003] ECR I-11613 .... 3.11

C-151/02 *Kiel v Jaeger* [2003] ECR I-8389 .... 2.1, 2.3

C-237/02 *Freiburger Kommunalbauten v Hofstetter* [2004] ECR I-3403 .... 7.4

C-281/02 *Andrew Owusu v NB Jackson et al* [2005] ECR I-1383 .... 5.12

C-442/02 *Caixa Bank France v Ministère de Finances* [2004] ECR I-8961 .... 1.11

C-19/03 *VZ HH v O2* [2004] ECR I-8183 .... 1.2

C-350/03 *Schulte* [2005] ECR I-9215 .... 4.21.

C-436/03 *EP v Council* [2006] ECR I-3733 .... 6.13

C-470/03 *AGM-COSMET* [2007] ECR I-2749 .... 3.8

C-540/03 *EP v Council* [2006] ECR I-5769 .... 2.4, 3.1

C-3/04 *Poseidon Chartering NV v Marianne Zeeship et al* [2006] ECR I-2505 .... 7.3

C-14/04 *Dellas* [2005] ECR I-10253 .... 2.3

C-94 + 202/04 *Frederico Cipolla et al v Rosaria Fazari, née Portolese et al* [2006] ECR I-1142 .... 1.10

C-131 + 257/04 *Robinson-Steele et al v Retail Services et al* [2006] ECR I-2531 .... 2.4

C-144/04 *Mangold v Helm* [2005] ECR I-9981 .... 0.3, **3.6**, 4.14

C-229/04 *Crailsheimer Volksbank* [2005] ECR I-9294 .... 4.21

C-295–298/04 *Vicenzo Manfredi et al v Lloyd Adriatico Asssicurazioni SpA et al* [2006] ECR I-6619 .... 4.5, **4.25**

C-344/04 *IATA and ELFAA v Department for Transport* [2006] ECR I-403 .... 6.4

C-465/04 *Honeyvem Informazioni Commerciali v Mariealla de Zoti*
    [2006] ECR I-2879 . . . . 7.3
C-479/04 *Laserdisken* [2006] ECR I-8089 . . . . 1.6
C-13/05 *Sonja Chacón Navas v Eurest Colectividades* [2006] ECR I-6467 . . . . 3.9
C-168/05 *E.M.M. Claro v Centro Movil Milenium* [2006] ECR I-10421 . . . . 4.15
C-277/05 *Société thermale d'Eugénie-les-Bains v Ministère de l'Économie,*
    des Finances et de l'Industrie [2007] ECR I-6428 . . . . 1.2
C-341/05 *Laval & partneri v Bygnadds* [2007] ECR I-11767 . . . . 3.3, **4.28, 5.12**
C-402 + 415/05P *Kadi et al v Council of the EU* [2008] ECR I-6351 . . . . 4.30
C-411/05 *Palacios de la Villa* [2007] ECR I-8531 . . . . 3.6
C-432/05 *Unibet v Justiekanslern* [2007] ECR I-2271 . . . . 4.30
C-438/05 *International Transport Workers Federation (ITW) and Finnish*
    Seamans Union (FSU) v Viking Line [2007] ECR I-10779 . . . . .3.3, 4.28, 5.12
C-99/06 *Mietz v Intership Yachting* [1999] ECR I-2277 . . . . 2.9
C-244/06 *Dynamik Medien Vertriebs GmbH v Avides Media AG* [2008] ECR I-505 . . . 5.18
C-275/06 *Productores de Música de España (Promusicae) v Telefónica*
    de España SAU [2008] ECR I-271 . . . . 1.6, 3.1., **5.1**
C-303/06 *S. Coleman v Attridge Law et al* [2008] ECR I-5603 . . . . 3.9
C-350 + 520/06 *Schulze-Hoff et al v DRB* [2009] ECR I-179 . . . . 2.4
C-353/06 *Grunkin and Paul* [2008] ECR I-7639 . . . . 3.11
C-404/06 *Quelle v Bundesverband der Verbraucherzentralen*
    [2008] ECR I-2685 . . . . 5.8, 6.17
C-412/06 *Annelore Hamilton v Volksbank Filder* [2008] ECR I-2383 . . . . . . .0.3, 5.9, 6.11
C-445/06 *Danske-Slagterier* [2009] ECR I-2119 . . . . .4.5, 7.11
C-47/07P *Masdar v Commission* [2008] ECR I-9761 . . . . 0.8
C-54/07 *Centrum voor gelijkheid van kansen en voor racismebestrijding*
    (CGKR) v Firma Feryn NV [2008] ECR I-5187 . . . . 3.4, 4.36
C-94/07 *Raccanelli* [2008] ECR I-5939 . . . . 3.3, 4.28
C-127/07 *Arcelor Atlantique and Lorraine et al* [2008] ECR I-9835 . . . . 3.1
C-169/07 *Hartlauer Handelsgesellschaft v Wiener Landesregierung et al*
    [2009] ECR I-1721 . . . . 5.4
C-205/07 *Gysbrechts* [2008] ECR I-9947 . . . . 1.9, 5.8, 7.19
C-518/06 *Commission v Italy* [2009] ECR I-3491 . . . . 1.10
C-316/07 *Markus Stoß* [2010] ECR I-8099 . . . . 1.5
C-402 + 432/07 *Sturgeon et al* [2009] ECR I-10923 . . . . 0.6
C-489/07 *Pia Messner v Firma Stefan Krüger* [2009] ECR I-7315 . . . . . 0.3, 5.9, 6.11, 7.10
C-531/07 *Fachverband der Buch- und Medienwirtschaft v LIBRO*
    Handelsgesellschaft [2009] ECR I-3717 . . . . 1.4
C-555/07 *Seda Kücükdevici v Swedex* [2010] ECR I-365 . . . . .0.7, 3.6, **4.14**
C-12/08 *Mono Car Styling* [2009] ECR I-6653 . . . . 4.30
C-40/08 *Asturcom v Christina Rodrigues Nogueria* [2009] ECR I-9579 . . . . 4.15
C-46/08 *Carmen Media* [2010] ECR I-8149 . . . . 1.5, 6.1
C-58/08 *Vodafone* [2010] ECR I-4999 . . . . 6.3
C-101/08 *Audiolux* [2010] ECR I-9823 . . . . 0.3, 3.22
C-137/08 *VB Penzügji Lizing v Schneider* [2010] ECR I-10847 . . . . 2.5, 4.15, 6.11, 7.5
C-147/08 *Jürgen Römer v Freie und Hansestadt Hamburg* [2011] ECR I-359 . . . . 3.8

C-215/08 *Friz* [2010] ECR I-2749 . . . . 0.3, 5.9, 6.11

C-238/08 *Ladbrokes Betting & Gaming Ltd et al v Stichting de Nationale Sportstotalisator* [2010] ECR I-4757 . . . . 6.4

C-243/08 *Pannon v Erzsébet Sustikné Győrfi* [2009] ECR I-4713 . . . . 4.15, 5.5

C-317/08 *Rosalba Alassini et al v Telecom Italia* [2010] ECR I-2214 . . . . 4.5, 6.21

C-381/08 *Car Trim v Key Safety* [2010] ECR I-1255 . . . . 6.15

C-403 + 429/08 *Football Association Premier League Ltd v QC Leisure et al* [2011] ECR I-9086 . . . . 1.11

C-484/08 *Caja de Ahorros y Monte de Piedad de Madrid v Asocación de Usuarios de servicios bancarios (Ausbanc)* [2010] ECR I-4785. . . . . 5.8

C-565/08 *Commission v Italy* [2011] ECR I-2101 . . . . 1.10

C-65 + 89/09 *Gebrüder Weber + Putz v Wittmer + Medianess El.* [2011] ECR I-5257 . . . . 2.5, **4.18**, 6.17, 7.10

C-203/09 *Volvo* [2010] ECR-10721 . . . . 7.3

C-236/09 *Ass. Belge Test-Achats et al* [2011] ECR I-773. . . . . **3.15**, 6.19

C-243/09 *Günter Fuß v Stadt Halle* [2010] ECR I-9849. . . . . 2.3

C-249/09 *S. Bulicke v DBS* [2010] ECR I-7003. . . . . 4.5

C-279/09 *DEB Deutsche Energiehandels- und Beratungsgesellschaft mbH v Bundesrepublik Deutschland* [2010] ECR I-13849. . . . . 3.2, 4.30

C-428/09 *Union Syndicale Solidaires Isère* [2010] ECR I-9961. . . . . 2.2

C-447/09 *R. Prigge et al v Lufthansa* [2011] ECR I-(13.09.2011). 3.6

C-214/10 *KHS v Winfrid Schulte* [2011] ECR I-(22.11.2011) **2.4**

C-282/10 *Dominguez v CICOA* [2012] ECR I-(24.01.2012). 2.1, 2.4

C-453/10 *Pereničová and Perenič v SOS financ* [2012] ECR I-(15.03.2012) . . .4.30, 6.16, 7.5

C-472/10 *Nemzeti Fogyaszróvédelni Hatóság v Invitel* [2012] ECR I-(26.04.2012) **4.15**, 4.30, 7.5

C-533/10 *CIVS v Receveur des Douanes de Roubaix* [2012] ECR I-(14.06.2012) 4.5

C-528 + 619/10 *Nelson et al v Lufthansa et al* [2012] ECR I-(24.10.2012). 0.6, 4.8

C-617/10 *Aklagaren v H.A. Fransson* [2013] ECR I-(26.03.2013). 3.2

C-618/10 *Banco Español de Credito v Camino* [2012] ECR I-(14.06.2012) 4.18

C-12/11 *D. McDonagh v Ryanair* [2013] ECR I-(31.01.2013). 2.1, 5.10

C -92/11 *RWE Vertrieb v Verbraucherzentrale NRW* [2013] ECR I-(21.03.2013) . . . 5.8, **7.4**

C-197 + C-203/11 *E. Libert et al v Gouvernement flamand* [2013] ECR I-(05.05.2013) 1.6

C-199/11 *Europese Gemeenschap v Otis et al* [2012] ECR I-(06.11.2012) 4.26, 4.30

C-202/11 *Anton Cas v PSA Antwerp* [2013] ECR I-(16.04.2013) 1.10

C-283/11 *Sky Österreich v Österreichischer Rundfunk* [2013] ECR I-(22.01.2013) 1.13, 3.21, 5.1

C-394/11 *Belov v CHEZ* [2013] ECR I-(31.01.2013) (opinion of AG Kokott of 20.09.2012) 3.13

C-415/11 *Mohamed Aziz v Catalunyacaixa* [2013] ECR I-(14.04.2013) 4.5

C-604/11 *Genil et al v Bankinter et al* [2013] ECR I-(30.05.2013) 7.10

C-81/12 *Asociatia ACCEPT v CNPCD* [2013] ECR I-(25.04.2013) **3.8**, 4.36

C-176/21 *Association de médiation sociale v CGT* (opinion of AG Cruz Villalón of 18.07.2013) 0.3

TABLE OF EU LEGISLATION

REGULATIONS

Council Regulation (EC) No 44/2001 of 22 December 2000 on jurisdiction and
the recognition and enforcement of judgments in civil and commercial
matters [2001] OJ L 12/1, 1. . . . . 2.9

Council Regulation (EC) No 1/2003 of 16 December 2002 on the implementation
of the rules on competition laid down in Articles 81 and 82 of the Treaty
[2003] OJ L 1. . . . . 1.14, 4.23

Regulation (EC) No 261/2004 of the EP and the Council of 11 February 2004 on
compensation and assistance to passengers in the event of denied boarding
and of cancellation and long delays of flights [2004] OJ L 46/1 . . . . 4.8, 5.10

Regulation (EC) No 864/2007 of the EP and the Council of 11 July 2007
on the law applicable to non-contractual obligations (Rome II)
[2007] OJ L 199/1 . . . . 4.12, 6.3

Regulation (EC) No 593/2008 of the EP and the Council of 17 June 2008
on the law applicable to contractual obligations (Rome I)
[2008] OJ L 176/6. . . . . 1.15, 4.12, 6.3,6.13–6.19

Commission Regulation (EU) No 330/2010 of 20 April 2010 on the application
of Article 101(3) TFEU to categories of vertical agreements and practices
[2010] OJ L 102/1 . . . . 1.16

Regulation (EU) No 1215/2012 of the EP and the Council of 12 December 2012
on jurisdiction and the recognition and enforcement of judgments in civil
and commercial matters [2012] OJ L 351/1. . . . . 2.9

DIRECTIVES

Council Directive 76/207/EEC of 9 February 1976 on the implementation of the
principle of equal treatment for men and women as regards access to
employment, vocational training and promotion, and working conditions
[1976] OJ L 039/40 . . . . 3.4, 4.12

Council Directive 85/374/EEC of 25 July 1985 on the approximation of the laws,
regulations and administrative provisions of the Member States concerning
liability for defective products [1985] OJ L 210/29 . . . . 7.14

Council Directive 85/577/EEC of 20 December 1985 to protect the consumer
in respect of contracts negotiated away from business premises
[1985] OJ L 372/31 (repealed by Directive 2011/83/EU) 2.9, 4.21, 5.9

Council Directive 86/653/EEC of 18 December 1986 on commercial agents [1986]
OJ L 382/17 . . . . , ...7.3, 7.21

Council Directive 90/314/EEC of 13 June 1990 on package travel, package
holidays and package tours [1990] OJ L 158/59 . . . . 7.14

Council Directive 93/13/EEC of 5 April 1993 on unfair terms in consumer
contracts [1993] OJ L 95/29 . . . . 2.5, 4.5, 4.15–4.17, 5.3–5.8, 7.5–7.8

Council Directive 93/104/EC of 23 November 1993 concerning certain aspects
of the organisation of working time [1993] OJ L 307/18 . . . . 2.1 ff

Directive 97/7/EC of the European Parliament and of the Council of 20 May 1997
on the protection of consumers in respect of distance contracts
[1997] OJ L 144/19 (repealed by Directive 2011/83/EU) 5.9

Directive 1999/44/EC of the EP and of the Council of 25 May 1999 on certain
aspects of the sale of consumer goods and associated guarantees
[1999] OJ L 171/12 . . . . 2.8, 4.18, 6.17, 6.23

Council Directive 2000/43/EC of 29 June 2000 implementing the principle
of equal treatment between persons irrespective of racial or ethnic
origin [2000] OJ L 180/22 . . . . 3.2, **3.5**, 3.12–**3.13**, **4.37**

Council Directive 2000/78/EC of 27 November 2000 establishing a general
framework for equal treatment in employment and occupation
[2000] OJ L 303/16 . . . . 3.2, **3.6–3.9**, **4.14**, **4.37**

Directive 2001/29/EC of the EP and the Council of 22 May 2001 on copyright
in the information society [2001] OJ L 167/10 . . . . .6.23

Directive 2002/22/EC of the EP and the Council of 2002 on universal service and
user's rights relating to electronic communications, networks and services
(Universal Services Directive) [2002] OJ L 108/51, amended by Directive
2009/136/EC of 19 December 2009 [2009] OJ L 337 . . . . 2.11, 3.19, 4.5

Directive 2002/65/EC of the EP and of the Council of 23 September 2002
concerning the distance marketing of consumer financial services and
amending Council Directive 90/619/EEC and Directives 97/7/EC and
98/27/EC [2002] OJ L 271/16 . . . . 2.7

Directive 2002/73/EC of the EP and of the Council of 23 September 2002
amending Council Directive 76/207/EEC on the implementation of the
principle of equal treatment for men and women as regards access to
employment, vocational training and promotion, and working conditions
[2002] OJ L 269/15 . . . . 4.34

Directive 2003/54/EC of the European Parliament and the Council of 26 June
2003 concerning common rules for the internal market for electricity
[2003] OJ L 176/37; for gas [2003] OJ L 176/57 . . . . 2.11, **3.19**

Working Time Directive 2003/88/EC of the EP and the Council of 4 November
2003 (recast) [2003] OJ L 299/9 . . . . 2.1 ff

Council Directive 2003/109/EC of 25 November 2003 concerning the status of
third-country nationals who are long-term residents [2004] OJ L 16/44 . . . . 3.12

Directive 2004/39/EC of the EP and the Council of 21 April 2004 on markets for
financial instruments (MIFID) [2008] OJ L 145/1 . . . . **7.10**

Council Directive 2004/113/EC of 13 December 2004 implementing the principle
of equal treatment between women and men in the access to and supply of
goods and services [2004] OJ L 373/37 . . . . 3.2, 3.12, **3.15–3.18**, 4.37

Directive 2005/29/EC of the EP and the Council of 11 May 2001 on unfair
commercial practices [2005] OJ L 149/22 . . . . 2.11

Recast Directive 2006/54/EC of the EP and the Council of 5 July 2006 on the
implementation of the principle of equal opportunities and equal treatment
of men and women in matters of employment [2006] OJ L 204/23 . . . . 3.4, 4.12

Commission Directive 2006/73/EC of 10 August 2006 (implementing the
MIFID) [2006] OJ L 241/26 . . . . 7.10

Directive 2007/64/EC of the EP and the Council of 12 December 2007 on
payment services in the internal market [2007] OJ L 319/36 . . . . 3.19a

Directive 2008/48/EC of the EP and the Council of 23 April 2008 on credit
agreements for consumers and repealing Council Directive 87/102/EEC
[2008] OJ 122/66 . . . . .2.7, 5.4, 7.9, 7.20

Directive 2008/122/EC of the EP and the Council of 14 January 2009 on the
    protection of consumers in respect of certain aspects of timeshare,
    long-term holiday products, resale and exchange contracts
    [2009] OJ L 33/10 . . . . 2.7

Directives 2009/72/EC and 2009/73/EC of the EP and the Council of 13 July 2009
    concerning common rules for the internal market of electricity and gas and
    repealing Directives 2003/54/EC and 2003/55/EC 2.11, 3.19

Directive 2010/13/EU of the European Parliament and the Council of 10 March
    2010 (Audiovisual Media Service Directive) [2010] OJ L 95/1 . . . . 3.21

Directive 2011/7/EU of the EP and the Council of 16 February 2011 combating
    late payment in commercial transactions (recast) [2011] OJ L 48/1 . . . 6.22, 7.4, 7.21

Consumer Rights Directive 2011/83/EU of the EP and the Council of 25 October
    2011 [2011] OJ L 304/64 . . . . .2.1, 2.6, 4.21, 5.9, 6.12–6.13, 6.16, 6.23, 7.1.

LIST OF ABBREVIATIONS

AcP	Archiv für die civilistische Praxis
AmericanJCompL	American Journal of Comparative Law
BGH(Z)	Bundesgerichtshof (German Federal Court), Zivilsachen (civil law reports)
BVerfG(E)	Bundesverfassungsgericht (Federal Constitutional Court, reports of cases)
CESL	Common European Sales Law
CISG	Convention on the International Sale of Goods
CMLR	Common Market Law Reports
CMLRev	Common Market Law Review
CRD	Consumer Rights Directive (2011/83/EU)
DCFR	Draft Common Frame of Reference
DJT	Deutscher Juristentag/German Law Associations Meeting
EBLRev	European Business Law Review
ECHR	European Convention of Human Rights
ECJ	Court of Justice of the EU
ECR	European Court Reports
ed(s)	Editor(s)
ELJ	European Law Journal
ELRev	European Law Review
EP	European Parliament
ERCL	European Review of Contract Law
ERPrL	European Review of Private Law
EuR	Europarecht
EWS	Europäisches Wirtschaftsrecht
EUI	European University Institute, Florence
EUVR	Zeitschrift für Europäisches Unternehmens- und Verbraucherrecht Journal of European Consumer and Market Law
EuZA	Europäische Zeitschrift für Arbeitsrecht
EuZW	Europäische Zeitschrift für Wirtschaftsrecht
GPR	Gemeinschaftsprivatrecht
JCP	Journal of Consumer Policy
Juridica Int.	Juridica International (Tartu, Estonia)
JZ	Juristenzeitung

KritJ	Kritische Justiz
ModLR	Modern Law Review
NJW	Neue Juristische Wochenschrift
OFT	Office of Fair Trading
OJ L/C	Official Journal of the EU, legislation or communication series
OJLS	Oxford Journal of Legal Studies
PECL	Principles of European Contract Law
PICL	Principles of International Contract Law
RabelsZ	Rabels Zeitschrift für ausländisches und internationales Privatrecht
RTDEur	Revue Trimestrielle du droit européen
S.I.	Statutory Instrument (UK)
TEU	Treaty on European Union
TFEU	Treaty on the Functioning of the EU
UKHL	UK House of Lords cases
UKSC	UK Supreme Court cases
VuR	Verbraucher und Recht
WiscIntLJ	Wisconsin International Law Journal
YEL	(Oxford) Yearbook of European Law
ZEuP	Zeitschrift für Europäisches Privatrecht
ZIP	Zeitschrift für Wirtschaftsrecht

INTRODUCTION

WHAT ARE GENERAL PRINCIPLES OF EU CIVIL LAW?

Contents

Bibliography 1
1. An ongoing debate: "principles" vs. "rules" 2
2. Some preliminary suggestions 6
3. The express recognition of general principles by the Charter 8
4. What do we mean by EU civil law: *acquis communautaire* vs.
   acquis commun 11
5. The competence dilemma of EU civil law 14
6. Why seven principles? 16

Bibliography

Acquis Group, *Principles of Existing EC Contract Law (Acquis Principles)*, Contract I 2007, Contract II 2009; C. von Bar et al. (eds.), *Principles, Definitions and Model Rules of European Civil Law – Draft Common Frame of Reference (DCFR)*, interim outline ed. 2008, outline ed. 2009, full ed. I-VI 2009; J. Basedow, 'The Court of Justice and civil law: vacillations, general principles, and the architecture of the European judiciary', ERPL 2010, 443; U. Bernitz et al. (eds.), *General Principles of EU Law in a Process of Development*, 2008; F. Cafaggi/H. Muir Watt (eds.), *Making European Private Law*, 2008; F. Cafaggi/H. Muir Watt (eds.), *The Regulatory Functions of European Private Law*, 2010; O. Cherednyshenko, *Fundamental Rights, Contract Law, and the Protection of the Weaker Party*, 2007; A. Ciacchi, 'The Constitutionalisation of European Contract Law: Judicial Convergence and Social Justice', ERCL 2006, 167; H. Collins, *The European Civil Code – The Way Forward*, 2008; M. Dougan, 'The Impact of the General Principles of Union Laws upon Private Relationships', in: D. Leczykiewicz/S. Weatherill (eds.), *The Involvement of EU Law in Private Law Relationships*, 2013, 71; R. Dworkin, *Taking Rights Seriously*, 1977; J. Esser, *Grundsatz und Norm in der richterlichen Fortbildung des Privatrechts*, 1956, 4th ed. 1968; J. Esser, *Vorverständnis und Methodenwahl in der Rechtsfindung*, 1970; X. Groussot, *General Principles of Community Law*, 2008; K. Gutman, *The Constitutional Foundations of European Contract Law*, 2011; A. Hartkamp, 'The General Principles of EU Law and Civil Law', RabelsZ 2011, 241; A. Hartkamp, *European Law and National Law*, 2012; M. Hesselink, 'If You Don't Like Our Principles We Have Others: On Core Values and Underlying Principles in European Civil Law: A Critical Discussion of the New Principles Section in the "Draft Common Frame of Reference"', in: R. Brownsword et al. (eds.), *The Foundations of European Civil Law*, 2011, 59; M. Hesselink, 'The general principles of civil law: their nature, role and legitimacy', in: D. Leczykiewicz/S. Weatherill (eds.), *The Involvement of EU Law in Private Law Relationships*, 2013, 131; K. Lenaerts/J. Gutierrez-Fons, 'The Constitutional Allocation of Powers and General Principles of

EU Law', CMLRev 2010, 1629; C. Mak, *Fundamental Rights in European Contract Law*, 2008; A. Metzger, *Extra legem, intra ius: Allgemeine Rechtsgrundsätze im Europäischen Privatrecht*, 2009; H.-W. Micklitz (ed.), *Constitutionalisation of Private Law*, 2013; H.-W. Micklitz (ed.), *The Many Concepts of Social Justice in European Private Law*, 2011; H.-W. Micklitz, 'The Visible Hand of European Regulatory Civil Law', YEL 2009, 3; F. Möslein, *Dispositives Recht*, 2011; L. Niglia (ed.), *Pluralism and European Private Law*, 2013; S. Peers/A. Ward (eds.), *The European Charter of Fundamental Rights*, 2004; P. Popelier/C. Van de Heyning/P. Van Nuffel (eds.), *Human rights protection in the European legal order: The interaction between the European and the national courts*, 2011; D. Pölzig, *Normdurchsetzung durch Privatrecht*, 2013; K. Purnhagen, 'The architecture of Post-National European Contract Law from a Phenomenological Perspective', RabelsZ 2013, 592; N. Reich, 'The Social, Political and Cultural Dimension of EU Civil Law', in: R. Schulze/H. Schulte-Nölke, *European Civil Law – Current Status and Functions*, 2011, 57; K. Riesenhuber, *Privatrechtsgesellschaft: Entwicklung, Stand und Verfassung des Privatrechts*, 2007; K. Riesenhuber, *Europäische Methodenlehre*, 2nd ed. 2010; H. Rösler, *Europäische Gerichtsbarkeit auf dem Gebiet des Zivilrechts*, 2012; M. Safjan/P. Miklaszewicz, 'Horizontal effect of the general principles of EU law in the sphere of civil law', ERPL 2010, 475; C. Schmid, *Die Instrumentalisierung des Privatrechts durch die EU*, 2010; E. Steindorff, *EG-Vertrag und Privatrecht*, 1996; T. Tridimas, *General Principles of EC Law*, 2nd ed. 2006; C. Twigg-Flesner (ed.), *European Private Law*, 2010; C. Twigg-Flesner, *A Cross-Border Regulation for Consumer Transactions in the EU – A Fresh Approach to EU Consumer Law*, 2012; S. Weatherill, 'The "principles of civil law" as a basis for interpreting the legislative *acquis*', ERCL 2010, 74.

1. AN ONGOING DEBATE: "PRINCIPLES" VS. "RULES"

0.1 "General principles" of EU law have long been recognised as part of unwritten law. They have been developed in a constant flow of case law of the now called Court of Justice of the EU (CJEU or simply ECJ) which takes its mandate from Article 19(1) TEU whereby "[i]t shall ensure that in the interpretation and application of the Treaty the law is observed." The law – *das Recht* – *le droit* – this formula was to be found already in the original EEC Treaty, and was taken over by what later became the EC Treaty after Amsterdam (Article 220 EC) and has not changed its wording in the latest Lisbon version. However, its "upgrading" from what is now called the Treaty on the Functioning of the EU (TFEU), formerly the EC Treaty, to the Treaty on European Union (TEU) containing the basic principles and institutions of the Union itself, shows its high standing and importance in the political and legal order.

The formula deliberately goes beyond a mere positivist concept of law. It obviously refers to the sources of the EU Treaties as "primary law" – now including the Charter of Fundamental Rights (the Charter) according to Article 6(1) TEU – and secondary law in the sense of Article 288 TFEU, namely regulations, directives and decisions. "General principles" seem to be in an "intermediary location" – something between primary and secondary law, even though they are, in the words of the ECJ, of *constitutional relevance*.[1] A number of such general principles – mostly relating to constitutional and administrative law – have been developed, described and analysed in the fundamental study of Tridimas.[2] They seem to be generally accepted by the ECJ, by its AGs, and by scholarship, even though there may be debates about their origin, scope and exact legal nature. However, principles of constitutional or administrative law will not be this book's focus, but rather principles of EU civil law.

0.2 In the above-mentioned discussion on the sources of EU law it was pointed out that the EU's respect for "the law" is inherent in a political organisation based on the rule of law (*Rechtsstaatlichkeit* or *état de droit*), a model to which the EU expressly subscribes. The authority to ensure respect for the law is vested in European courts – including all courts in the EU – and in particular in the ECJ. Ensuring respect for the law is done by "discovering" and developing general principles which guide the application and interpretation of EU primary and secondary law as "positive law". Therefore, EU law is characterised by a distinction between "rules" and "principles", the first being the provisions of positive EU law, the second the more general concepts which guide law interpretation and application. *Rules* – if they are specific and unconditional enough – create rights and impose obligations on parties to a civil transaction; in EU law, the entire theory of "direct effect" is based on this condition of the application of rules, although it makes allowance for exceptions to the effect of directives between civil parties (so called absence of "direct horizontal effect").[3] *Principles*, on the other hand, do not have this specific legal effect because they are much broader, more flexible, quite unspecific and need judicial implementation in order to become part of the legal regime of a civil law obligation or transaction. Their importance can be found in their methodological impact on law interpretation and application. They are linked to rules, but are not rules themselves.

This fundamental distinction between "rules" and "principles" has been developed in legal theory and methodology in Germany by Josef Esser, and in the US by Ronald Dworkin; it is also useful for an understanding of the process of evolution of EU law and the binding effect of rulings of the ECJ beyond a formal *stare decisis* doctrine.[4] Josef Esser in his 1960s studies, *Grundsatz und*

---

[1]   K. Lenaerts/J. Gutierrez-Fons, CMLRev 2010, 1629 at 1641: "status of primary law"; at 1647: "constitutional status" based on the case law of the ECJ.
[2]   T. Tridimas, *The General Principles of EU Law*, 2nd ed. 2006.
[3]   See for details S. Prechal, *Directives in EU Law*, 2nd ed. 2006; N. Reich et al., *Understanding EU Internal Market Law*, 3rd ed. forthcoming, paras 2.5–2.13.
[4]   For a detailed discussion see N. Reich, in: R. Brownsword et al. (eds.), *The Foundations of European Civil Law*, 2011, 221 at 225.

Norm ("Principle and Norm")[5] and *Vorverständnis und Methodenwahl* ("Pre-understanding and Choice of Methods"),[6] which are still valuable today, refers to the importance of legal principles which must be integrated into the finding and assessment of "rules". Esser rejects the theory of *Wertfreiheit* (absence of value judgments) in legal thinking as "ideology". Instead he talks of a *Vorverständnis* in legal thinking and interpretation, namely as "conceptualising" the understanding of legal texts whereby a just result is – or should be – the final objective.

For US law, Ronald Dworkin[7] insisted on the difference between "rules", which have an imperative character, allow only "yes" and "no" answers and are applicable in an "all-or-nothing fashion",[8] and "principles" (or standards), which should be respected "because it is a requirement of justice or fairness or some other element of morality".[9] He goes on to insist that "[p]rinciples have a dimension that rules do not – the dimension of weight or importance. When principles intersect [...] one who must resolve the conflict has to take into account the relative weight of each. [... I]t is an integral part of the concept of a principle that it has this dimension, that it makes sense to ask how important or how weighty it is. Rules do not have this dimension."[10]

It will be shown throughout this study that the main development of EU law has been achieved by the insistence of the ECJ on these general principles as part of a "judicial law discovery" in the sense of Esser and Dworkin. This has been demonstrated in the monograph by Tridimas in which he develops a theory of "the General Principles of EU Law", explicitly referring to Dworkin.[11] Once these principles have evolved and been recognised, particularly by repeated application, they become part of "the law". Usually the ECJ will be required to apply partially conflicting, partially overlapping principles, for example legal certainty on the one hand and substantive justice on the other, or recognition of party autonomy in EU contract law versus how it is limited by the principle of non-discrimination, or the protection of fundamental freedoms versus respect for fundamental rights. The EU theory of adjudication is to a large extent based on this balancing of "intersecting principles" in the words of Dworkin, or the search for *Sachgerechtigkeit* (substantive justice) as Esser puts it. The concept of

---

[5]   J. Esser, *Grundsatz und Norm in der richterlichen Fortbildung des Privatrechts*, 1956, 4th ed. 1968.

[6]   J. Esser, *Vorverständnis und Methodenwahl in der Rechtsfindung*, 1970; a popular pocket edition was published in 1972.

[7]   R. Dworkin, *Taking Rights Seriously*, 1977.

[8]   Ibid., at 24.

[9]   Ibid., at 22.

[10]   Ibid., at 26.

[11]   Ibid., at 2.

balancing will be looked at in a separate part of this book (Chapter 5). As the prominent authors Lenaerts and Gutiérrez-Fons from the ECJ itself write:[12]

> "Hence, by having recourse to balancing criteria enriched by different, albeit converging, legal, moral, or political theories, the ECJ ensures a case-by-case, flexible construction of the EU legal order, expressed inter alia in the various general principles of EU law."

On the other hand, one may question whether this sharp distinction between rules and principles is always appropriate for the emerging EU legal order. Principles seem to be binding according to Tridimas and Lenaerts, who mostly refer to the case law of the Court. EU rules on the other hand frequently lack the precision and specificity demanded by Dworkin and Esser. Both need to be "discovered" and recognised by judicial practice and made manageable for interpreting and applying EU law. The dividing line between "rules" and "principles" is not always easy to draw in practice when applying such general documents as the Charter of Fundamental Rights in the EU, which will be the main object of this study as regards its relations to EU civil law.

0.3   Much less advanced is the debate in EU civil law – a concept which will be defined later (0.9). The reason may be historical: originally EU law was mostly concerned with administrative law, so-called "vertical relations" between citizens and Member States under the impact of EU freedoms and other normative acts, and also with constitutional questions of a division of "horizontal" and "vertical" distribution of powers and competences in the EU. Civil law matters – so-called "horizontal relations" – became part of the EU agenda mostly after the adoption of the Maastricht Treaty in such "new subject matters" as non-discrimination and protection of employees and consumers, and even some commercial relations like late payments (6.22) by more powerful businesses and state procurement agencies in particular to the detriment of small and medium undertakings (SMU). Competition law had a hybrid character – enforced mostly "vertically" via the Commission, later also by Member State authorities – with an impact on commercial contracts via the nullity provision of Article 101(2) TFEU, but without any express remedy of compensation (see 1.14) as this was only later added by case law of the ECJ (4.25).

The debate on general principles was pushed forward by seemingly conflicting lines of argument by the ECJ. To give some very preliminary examples:

– An activist, for some observers almost aggressive, ECJ case law concerning non-discrimination principles based on nationality and gender, later also on

---

[12]   K. Lenaerts/J. Gutiérrez-Fons, CMLRev 2010, 1629 at 1653 (also referring to the limits of such balancing).

other inherent characteristics such as race and age, with an impact on civil law ("horizontal") relations conflicting with the principle of contractual autonomy. This will be analysed in detail in Chapter 3. The most prominent and most controversial case has been *Mangold* (3.6).[13]

- A reference by the ECJ to (general) principles of civil law, mostly concerning the interpretation of consumer law directives (5.9). The judgments in *Hamilton*,[14] *Messner*[15] and *Friz*[16] referred expressly to "the (general) principles of civil law" such as good faith, unjust enrichment, satisfactory balancing and a fair division of risks among the various interested parties. A quite controversial debate arose out of the importance of these pronouncements,[17] which will be set out in some detail in Chapter 5.

- In *Audiolux*[18] the ECJ, based on the detailed analysis of AG Trstenjak of 30 June 2009, flatly denied the existence of a general principle of equal treatment of shareholders (3.22).

2. SOME PRELIMINARY SUGGESTIONS

0.4 At first sight, there seems to be some confusion over the origin, existence and function of general principles in EU civil law. The legal scholarship is divided between those who are sceptical of, even hostile towards, the place of these principles in civil law. From the point of view of an English lawyer, Weatherill[19] voiced the following concerns:

"Even if one is prepared to engage in the quest of 'systematisation' of the EU's legislative *acquis,* the consequence of success in such a quest is unavoidably that limits are placed on national autonomy in the area touched – incrementally, as a 'patchwork' – by the EU. A more coherent system at EU level may lead to a less

---

[13] Case C-144/04 *Mangold v Helm* [2005] ECR I-9981.

[14] Case C-412/06 *Annelore Hamilton v Volksbank Filder* [2008] ECR I-2383, para 24.

[15] Case C-489/07 *Pia Messner v Firma Stefan Krüger* [2009] ECR I-7315, para 26.

[16] Case C-215/08 *Friz* [2010] ECR I-2749, paras 48–49.

[17] For an comprehensive analysis of this development see M. Hesselink, in: D. Leczykiewicz/ S. Weatherill (eds.), *The Involvement of EU Law in Private Law Relationships*, 2013, 131; S. Weatherill, 'The "principles of civil law" as a basis for interpreting the legislative acquis', ERCL 2010, 74; J. Basedow, 'The Court of Justice and civil law: vacillations, general principles, and the architecture of the European judiciary', ERPL 2010, 443; M. Safjan/P. Miklaszewicz, 'Horizontal effect of the general principles of EU law in the sphere of civil law', ERPL 2010, 475; A. Hartkamp, 'The General Principles of EU Law and Civil Law', RabelsZ 2011, 241; for a narrower view by limiting general principles to constitutional and administrative law: M. Dougan, in: D. Leczykiewicz/S. Weatherill (eds.), *The Involvement of EU Law in Private Law Relationships*, 2013, 71 at 81. For detailed analysis of the relevance of "principles" in Art 52(5) of the Charter for EU civil law see now the opinion of AG Cruz Villalón of 18 July 2013 in case C-176/12 *Association de médiation sociale v CGT*, conforming to the principles advanced in this book.

[18] Case C-101/08 *Audiolux* [2010] ECR I-9823.

[19] *Supra* note 5, at 80.

coherent system at national level. Such a starkly destructive outcome is not inevitable, but this is where the Court's use of general principles may lead, and it is one reason why it is troubling."

Whether such judgment is correct or not will be discussed later in this book. Another criticism has been voiced by Hesselink who wonders how from a "patchwork" of contractual regulations in the EU some general principles can be derived; the "Court simply postulates the principles without providing any evidence".[20] He suggests that only principles of an "intermediate level" can be found in EU contract law. Basedow,[21] in discussing the seemingly divergent arguments in the ECJ judgments of *Mangold* and *Audiolux*, points out that the discovery of general principles like "equality" or "equal treatment" is always based on a value judgment and it may therefore be difficult to give broader application to that principle. Metzger[22] in his mostly methodological approach finds that there are only "few legal principles in the case law" ("*kaum Rechtsgrundätze in der Rechtsprechung*"), a statement which will be challenged throughout this study.

0.5 A useful methodological approach to the place of "general principles" in EU civil (company) law has been offered in the opinion of AG Trstenjak in *Audiolux*. She makes a clear distinction between the more general questions of the existence of such principles on the one hand, and the more specific question of its impact on the dispute before the ECJ in *Audiolux*. She notes the importance of such principles in the "developing Community legal order" for filling gaps as an aid to interpretation (para 68). She thereby refers to the work of Tridimas[23] who insists on the need to fill gaps in Community law which result from the fact that "the Community legal order is a new and young legal order which needs to be developed further". Some of these gaps, for example state liability, result from the "general principles common to the laws of the Member States" (Article 340(2) TFEU) and may become principles of EU law by their integration and application into the Union legal order, including its extension to state liability.[24] Others may be specific to EU law itself, for example the principle of sincere cooperation according to Article 4(3) TEU (ex Article 10 EC), and will remain without any impact on civil law.

As far as civil law principles are concerned, there is no reason to exclude them from this process of "principalisation" of EU law.[25] As Hartkamp has shown, they are necessary both for gap filling and for interpretative purposes.

---

[20]   M. Hesselink, *supra* note 17, at 17 and 1730.
[21]   J. Basedow, *supra* note 17.
[22]   A. Metzger, *Extra legem – intra jus*, 2009, at 352.
[23]   T. Tridimas, *supra* note 2, at 1729.
[24]   T. Tridimas, *supra* note 2, at 502.
[25]   See X. Groussot/H. Lidgard, in: U. Bernitz et al. (ed.), *General Principles*, 2008, 155.

He even goes further and suggests their use for "assessing the legality of national legislation in the light of general principles of EU law".[26] This can be justified by their "constitutional character" as interpreted by Lenaerts and Gutierrez-Fons, who insist on their gap-filling function.[27]

3. THE EXPRESS RECOGNITION OF GENERAL PRINCIPLES BY THE CHARTER

0.6   The debate on "general principles" in EU law as such in civil law which is important for this book has to some extent found its solution in the Charter. It has been overlooked by many observers that the Charter contains not only "Fundamental Rights" but also (fundamental) "Principles" which "may be implemented by legislative and executive acts by institutions, bodies, offices and agencies of the Union, and by acts of Member States when they are implementing Union law, in the exercise of their respective powers. They are judicially cognisable only in the interpretation of such acts and in the ruling of their legality" (Article 52(5)).

In the Explanations of the Praesidium of the Convention attached to this Article,[28] the distinction refers to "subjective rights which shall be respected, whereas principles shall be observed (Art. 51 (1) Charter); [...] accordingly, they become significant to the Courts only when such acts are interpreted or reviewed". The interpretative and review function of principles has therefore been expressly recognised by the Charter; principles may not be placed on the highest level in the hierarchy of constitutional norms, but they are still of *constitutional relevance*. The "gap-filling function" mentioned by Trstenjak and Hartkamp has not been expressly mentioned, but since it is part of the process of interpretation,[29] and since this interpretation must take principles into account, there is no need to exclude gap-filling from the normative function of principles. In its recent *Nelson* judgment of 23 October 2012, in justifying the extension of compensation under the Air Passenger Regulation (EC) 261/2004 from cancelled flights to those delayed by more than three hours, the ECJ wrote:[30]

> "[I]t should be noted that the principle of equal treatment requires that comparable situations must not be treated differently and that different situations must not be treated in the same way unless such treatment is objectively justified."

---

[26]   *Supra* note 17, at 245.

[27]   K. Lenaerts/J. Gutiérrez-Fons, *supra* note 1, at 1631; criticized by M. Dougan, *supra* note 17, at 83: "gap filling" left to the legislator.

[28]   OJ C-303/17 of 14.12.2007, at 35.

[29]   See J. Neuner, in: K. Riesenhuber, *Europäische Methodenlehre*, 2nd ed. 2010, 385, who mentions it under the heading of "Rechtsfinding praeter legem" (finding the law beyond the law).

[30]   Joined Cases C-528 + 619/10 *Nelson et al v Lufthansa et al* [2012] ECR I-(23.10.2012), para 33.

This clearly amounts to an express recognition of the function of general principles like equal treatment in providing an analogy for the interpretation of Union law in terms of filling a gap left by the Regulation in seemingly excluding departures that suffer long delays, and the filling of that gap is thereby justified under Article 52(5) of the Charter. On the other hand, it is not surprising that the existence of such a "gap" has been contested by many authors and many Member State courts against the prior *Sturgeon* judgment of the ECJ,[31] insisting that legislator made a deliberate choice to exclude long delays from compensation.[32]

On the other hand, the differentiation between "principles" and "rights" in Article 51 of the Charter should not be exaggerated. Rights must be "respected" ("*achten*"), principles "observed" ("*sich halten an*") – but what is the difference between these two rather vague concepts? "Rights" shall be "exercised under the conditions and within the limits defined by those Treaties", according to Article 52(2). They are not "free standing rights" and do not enjoy direct effect in favour of individuals, as AG Trstenjak correctly found in her opinion of 8 September 2011 in *Dominguez*.[33] On the other hand, just like principles, the rights included in the Charter can be used to interpret EU law and Member State law that implements EU law, and may even allow a "negative direct horizontal effect" in conjunction with existing directives, as the *Kücükdevici* case has demonstrated (2.6)[34] – an effect that can be extended to other fundamental rights and principles guaranteed by the Charter which in practice do not seem to lead to different results.

0.7 When arguing for a concept of general principles which can be based on the Charter, one can go back to earlier EU legislation and ECJ case law in which these principles are already recognised. The Charter to some extent only consolidates the existing EU *acquis* as regards general principles of civil law and "upgrades" them to having a constitutional status, as will be shown in more detail throughout this study. The following subjects will be covered in this book, keeping in mind that some Articles of the Charter may contain both rights and principles according to the Explanations.

–   The principle of "*framed*" autonomy – already present in the free movement and competition rules of primary law – is now grounded in Article 16 of the

---

[31]   Joined Cases C-402/07 + C-432/07 *Sturgeon et al* [2009] ECR I-10923; J. Neuner, *supra* note 29, regards this as "den klassischen Analogieschluss" (traditional analogy argument); the ECJ does not seem to use this methodological argument because Article 220 EC (now Article 19(1) TEU) only refers to "interpretation".

[32]   K. Riesenhuber, 'Comment on Sturgeon', ERCL 2010, 384; AG Bot in his opinion in *Nelson* unfortunately does not discuss these objections.

[33]   Case C-282/10 *Dominguez v CICOA* [2012] ECR-I-(24.01.2012), para 83.

[34]   Case C-555/07 *Seda Kücükdevici v Swedex* [2010] ECR I-365, at para 22 referring to Article 21 of the Charter, though in the end not arguing with the existence of a "right", but rather of a "general principle of equality", at paras 50–53.

Charter on the "freedom to conduct a business" and in Article 17 on the protection of property. This autonomy is not "self-sufficient" but may and must be regulated by EU and national law – it is *framed* by countervailing legal principles which are discussed in Chapters 2 to 7. The general issues of autonomy will be covered in Chapter 1.

- The principle of *protection of weaker parties* in employment and consumer contract law has its constitutional confirmation in Articles 31 and 38 of the Charter; it has been recognised by several Directives that have been interpreted as *pro-worker* and *pro-consumer* by the ECJ in the spirit of an individualistic understanding of EU civil law, to be discussed in Chapter 2.
- The principle of *non-discrimination* in Article 21 and in Article 23 of *"equality between men and women"* was already present before the enactment of the Charter; earlier instruments in particular prohibited discrimination based on gender (Article 157 TFEU and predecessors) or (EU) nationality (Article 18 TFEU). This was later extended by secondary law with a "constitutional relevance" to such inherent characteristics as race, disability, age and sexual orientation, with a substantial impact on civil autonomy, as is discussed in Chapter 3.
- The principle of *effective legal protection* is now written into Articles 47(1) and 19(1) TEU, although its relevance was first established in Article 6/13 of the European Convention on Human Rights as applied by the ECJ to EU law. Its importance for the substance and procedures of EU civil law will be explored in Chapter 4.
- The principle of *balancing opposing interests* in civil law relations is indirectly found in Articles 51, 52 and 54 of the Charter. This principle has both an individual and a collective dimension, and may also be used to limit the exercise of EU granted rights. It will be considered as an important interpretative principle for civil law relations in the discussion on the impact of EU law in Chapter 5.
- Chapter 6 is concerned with the principle of *proportionality* in conjunction with Article 5(4) TEU and Article 52(1) of the Charter whereby the "content and form of Union action shall not exceed what is necessary to achieve the objectives of the Treaty". Proportionality should not only be regarded as a "negative" principle concerning the use of EU powers, but also as a "positive" principle requiring EU action where necessary. An examination of this principle will allow us to question current EU initiatives for a "codification", "consolidation" or "optionalisation" of civil law in the EU. An argument will be made for more flexible instruments like the "open method of coordination and convergence" in the development of a multi-layered EU civil law instrument limited to the scope of application of the Treaties, together with mandatory provisions in fields where action seems necessary.

– Chapter 7 will explore whether a general principle of *good faith*, a duty to loyal cooperation coupled with a prohibition on abuse of rights, is emerging in EU civil law despite substantially different approaches in Member State law, in particular between civil and common law countries. We will examine whether Article 54 of the Charter on "prohibition of abuse of rights" can be meaningful in this context.

4. WHAT DO WE MEAN BY EU CIVIL LAW: *ACQUIS COMMUNAUTAIRE* VS. *ACQUIS COMMUN*

0.8 This study is limited to civil law relations and consequently looks at principles that have an explicit relevance for and impact on civil law. Can one distinguish in EU law between "civil" (private) and "public" (administrative) law? This seems difficult considering the specific functions of EU law as regards the internal market and the achievement of the specific (and limited) objectives of the Treaty especially in the field of social policy.[35] In this context it is suggested that we take an hermeneutical approach because of the different criteria used in the Member States to explain this distinction, and because there is no such thing as a systematic and coherent body of EU civil law. This study, however, will have to exclude such important yet somewhat specialised matters as conflict of laws, company law and intellectual property law.

This study is concerned mostly with *contract law and civil liability*. Two criteria to conceptualise this concern can be found in the legal literature:

– the concept of *horizontal relationships* in contrast to vertical ones, the first relating to those between civil parties (businesses and consumers (B2B, B2C, C2C), employees and employers, etc.), and the second involving the position of the individual towards a Member State and the Union respectively, which may be put under the heading of "administrative" law; and
– the concept of *remedies*, used especially in the study by Hartkamp:[36] civil law remedies include compensation, recovery of unjust enrichment, avoidance of a contract clause, etc., which are also possible against the state, in contrast to prohibition orders, administrative sanctions, etc., which are penalties reserved for state institutions (including courts of law).

---

[35] For an overview see N. Reich, 'The public/private divide in European law', in: F. Cafaggi/ H.-W. Micklitz, *European Private Law after the Common Frame of Reference*, 2011, 56; the importance of the principle of "social justice" has been discussed by Micklitz and others in H.-W. Micklitz (ed.), *The Many Concepts of Social Justice in the EU*, 2011. The market-creation value of European contract law, including consumer protection and social justice, has recently been stressed by K. Purnhagen, RabelsZ 2013, 592 at 611.

[36] A. Hartkamp, *European Law and National Private Law*, 2012, paras 79 and 84.

In practice there will be a great deal of overlap, especially in relations involving civil parties, EU law and the state. A good example is the *Unilever* case.[37] It concerned an action for breach of contract where the Italian importer of olive oil (Central Food) denied payment to the seller (Unilever) because the oil had not been packaged and labelled according to a new Italian regulation. Since the Commission had not been properly notified of this regulation according to an EU Directive, it could not be invoked in civil proceedings before the Italian court.[38] The real issue concerns the effect of an EU instrument that had not been properly implemented by a Member State (a "vertical relation") in a civil law action between the parties ("horizontal effects"). The opposite case is that of *Masdar*,[39] which concerned the civil law remedy of unjust enrichment in a "vertical" action of a civil party against the Commission for compensation without fault.

0.9   This study will not develop any specific theory of "civil law" as conceptually distinct from "public" EU law, but instead will take as a starting point civil law's specific characteristic, namely the concept of "regulatory civil law" as developed by Micklitz.[40] In sharp contrast to the civil law of Member States, this consists of a body of mostly *mandatory provisions and rules* that aim at specific objectives written into the EU Treaties, the most important of which relate to the establishment and functioning of the internal market (Article 114(1) TFEU) but also extend to the field of social policy (Article 153) and to non-discrimination (Articles 19 and 157 TFEU; Articles 13 and 21 of the Charter). Even in cases where the EU has regulated certain commercial relations, mandatory provisions are included, for example the protection of self-employed commercial agents by Article 19 of Directive 86/653/EEC[41] concerning the indemnity to be paid in case of termination of the contract, and by Article 7 of Directive 2011/7/EU of 16 February 2011[42] on combating late payments by prohibiting "grossly unfair terms" in payment clauses that are to the detriment of the creditor. This will of course not exclude the fact that *default provisions* may also be found in many secondary EU legal acts,[43] but such provisions do not seem to be characteristic of EU civil law, in clear contrast to Member State contract law where the

---

[37]   Case C-443/98 *Unilever Italia v Central Food* [2000] ECR I-7535; critique S. Weatherill, in: D. Leczykiewicz/S. Weatherill (eds.), *The Involvement of EU Law in Private Law Relationships*, 2013, 9 at 17.

[38]   See case C-194/94 *CIA Security International SA v Signalson SA and Securitel SPRL* [1996] ECR I-2201.

[39]   Case C-47/07P *Masdar v Commission* [2008] ECR I-9761.

[40]   H.-W. Micklitz, YEL 2009, 3 at 33.

[41]   [1986] OJ L 382/17.

[42]   [2011] OJ L 48/1.

[43]   For a general discussion see F. Möslein, *Dispositives Recht*, 2011, referring to the function-oriented EU competence in contract law at 349 ff., but exaggerating the discretion of Member States in transposing mandatory EU directives also via default rules, at 363.

relationship between default and mandatory provisions is just the opposite, with default provisions providing the rule and mandatory provisions the exception.

EU civil law, to the regret of many observers who do not seem to understand the competence limits of the EU under the principle of conferral (Article 5(1) and (2) TEU), consists of a number of not always systematic and in many cases incoherent provisions of mandatory and exceptionally default nature. The development of "general principles" must therefore take this somewhat haphazard nature of EU civil law as *function-oriented regulatory law* into account. It does not however mean that there are no general characteristics which could not be used to interpret these provisions and to fill gaps in the sense mentioned above. Caution however is necessary: the principles must not be used to extend the scope of application of the "generalised provisions". The Charter makes it clear that the rights to be respected and the principles to be observed therein may not be used to establish new powers or to modify the EU's existing ones (Article 51(2)). This of course does not exempt both EU and implementing Member State law from conforming to these principles and being subject to judicial control, as mentioned above (0.6).

0.10   This study is deliberately limited to the *acquis communautaire*, that is to general principles not of civil law in the EU or of "principles common to the Member States" based on a comparative analysis (the so-called *acquis commun*),[44] but to the specific contribution of civil law provisions of EU law, whether primary or secondary law in the "shadow" of the EU Charter of Fundamental Rights. The *acquis commun* has been intensely developed through a number of initiatives of European and international civil and comparative law scholars and institutions. Of particular note are the so-called Principles of European Contract Law (PECL) which were elaborated under the chairmanship of the well-known Danish law professor Ole Lando.[45] In the international arena, UNIDROIT developed its Principles of International Commercial Contracts (PICL) and published a third edition in 2010.[46] Finally, because of its role in advocating the development of an EU civil law, and as a sort of much-extended follow-up to PECL and PICL, a Study Group on a European Civil Code, together with the Acquis Group, was invited by the EU Commission to prepare a Draft Common Frame of Reference (DCFR) (details at 6.6). Under the chief editorship of Christian von Bar, an interim outline edition was published in 2008 and an

---

[44]   For an explanation of this difference see N. Jansen, 'Legal Pluralism in Europe', in: L. Niglia, *Pluralism and European Private Law*, 2013, 109 at 121.

[45]   O. Lando/H. Beale (eds.), *Principles of European Contract Law*, Vols I and II, 2000; O. Lando et al. (eds.), *ibid.*, Vol III, 2003.

[46]   S. Vogenauer, 'Die UNIDROIT-Grundregeln von 2010', ZEuP 2013, 7; for a comment on earlier versions see S. Vogenauer/J. Kleinheisterkamp (eds.), *Commentary on PICL*, 2009.

outline edition, complemented by a full edition, in 2009.[47] Jansen[48] comments on these different initiatives as follows:

> "[T]here can be no doubt anymore that there is a new European law emerging from these two processes. It is a matter of standpoint whether the Europeanisation of private law is seen primarily as the introduction of a new – pointillist, though formally binding – *supra*-national system of private law (*acquis communautaire*), or whether it is understood as an informal reconstructive continuation of former private law discourses of the European *ius commune (acquis commun)*."

Emphasis in the following study will be put on the *acquis communautaire*, in particular with the intention of developing general principles with constitutional value of their own, and which may be used to interpret existing EU civil law, to fill gaps and to eventually review its legality. This does not preclude references to the *acquis commun* as described by Jansen, for example in developing an EU-specific "good faith" principle (see Chapter 7); however, the competence limits for creating a genuine, fully fledged EU civil law must be respected in this context, to which I will now briefly turn.

5. THE COMPETENCE DILEMMA OF EU CIVIL LAW

0.11 There is agreement that there is no general competence for the EU to regulate civil law matters, for instance by adopting a general contract law, a code of obligations, or even a general civil code.[49] EU competence is function- and not topic- or system-oriented. As far as elements of civil law in the context of this study of EU contract law and civil liability are concerned, the four most important enabling provisions under the TFEU with respect to the preceding parallel or modified provisions under the Maastricht and Amsterdam regimes have been used:

- Article 114 TFEU concerning the establishment and function of the internal market, mostly with relation to consumer contracting, but also in a much more limited scope in relation to some B2B contracts;
- Article 153 TFEU on social policy;

---

[47]   C. von Bar/E. Clive/H. Schulte-Nölke (eds.), *Principles, Definitions and Model Rules of European Private Law*, Vols I-VI, 2009.

[48]   *Supra* note 44, at 125.

[49]   S. Weatherill, 'Competence and European Private Law', in: C. Twigg-Flesner (ed.), *European Union Private Law*, 2010, 58, referring to "competence sensitivity" at 65 and insisting on the "constitutional constraints" of the proponents of a "European private law" at 69. More ambitious is H. Collins, *The European Civil Code*, 2008, ignoring questions of competence and trying to develop common principles of private law based on a "European Economic Constitution" linked to social justice, at 89. However, this is not the place to go into a deeper argument about this project.

- Article 157/19 TFEU concerning provisions on non-discrimination in employment and consumption; and
- Article 81 concerning conflict of law regulations under the heading of "judicial cooperation on civil matters".

It is not the intention of this study to go deeper into the very controversial and in fact redundant competence discussion. Suffice to say that the measures referred to in this study have withstood judicial challenge despite some criticism in the literature, for example on a "competence creep" in consumer protection[50] and on limiting working time as part of social policy (2.2).[51] The "warning" in the tobacco advertising judgment[52] of an overly broad extension of EU competences should however be remembered, even if the case itself was not directly concerned with EU civil law:

> "To construe that article [100a EEC, now Article 114 TFEU] as meaning that it vests in the Community legislature a general power to regulate the internal market would not only be contrary to the express wording of the provisions cited above but would also be incompatible with the principle embodied in Article 3b of the EC Treaty [now Article 5 TEU] that the powers of the Community [Union] are limited to those specifically conferred on it. Moreover, a measure adopted on the basis of Article 100a of the Treaty must genuinely have as its object the improvement of the conditions for the establishment and functioning of the internal market. If a mere finding of disparities between national rules and of the abstract risk of obstacles to the exercise of fundamental freedoms or of distortions of competition liable to result there from were sufficient to justify the choice of Article 100a as a legal basis, judicial review of compliance with the proper legal basis might be rendered nugatory. The Court would then be prevented from discharging the function entrusted to it by Article 164 of the EC Treaty (now Article 220 EC) of ensuring that the law is observed in the interpretation and application of the Treaty."

The Court's "warning" can also be extended to legislation on general civil law matters. Under the measures discussed in this study, there seems to be no danger in this regard. However, even where competence exists, its use must still obey certain general constitutional principles, in particular the proportionality principle of Article 5(4) TEU and Article 52(1) of the Charter. This will be discussed further in relation to recent initiatives on a Common European Sales Law (CESL) in Chapter 6 (6.12–6.19).

---

[50] S. Weatherill, *EU Consumer Law and Policy*, 2005, 14 and 72, on the problem of a "competence creep" of the EU.

[51] See case C-84/94 *UK v Council* [1996] ECR I-5755.

[52] Case C-376/98 *Germany v Parliament and Council* [2000] ECR I-8419, paras 83–84.

6. WHY SEVEN PRINCIPLES?

0.12   The reader may wonder why this study has discovered *seven* principles of EU civil law? I am not attached to any magical number like T.E. Lawrence's "Seven Pillars of Wisdom", nor would I contest any criticism telling me that there are more or fewer principles. It should not be forgotten that the structure and content of these principles are somewhat different, which may be explained by their origin and function, even if they can now be more or less found in the Charter.

–   Principle 1 (framed autonomy), principle 2 (protection of the weaker party) and principle 3 (non-discrimination) are part of substantive EU law, mainly contract law. They may to some extent contradict each other, as will be explained in more detail in the relevant chapters, and may need to be balanced against each other, notably the concept of autonomy vs. the need to protect the weaker party and to avoid discrimination in contracting.
–   Principle 4 (effectiveness), together with the principle of equivalence, which is an "old acquaintance" of EU law, has mostly to do with procedural matters but can also – in my opinion should be – extended to cover substantive and remedial matters.
–   Principle 5 (balancing) and principle 6 (proportionality) are primarily concerned with methodological questions. The first has more to do with judicial interpretation and application of EU civil law, the second with legal-political questions on the future of a (questionable) codified or optional EU civil law, in particular sales law, both in a critical and in a positive sense.
–   Principle 7 (good faith) may only be an emerging principle – or may not be a principle at all. But there are already, in my opinion, elements to it that may one day develop into a more coherent principle, depending on the further development of EU civil law, in particular the case law of the ECJ.

CHAPTER 1

THE PRINCIPLE
OF "FRAMED" AUTONOMY

Contents

Bibliography 17
1. Freedoms framed by law. 18
2. Fundamental freedoms, autonomy and public interest restrictions 21
   2.1. Free movement of goods and freedom of contract. 21
   2.2. Freedom to provide services 22
   2.3. Free movement of capital 23
   2.4. Free movement of persons and freedom of contract 24
   2.5. Limitations on the guarantee of autonomy under primary
        Union law 24
   2.6. The public interest proviso allowing limitations on the free
        movement provisions by Member State: some examples 25
3. Freedom of contract as fundamental yet limited right and principle. 28
   3.1. Recognition of freedom of contract as a fundamental right
        before the adoption of the Charter 28
   3.2. EU Charter of Fundamental Rights 29
4. Competition law and autonomy 30
   4.1. Provisions against restrictions of competition by contract 30
   4.2. Contractual effect of nullity under Article 101(2) 30
   4.3. Enforcing cooperation agreements as a precondition of
        competition. 31
   4.4. Limited scope of application of competition rules. 32
   4.5. Competition law and collective autonomy 32
5. Conclusion: framing of autonomy under welfarism aspects – going
   beyond the traditional approach? 34

Bibliography

G. Alpa, 'Party autonomy and freedom of contract today', EBLRev 2010, 119; C. Barnard, *EU Employment Law*, 4th ed. 2012; J. Baquero Cruz, 'Free movement and private autonomy', ELRev 1999, 603; J. Basedow, 'Freedom of Contract in the EU', ERPrL 2008, 901; J.M. Broeckman, *A Philosophy of European Law*, 1999; D. Caruso, 'Black Lists and Private Autonomy in EU Contracts Law', in:

D. Leczykiewicz/S. Weatherill (eds.), *The Involvement of EU Law in Private Law Relationships*, 2013, 291; H. Collins, 'The constitutionalisation of European private law as a path to social justice?', in: H.-W. Micklitz (ed.), *Social Justice in EU Private Law*, 2011, 133; H. Collins, 'Social Dumping, Multi-level Governance and Private Law Employment Relationships', in: D. Leczykiewicz/S. Weatherill (eds.), *The Involvement of EU Law in Private Law Relationships*, 2013, 223 A. Colombi Ciacci, 'Party autonomy as a fundamental right in the European Union', ERCL 2010, 303; G. Davis, 'Freedom of Contract and the Horizontal Effect of Free Movement Law', in: D. Leczykiewicz/S. Weatherill (eds.), *The Involvement of EU Law in Private Law Relationships*, 2013, 53; S. Grundmann/W. Kerber/ S. Weatherill (eds.), *Party Autonomy and the Role of Information in the Internal Market*, 2001; A. Hartkamp, *European Law and National Private Law*, 2012; N. Helberger et al., 'Digital Content Contracts for Consumers', JCP 2013, 37; M. Hesselink, 'The General Principles of Civil Law: Their Nature, Role and Legitimacy', in: D. Leczykiewicz/S. Weatherill (eds.), *The Involvement of EU Law in Private Law Relationships*, 2013, 131; H.-W. Micklitz (ed.), *Social Justice in EU Private Law*, 2011; H.-W. Micklitz, *Brauchen Unternehmen und Verbraucher eine neue Architektur, Gutachten 69. Dt.-Juristentag München*, 2012; H.-W. Micklitz/N. Reich/P. Rott, *Understanding EU Consumer Law*, 2009; L. Moccia (ed.), *The Making of European Private Law: Why, How, What, Who*, 2013; P.-C. Müller-Graff (ed.), *Gemeinsames Privatrecht in der Europäischen Gemeinschaft*, 1999; L. Niglia (ed.), *Pluralism and European Private Law*, 2013; N. Reich, *Bürgerrechte in der Europäischen Union*, 1999; N. Reich, 'Crisis or Future of European Consumer Law?', in: *Yearbook of Consumer Law 2009*, 2010, 3; N. Reich, 'The public/private divide in European law', in: H.-W. Micklitz/F. Cafaggi, *European Private Law after the Common Frame of Reference*, 2010, 56; O. Remien, *Zwingendes Vertragsrecht und Grundfreiheiten des EG-Vertrages*, 2003; K. Riesenhuber, *Europäisches Privatrecht*, 2nd ed. 2006; K. Riesenhuber, *European Employment Law*, 2012: V. Roppo, 'From Consumer Contracts to Asymmetric Contracts', ERCL 2009, 304; D. Schiek, *Economic and Social Integration*, 2012; R. Schulze/H Schulte-Nölke, *European Private Law – Current Status and Perspectives*, 2011; A. Somek, *Individualism: An essay on the authority of the European Union*, 2008; E. Steindorff, *EG-Vertrag und Privatrecht*, 1996; Study Group on Social Justice in European Private Law, Social Justice in European Contract Law: A Manifesto, ELJ 2004, 653; K. Tonner/K. Fangerow, 'Directive 2011/83 on consumer rights: a new approach to European consumer law?', EUVR 2012, 67; S. Weatherill, *EU Consumer Law and Policy*, 2005, 2nd ed. 2013; C. Wendehorst, 'The "Legal Basis" of European Private Law in the Light of EU Constitutionalisation', in: L. Moccia (ed.), *The Making of European Private Law: Why, How, What, Who*, 2013, 33; T. Wilhelmsson et al. (eds.), *Private Law and the Many Cultures of Europe*, 2007; T. Wilhelmsson, 'Varieties of Welfarism in European Contract Law', ELJ 2004, 712.

1. FREEDOMS FRAMED BY LAW

1.1 Primary European Union law originally did not expressly guarantee the autonomy of economic actors (the active market citizen), but it presupposed it in its legal rules.[1] Article 3(3) TFEU requires as the basis for the internal market "a highly competitive social market economy". European Union law is not a comprehensive legal order, but builds on the legal systems of the Member States. Every liberal legal order has the autonomy of private parties as its basic

---

[1]   P.-C. Müller-Graff, in: S. Grundmann et al., *Party autonomy and the role of information in the internal market*, 2001, 135–150; A. Hartkamp, *European Law and National Private Law*, 2012, §139.

philosophy,[2] and it had therefore not been necessary for the ECJ to define autonomy explicitly as a fundamental principle. An open market economy can only exist if actors can freely decide whether to enter markets or not, and, if so, when and how. On the other hand, on the demand side, potential customers (whether businesses or consumers) should be free to choose the products, services and suppliers at the prices and conditions they prefer. *Freedom of decision* for active market citizens and *freedom of choice* for consumers and customers are two of the governing principles of a liberal market system.

These freedoms are supplemented by the *freedom of contract*, now recognised as a fundamental right (1.13). Freedom of contract as framed by EU law has positive and negative aspects.

It is *positive* insofar as freedom of contract implies the freedom to choose with whom one wants to enter into contractual negotiations (and ultimately contracts) and freedom as to the terms of the contract (such matters as price and the quality of products and services offered and purchased, and the freedom to decide what will constitute valid performance of the contract).

However, it is *negative* insofar as (in contrast to formerly socialist economies)[3] one cannot normally be forced to enter into any contract; parties may opt out of Member State contract law by means of choice of law and jurisdiction clauses (at least to the extent that the rules of the relevant Member State legal system of contract law are not mandatory), and usually the content of their contracts will not be prescribed by the state or other third party.[4]

1.2 Freedom of contract is a general principle in the national laws of the Member States, and underlies (though it is not explicitly stated to underlie) primary Union law. This is due to the historical development of the Union from an economic Community, and to Union law not being a complete and coherent system of law based, in part at least, on the common legal traditions of the Member States.

If a party who is in breach of contract is forced by law to make specific performance of its contractual obligations or to pay the other party compensation (damages) for the breach, this consequence is not determined by an imposed rule, but is the logical result of the free will of the parties. Therefore, *pacta sunt servanda* as a fundamental rule of contract law is not the imposition

---

[2] K. Riesenhuber, *Europäisches Vertragsrecht*, 2006, §4, II.

[3] For a discussion in the historical perspective cf. N. Reich, *Sozialismus und Zivilrecht*, 1972; for an analysis of developments after the fall of socialism, see N. Reich, *Transformation of contract law in new Member countries*, 2004, and O. Remien, *Zwingendes Vertragsrecht und Grundfreiheiten des EG-Vertrages*, 2003.

[4] Other than in very limited cases, as in the case of electricity distributors, telecommunications services providers, etc. where, for reasons of user protection, there will be a universal service obligation including a right to non-discriminatory access, and contract terms to be applied by the providers of such services will generally be prescribed by law; see 3.19.

of a mandatory rule, but is the realisation of the free will of the parties themselves. In *Société thermale*,[5] the Court explicitly referred to the general principles of civil law:

> "In accordance with the general principles of civil law, each contracting party is bound to honour the terms of its contract and to perform its obligations thereunder. The obligation to fulfil the contract does not therefore arise from the conclusion, specifically for that purpose, of another agreement. Nor does the obligation of full contractual performance depend on the possibility that otherwise compensation or a penalty for delay may be due, or on the lodging of security or a deposit: that obligation arises from the contract itself."

In *VZ Hamburg/O2*,[6] which concerned rounding rules disadvantaging the consumer on the occasion of the transition to the euro, the Court insisted on the "principle of continuity of contracts" unless otherwise agreed by the parties.

Whilst the *Acquis* Principles (0.11) define the term "contract" in Article 4:101 and the "conclusion" of a contract in Article 4:102, autonomy is not mentioned explicitly. The Draft Common Frame of Reference (DCFR: 0.12), however, which is based on the legal systems of the Member States as well as the existing *acquis*, refers to freedom of contract as a general principle in rule II. – I:102, restricted only by good faith, fair dealing and other mandatory rules (7.15).

1.3 Autonomy and its corollary, freedom of contract, are "framed"[7] by EU civil law by being both guaranteed and limited. "Autonomy" is a general principle of EU law, as will be shown later (1.13), but is to some extent limited by legal rules of primary and secondary law protecting objectives which are regarded as having a higher or at least equal ranking. The most important ones are imposed on the one hand by *EU competition law* (1.14), and on the other hand by the laws protecting the *weaker party to a contract* mostly in EU labour and consumer law as part of the "social"[8] in the market economy according to Article 3(3) TEU (2.1), as well as by legislation *combating discrimination in civil law relations* (3.1). In addition, national law which restricts autonomy must be considered in this respect, in particular laws that relate to the fundamental freedoms which presuppose freedom of contract for the parties, but that can be restricted by Member States under the non-discrimination, public interest and proportionality

---

5   Case C-277/05 *Société thermale d'Eugénie-les-Bains v Ministère de l'Économie, des Finances et de l'Industrie* [2007] ECR I-6428, para 24; for a discussion, see M. Hesselink, 'The General Principles of Civil Law: Their Nature, Role and Legitimacy', in: D. Leczykiewicz/S. Weatherill (eds.), *The Involvement of EU Law in Private Law Relationships*, 2013, 131 at 133.

6   Case C-19/03 *VZ HH v O2* [2004] ECR I-8183, para 54.

7   The concept of framing goes back to a seminal paper by E. Goffman, *Frame Analysis – An Essay on the Organisation of Experience*, 1974, 345: "All frames involve expectations of a normative kind".

8   See contributions to H.-W. Micklitz (ed.), *Social Justice in EU Private Law*, 2011; D. Schiek, *Economic and Social Integration*, 2012.

tests (1.9). More precisely, the *general principle of autonomy* cannot be theoretically and practically conceived without the existence of the *countervailing principles of its limitations* under public interest criteria which try to avoid abuses by a unilateral exercise of these freedoms by the stronger party to a contract, or to the detriment of competition and open markets. The task of the legal order will be to find the right balance between these two principles (Chapter 5). This is a permanent challenge to both EU and Member State law, led by the case law of the ECJ, which will be of particular interest in this context and will be analysed throughout this study.

2. FUNDAMENTAL FREEDOMS, AUTONOMY AND PUBLIC INTEREST RESTRICTIONS

2.1. FREE MOVEMENT OF GOODS AND FREEDOM OF CONTRACT

1.4   As is well known, Article 34 TFEU (ex-Article 28 EC) is one of the fundamental rules of the European economic constitution in imposing the principle of open markets for products against unreasonable and disproportionate Member State restrictions. The Article says nothing about freedom of contract; it simply takes it for granted. Freedom of contract is a necessary precondition for the free movement of goods. To enable the free movement of goods, an economic actor must be free to choose contractual partners in another Member State. If s/he were not able to negotiate the contents of the contract, its price or the terms of the agreement, as well as the applicable law and jurisdiction in case of disputes, then there would be no free movement of goods purchased under any contract. Ownership of goods (in a commercial context, at least) can only be transferred by contract. Union law is therefore in principle hostile to any restrictions on the contractual freedom of the parties if these restrictions come into the scope of application of the EU. One example is the *Libro* case, which concerned Austrian provisions of the obligation of importers to sell books at prices fixed in the country of publication (Germany); they were held to be in violation of Article 28 EC (now Article 34 TFEU).[9]

On the other hand, the ECJ has said that the free movement rules do not prevent contracting parties from taking legitimate steps to avoid the applicability of some system of Member State law which restricts their contractual freedom. In the *Alsthom* case,[10] the Court was concerned with the question of whether the

---

[9]   Case C-531/07 *Fachverband der Buch- und Medienwirtschaft v LIBRO Handelsgesellschaft* [2009] ECR I-3717.

[10]   Case C-339/89 *Alsthom Atlantique v Compagnie de construction mécanique Sulzer SA* [1991] ECR I-107, para 17.

French rules in the sale of goods law, which impose strict liability on the seller for defects in a product in the chain of distribution, amount to a restriction on free movement of goods in the sense of Articles 34 TFEU (ex-Article 28 EC) and 35 TFEU (ex-Article 29 EC). The Court insisted that the parties in an international business-to-business (B2B) sale of goods contract are generally free to choose the system of law applicable to their contractual relations, and can thus avoid being subject to strict French law on liability in a chain of contracts (*action directe*). This amounts to an implicit recognition of the parties' freedom to contract, at least in a commercial context. If the parties are free to avoid a Member State rule restricting their freedom to contract as regards applicable terms (which in the *Alsthom* case the ECJ said they were, as they were free to choose that their contract should be governed by the law of some other Member State which did not contain such rules), there is no need for Union law intervention. On the other hand, where Member State law imposes mandatory rules which cannot be avoided by choosing a more liberal law, there may be a conflict with the freedom of movement rules.[11] Such mandatory rules are only permissible, however, if they protect an overriding public interest which must be applied by respecting the proportionality principle, for example restrictions imposed on the sale of certain types of goods (1.9).

2.2. FREEDOM TO PROVIDE SERVICES

1.5   The Union law rules on the freedom to provide services are closer to the general principle of freedom of contract, because the contents of a service (and especially in the case of financial services), are usually determined by the contract itself. The only requirement of Union law is that it will only apply if the service is being provided in return for remuneration,[12] although it is not necessary that this remuneration be part of the contract itself if a third party is financing the service.[13] If Member State law contains mandatory rules on the contents of certain services, or restricts the provision of or access to certain cross-border services by giving a monopoly on them to state-run bodies (e.g. lotteries),[14] or imposes requirements on the qualification of service providers, for

---

[11]   In case C-93/92 *CMC Motorradcenter v P.B.* [1993] ECR I-5009, the Court found that the (mandatory) German principle of *culpa in contrahendo* as developed by case law cannot be regarded as an impediment to the free movement of goods, even if they force the seller to inform the consumer about the difficulties of enforcing contractual guarantees for a motor cycle imported from another EU country by way of parallel trade.

[12]   Case C-159/90 *The Society for the Protection of Unborn Children v Grogan* [1991] ECR I-4685.

[13]   Case 352/88 *Bond van Adverteerders v The Netherlands State* [1988] ECR I-2085, concerning broadcasting services.

[14]   Cases C-316/07 *Markus Stoß* [2010] ECR I-8099; C-46/08 *Carmen Media* [2010] ECR I-8175, concerning the German state monopoly on lotteries; these restrictions may however be justified by proportionate and coherent public policy reasons, which the ECJ found absent in

example that the provider must have a prior authorisation, registration or licence of some sort, then this amounts *both* to a restriction on the free provision of services according to Article 46 TFEU (ex-Article 49 EC) *and* to a restriction of freedom to contract usually governed by Member State law unless justified under a proportionate public interest test (1.9). The rules on open markets and on freedom to contract coincide whenever an economic activity is concerned. The freedom to provide services is not only granted in the objective interest of establishing an internal market, but also as a *subjective right of the economic actors* themselves. Union law therefore contains an indirect yet powerful tool to recognise the freedom of contract (including the freedom to enter into a contract, to negotiate price and other conditions).

2.3. FREE MOVEMENT OF CAPITAL

1.6   Although the original EEC Treaty contained provisions relating to the free movement of capital, the rules were not directly applicable.[15] On the other hand, from an early stage the Court recognised *freedom of payment* as a necessary corollary to the free movement of goods and services.[16] This is of course in line with the general yet implicit recognition of freedom of contract. If one party is to be free to offer its goods and services for sale and to agree to provide them, the other party must be free not only to accept (or reject) these at a negotiated price, but must also be permitted to actually pay the negotiated price for what that party has agreed to buy. Free movement of goods and services would be paralysed if it were not supplemented by the freedom to make payment. Member State restrictions on the free flow of payments to fulfil cross-border transactions are contrary to the free movement rules themselves. However, this ancillary freedom is only concerned with the performance of existing contracts (e.g. contracts for the sale and purchase of goods), not the free flow of capital as such for investment and/or speculation purposes.

Directly applicable rules on free movement of capital have only been introduced into primary Union law relatively recently. The Maastricht Treaty rephrased Article 73b, now Article 63 TFEU (ex-Article 56 EC) and introduced directly applicable rules on the free movement of capital. This includes all investment and monetary transactions on capital markets.[17] It implies, furthermore, the freedom to purchase and sell real estate property in any

---

the German case; see the abundant and not always clear case law in N. Reich et al., *Understanding EU Internal Market Law*, 3rd ed. forthcoming, para 7.19.

[15]   Case 203/80 *Casati* [1981] ECR 2595.

[16]   Cases 26 and 286/83 *Luisi and Carbone v Ministero del Tesoro* [1984] ECR 377.

[17]   Case C-478/98 *Commission v Belgium* [2000] ECR I-7587.

Member State[18] unless certain restrictions are exceptionally allowed by the Treaty. Most of the Accession Treaties for new member countries contain restrictions on the acquisition of agricultural land, limiting it to nationals of the acceding state. Other than for exemptions of that type (which represent "one-off" political compromises), the right to hold property (including intellectual property) is recognised as a fundamental right, which is protected as a general principle of Union law[19] and as an explicit right in the Charter of Fundamental Rights in Article 17 (1.13).

2.4. FREE MOVEMENT OF PERSONS AND FREEDOM OF CONTRACT

1.7   The right of free movement granted to citizens of the Union implies the right to enter into any contractual relationship in order to make the right to free movement effective. Conversely, it forbids all discrimination based on nationality, even if imposed by collective agreements based on private law.[20] The main area this freedom is concerned with is employment contracts, but it can be extended to ancillary agreements such as agreements in relation to housing, maintenance, education, etc. If a Member State's law or a collective agreement imposes a language requirement on candidates for employment, they cannot force those candidates to take the language test only through an institution accredited in that state.[21] This case shows very clearly the close link between open markets, freedom of choice and freedom of contract.

2.5. LIMITATIONS ON THE GUARANTEE OF AUTONOMY UNDER PRIMARY UNION LAW

1.8   Stemming from the development of the Union as an economic community, primary Union law is mostly concerned with the economic aspects of autonomy, not with the personal and philosophical aspects.[22] However, it can be shown that the broad interpretation of Union freedoms also contains a personal element. This can be seen as an individualistic concept of law and not just an economic

---

18   Case C-423/98 *Albore* [2000] ECR I-5965: for a recent application see joined cases C-197 + C-203/11 *E. Libert et al v Gouvernement flamand* [2013] ECR I-(05.05.2013) concerning national (Flemish) legislation making the transfer of land subject to the condition that there exists a "sufficient connection" between the prospective buyer and the target commune with a critical analysis of this requirement under proportionality aspects,.

19   Case C-479/04 *Laserdisken* [2006] ECR I-8089, para 65; Case C-275/06 *Productores de Música de España (Promusicae) v Telefónica de España SAU* [2008] ECR I-271, para 62.

20   Case C-415/93 *ABSL v Bosman* [1995] ECR I-4921.

21   Case C-281/98 *Roman Angonese v Casa di Risparmio di Bolzano* [2000] ECR I-4139.

22   J.M. Broeckman, *A Philosophy of European Law*, 1999, 106 ff.

one.[23] The right of Union citizens to free movement contains an implicit recognition of contractual autonomy, without which this right would, as has been pointed out above, be economically worthless. Restrictions of this right need a specific justification under Union law.

This autonomy is not only guaranteed in B2B (business-to-business) relations, but also in B2C (business-to-consumer) relations. It is mostly concerned with cross-border transactions, and therefore does not usually apply to "purely internal situations" – a somewhat confused concept due to the ongoing integration of national markets in the EU (example at 1.10).[24] But it is hardly conceivable that Member States would deny their own citizens such essential rights as autonomy when they are obliged to guarantee those for citizens of other EU Member States. However, so-called "reverse discrimination" does not come under the scope of application of Union law,[25] unless the restrictive Member State rule tends to discourage citizens from other EU countries from making investments in this country.[26]

2.6. THE PUBLIC INTEREST PROVISO ALLOWING LIMITATIONS ON THE FREE MOVEMENT PROVISIONS BY MEMBER STATE: SOME EXAMPLES

1.9 Member State law may contain limitations on the freedom of contract that may contradict the fundamental freedoms as described above if they have a cross-border element. These limitations may concern the object of the contract and its price, the persons contracting, the fairness of contract terms, resolution of disputes and the like. EU law will in many cases not have harmonised nor have set uniform rules on standards for defining the objectives and inherent limitations for the entire internal market. Member State law will be called upon to justify such restrictions if they have an impact on the internal market.

A large part of the ECJ case law has been charged with the never-ending task of defining the criteria for allowing such restrictions. This is not the place to go into detail about cross-border contracting in the EU. The basis for this case law is still the ECJ's so-called *Gebhard* test:[27]

> "It follows, however, from the Court's case law that national measures liable to hinder or make less attractive the exercise of fundamental freedoms guaranteed by the Treaty must fulfil four conditions: they must be applied in a non-discriminatory

---

23   N. Reich, *Bürgerrechte*, 1999, 158 ff.
24   Case C-332/90 *Steen v Deutsche Bundespost* [1992] ECR I-341.
25   Case 14/68 *Walt Wilhelm and others v Bundeskartellamt* [1969] ECR 1; Case 355/85 *Driancourt v M. Cognet* [1986] ECR 3231, para 10.
26   See the *Libert* case, *supra* note 18 at para 47.
27   Case C-55/94 *Gebhard v Consiglio dell'Ordine degli Advocati e procuratori di Milano* [1995] ECR I-4165, para 37.

manner; they must be justified by imperative requirements in the general interest; they must be suitable for securing the attainment of the objective which they pursue; and they must not go beyond what is necessary in order to attain it."

This test has in particular been used to justify restrictions on contractual autonomy in order to protect the weaker party as a justified public interest, unless this protection is already guaranteed exhaustively by EU law. The main criteria for determining the legitimacy of such restrictions has been the *proportionality test*. Even if a directive provides for minimum harmonisation, any extension by Member States must still respect fundamental freedoms, as the Court expressly stated in the *Gysbrechts* case,[28] in doing so precluding state legislation that did not allow the trader to take the credit card number of the consumer as security before the lapse of the withdrawal period in a distance contract; however the prohibition of prepayment of the purchase price was said to be in accordance with EU law.

1.10 Another example concerning the freedom to provide services and its impact on contracting has been *Cipolla*.[29] That case concerned the compatibility of Italian minimum fees for lawyers with Article 49 EC (now Article 56 TFEU) and indirectly was a matter of the extent and limitations of contractual freedoms. Even though the reference only concerned a "purely internal matter", the Court found that minimum rates may deter foreign lawyers from entering the Italian market, and potential clients from asking services from them, thus limiting their freedom of choice (para 60). This restriction may however be justified by overriding concerns of protection of consumers, in particular recipients of legal services, and the safeguarding of the proper administration of justice. The question of proportionality has to be decided by the national court based on a number of factors outlined by the ECJ, for example the asymmetry of information between 'client-consumers' and lawyers which makes a judgment on the quality of service difficult (para 68). In the later case *Commission v Italy* the Court found the Commission did not show that the Italian provisions on maximum fees for lawyers were an impediment to foreign lawyers' market access.[30]

Another example concerns Member State regulation imposing mandatory insurance. A case brought by the Commission against Italy[31] centred on an Italian law imposing an obligation on (foreign) car insurance providers to conclude a contract of third party cover with car owners in Italy. Even though this obligation to contract, applying without distinction to Italian and foreign insurance companies, was regarded as a restriction in the sense of Articles 43

---

[28]   Case C-205/07 *Gysbrechts* [2008] ECR I-9947.
[29]   Cases C-94 and 202/04 *Frederico Cipolla et al v Rosaria Fazari, née Portolese et al* [2006] ECR I-11421.
[30]   Case C-565/08 *Commission v Italy* [2011] ECR I-2101.
[31]   Case C-518/06 *Commission v Italy* [2009] ECR I-3491.

and 49 EC (now Article 49/56 TFEU) because it affected market access for undertakings from other member countries (para 64), it could still be justified by "social protection objectives", namely to protect potential victims of car accidents who should not be forced to rely on a guarantee fund. The Court went on to say:[32]

> "The situation relating to road traffic, and to the relevant public interest objectives in that area, varies from one Member State to another. Consequently, Member States must be recognised as having some discretion in that area. Whilst it is true that it is for a Member State which relies on an imperative requirement to justify a restriction within the meaning of the EC Treaty to demonstrate that its rules are appropriate and necessary to attain the legitimate objective being pursued, that burden of proof cannot be so extensive as to require the Member State to prove, positively, that no other conceivable measure could enable that objective to be attained under the same conditions."

Language requirements as a condition for the validity of an employment contract may be justified by the concern to protect the local language, but they must still be proportionate, as the Court said in *Cas*:[33]

> "However, parties to a cross-border employment contract do not necessarily have knowledge of the official language of the Member State concerned. In such a situation, the establishment of free and informed consent between the parties requires those parties to be able to draft their contract in a language other than the official language of that Member State."

1.11   Within the broad concept of a restriction to the right of establishment, EU law as interpreted by the ECJ is opposed to any national rule that makes more difficult or less profitable the business exercise of a company established under Article 49/54 TFEU and that thereby restricts contracting. In *Caixa*[34] the Court first restated its principal approach to the freedom of establishment:

> "Article 43 EC requires the elimination of restrictions on the freedom of establishment. All measures which prohibit, impede or render less attractive the exercise of that freedom must be regarded as such restrictions."

This freedom is restricted by forbidding the newly established company from using a certain business model which thereby means that it cannot compete more effectively for customers, namely to pay remuneration for sight accounts. Even though this prohibition was not covered by secondary law, this business practice nevertheless comes under the protection of Article 43 EC (now Article 49 TFEU) unless such prohibition is justified "where it serves overriding

---

[32]   Ibid., para 84.
[33]   Case C-202/11 *Anton Cas v PSA Antwerp* [2013] ECR I-(16.04.2013), para 31.
[34]   Case C-442/02 *Caixa Bank France v Ministère de Finances* [2004] ECR I-8961, para 11.

requirements relating to the public interest, is suitable for securing the attainment of the objective it pursues and does not go beyond what is necessary in order to attain it".[35] The Court rejected the arguments of the French government relating to consumer protection and encouragement of medium- and long-term saving because a total ban on remuneration for sight accounts went beyond what was necessary to attain this objective. The Court insisted on the free choice of the consumer who could be offered sight accounts either without remuneration at no cost for banking services, or with remuneration but with charges for services previously provided free of charge, for example the issuing of cheques or bank cards. This choice is made impossible by the French regulation.

3. FREEDOM OF CONTRACT AS FUNDAMENTAL YET LIMITED RIGHT AND PRINCIPLE

3.1. RECOGNITION OF FREEDOM OF CONTRACT AS A FUNDAMENTAL RIGHT BEFORE THE ADOPTION OF THE CHARTER

1.12 There has been a debate as to whether the principle of freedom of contract can be regarded as a fundamental right in the sense of Article 6(2) TEU (ex-Article 6(2) EC). The ECHR does not expressly mention freedom of contract, and therefore has had little impact on contract law theory.[36] However, the ECHR protects property in Protocol No. 1. In doing so, it implicitly regards a contractual disposition of ownership as the normal legal way to acquire and use property. Property is not merely protected in a static sense, but also in the dynamic sense of its acquisition and use under contract. Protection of property would be very seriously lacking if contractual engagements undertaken in relation to property were not respected. The Court has in *Promusicae* expressly stated that fundamental rights do not just include the rights guaranteed in the Charter, but also "other general principles of Community law, such as the principle of proportionality".[37]

---

[35] Ibid., para 17.
[36] O. Remien, *supra* note 3, at 172–177.
[37] Case C-275/06 *Promusicae*, *supra* note 19, para 68; recently, this problem has also been analysed in the opinion of the Advocate General of 3 February 2011 in case C-403/08, paras 165 ff; in its judgment the Court does not refer to proportionality as a principle, but applies it: Joined Cases C-403/08 *Football Association Premier League Ltd v QC Leisure* and C-429/08 *Murphy v Media Protection Services Ltd* [2011] ECR I-9083.

3.2. EU CHARTER OF FUNDAMENTAL RIGHTS

1.13   Chapter II of the EU Charter is concerned with "freedom" and guarantees freedom of association (Article 12), the freedom to choose an occupation and the right to engage in work (Article 15), the freedom to conduct a business (Article 16), and the right to property (Article 17). All these freedoms are exercised by contractual engagements. Contracts are the dynamic form of putting to work the freedoms of economic and civil actors, whether they use their right to engage in work, to conduct a business, or to possess and use property.

Particularly interesting in this respect is the broad guarantee of the right to property which gives "everybody […] the right to own, use, dispose of and bequeath his or her lawfully acquired possessions". This right would be worthless without the dynamic element inherent in the freedom of contract as freedom to acquire goods and immovables, freedom to dispose of them by contract, freedom to enter into contracts and to refuse to contract with any person at the will of the owner. Expropriation, that is, the taking of property without contract, is strictly regulated and limited by a public interest test subject to fair compensation.

So, although there is no express mention of freedom of contract as a fundamental right, once again one finds that certain explicitly recognised freedoms assume that it exists and is respected. In this spirit, the ECJ it its *Sky* judgment wrote:[38]

> "The protection afforded by Article 16 of the Charter covers the freedom to exercise an economic or commercial activity, the freedom of contract and free competition, as is apparent from the explanations relating to that article, which, in accordance with the third subparagraph of Article 6(1) TEU and Article 52(7) of the Charter, have to be taken into consideration for the interpretation of the Charter. […] In addition, the freedom of contract includes, in particular, the freedom to choose with whom to do business, […] and the freedom to determine the price of a service."

This freedom of contract as a fundamental right and as a fundamental principle of EU law is subject to restrictions under the general clause of Article 52(1) of the Charter. Some of these potential restrictions are already inherent in EU law and the Charter itself, as will be shown in the following sections concerning competition law as well as the discussion of protection of weaker parties like workers and consumers in Chapter 2. It is therefore justified to talk of a principle of "*framed autonomy*" in EU civil law, to be elaborated in detail by a balancing test against possible restrictions and limitations both by the Union and by Member States. This framework exists within the EU system of fundamental freedoms, fundamental rights and general principles which also balance

---

[38]   Case C-283/11 *Sky Österreich v Österreichischer Rundfunk* [2013] ECR I-(22.01.2013), paras 42–43.

autonomy against privately imposed restrictions and have a deep impact on EU civil law, in particular contract law.

4. COMPETITION LAW AND AUTONOMY

4.1. PROVISIONS AGAINST RESTRICTIONS OF COMPETITION BY CONTRACT

1.14 Article 101 TFEU (ex-Article 81(1) EC) is the fundamental rule on the protection of competition. If this rule is violated by anti-competitive agreements, concerted practices or decisions of associations of undertakings and they do not fulfil the Article 101(3) exemption criteria, any contract or practice with this object or effect is said to be automatically void.[39] On the other hand, contracts promoting competition, for example by cooperation agreements on research and development, are in principle valid. One might say that the competition rules thereby contain an implicit (negative) recognition of the autonomy principle, insofar as the enforceability of contracts that do not serve anti-competitive purposes or have anti-competitive effects is concerned.

4.2. CONTRACTUAL EFFECT OF NULLITY UNDER ARTICLE 101(2)

1.15 The ECJ has made it clear that where the parts of an agreement that make it anti-competitive by object or effect can be separated from other parts that are not in breach of Article 101, the parts that are not affected should be allowed to stand and not be affected by a nullity under Article 101(2), provided they can be effectively separated.[40] The ECJ has also stated in clear terms that it is for national law (the applicable law of the contract under private international law provisions)[41] to decide whether, and if so how, that separation (or severance) of the "good" from the "bad" parts in the agreement should be achieved.[42] In limiting in that way the effects of the ban on anti-competitive agreements to merely a partial nullity of such agreements (where such separation is possible),[43] the ECJ tries to respect the contractual will of the parties so far as it considers it to be lawful. It will normally follow that all subsequent contracts concluded on

---

[39] Article 101(2) TFEU (ex-Article 81(2) EC); on its *ex officio* application see A. Hartkamp, *European Law and National Private Law*, 2012, para 127.
[40] Case 56/65 *Société Technique Minière v Maschinenbau Ulm* [1966] ECR 235; Case 319/82 *Société de Vente de Ciments et Bétons v Kerpen & Kerpen* [1983] ECR 4173, paras 11–12.
[41] Regulation Rome I No. 593/2008 [2008] OJ L 177/6.
[42] Case 56/65 *Société de Vente de Ciments*, *supra* note 40, paras 11–12.
[43] Case C-234/89 *Delimitis v Henninger-Bräu* [1991] ECR I-935, para 40.

the basis of anti-competitive agreements will be valid. Where there is no specific legislation in place, Union law interferes as little as possible with the contractual freedom of the parties and the principles of *pacta sunt servanda*, especially in B2B contracts.

4.3. ENFORCING COOPERATION AGREEMENTS AS A PRECONDITION OF COMPETITION

1.16 Competition law not only takes a negative view vis-à-vis contracts restraining competition, but either indirectly or directly exempts (within certain limits) certain horizontal or vertical cooperation agreements, sometimes even those made between competitors, from the competition rules. It has used the technique of so-called block exemptions to give cooperation partners, particularly in exclusive or selective distribution agreements as well as in franchising systems, a scheme to put their contracting out of reach of competition law sanctions, for example being annulled under Article 101(2) TFEU. Most of these "vertical agreements" will be exempt if they come under a certain market share threshold of 30%.[44] Only certain particularly relevant restrictions are black- or grey-listed: Article 4 black lists vertical price maintenance clauses, territorial restrictions and the like, while Article 5 grey lists conditional non-compete obligations. Recitals 10 and 11 justify this with the following words:

> "[V]ertical agreements containing certain types of severe restrictions of competition such as minimum and fixed resale-prices, as well as certain types of territorial protection, should be excluded from the benefit of the block exemption established by this Regulation irrespective of the market share of the undertakings concerned. In order to ensure access of or prevent collusion on the relevant market, certain conditions should be attached to the block exemption. To this end, the block exemption of non-compete obligations should be limited to obligations which do not exceed a defined duration."

As recital 7 makes clear, the exemptions and their limitations in Articles 4 and 5 are based on a balancing of "efficiency-enhancing effects" as long as they outweigh "any anti-competitive effects".

The express or implied exemption of certain types of cooperation agreements from the competition rules has been going on for some time and cannot be analysed in detail here. Not only is a new economic reasoning responsible for

---

[44] Regulation (EU) No. 330/2010 of 20 April 2010 [2010] OJ L 102/1; its importance for EU competition policy has been analysed by R. Wish/D. Bailey, 'Regulation 330/2010: The Commission's New Block Exemption for Vertical Agreements', CMLRev 2010, 1757.

this paradigm shift, but also a new understanding of autonomy.[45] Economic actors are given more freedom to regulate their relations between themselves, even if this provokes some – allegedly consumer-welfare enhancing – anti-competitive effects, while competition law is not seen as a limit on autonomy, but rather as a "long stop" against certain practices where freedoms are clearly used against public or third-party interests. Therefore, modern competition law is increasingly applied so as to limit its role to fighting certain hardcore restrictions such as price-fixing and market partitioning. At the same time, it leaves to the parties the freedom to determine their modes of cooperation themselves by autonomously limiting their freedom of action through anti-competition and exclusivity clauses.

4.4. LIMITED SCOPE OF APPLICATION OF COMPETITION RULES

1.17   Even when the competition rules apply against unilateral anti-competitive behaviour, the principle of freedom of contract is still respected. Thus under Article 102 TFEU it is not the existence of a business in a dominant position that is prohibited, but only certain types of behaviour of a dominant business. There has been some variation down the years as to the essence of what is permitted behaviour for a dominant undertaking: the Court in *Hoffmann-LaRoche* talked about one form of abuse being methods of trading "different from those which condition normal competition [...] on the basis of the transactions of commercial operators",[46] while the CFI (now General Court) in *Irish Sugar* referred to the right of the dominant business to take reasonable steps to protect its own commercial interests when they are attacked, but added that "[such protective action] must, at the very least, in order to be lawful, be based on criteria of economic efficiency and consistent with the interests of consumers".[47] The acknowledgement of autonomy within limits for the dominant business is, however, clear.

4.5. COMPETITION LAW AND COLLECTIVE AUTONOMY

1.18   Another field in which the interplay between autonomy and competition has been discussed is that of collective bargaining and the issue of whether

---

[45]   See D. Caruso, 'Black Lists and Private Autonomy in EU Contracts Law', in: D. Leczykiewicz/ S. Weatherill (eds.), *The Involvement of EU Law in Private Law Relationships*, 2013, 291 at 303.

[46]   Case 85/76 *Hoffmann-La Roche v Commission* [1979] ECR 461, para 91.

[47]   Case T-228/97 *Irish Sugar PLC v Commission* [1999] ECR II-2969, paras 112 and 189.

competition law applies in that field. The *Albany* case[48] concerned an obligation under a collective agreement of employers to provide supplementary pensions for all their relevant employees by means of compulsory affiliation to a sectoral pension scheme set up under the collective agreement and to which affiliation was in principle made compulsory under Dutch law. The question in that case was whether the agreement was compatible with competition rules. The arrangement prevented employers in the sector from offering more favourable pension arrangements than those provided by the collective scheme, and prevented other pension providers (e.g. insurance companies) from selling pensions in the sector. In a lengthy opinion based on comparative law analysis, AG Jacobs noted that there is no specific provision in the EC Treaty to exclude collective bargaining from the competition rules (as there is, for example, for certain agreements in the agriculture sector, for certain agreements relating to defence, etc.) nor that was Article 101(3) TFEU (ex-Article 81(3) EC) appropriate for the purpose. On the other hand, there are Treaty rules that encourage and support collective bargaining, which, he reasoned, make no sense unless there is also an underlying assumption that collective bargaining is in principle lawful under the competition rules. He reasoned, therefore, that Article 101 cannot have been intended to apply to collective agreements between employers and employees, at least when they are agreeing on the "core subjects" one would expect collective bargaining to deal with (wages, employment terms, the workplace environment, redundancies, etc.). In his view, therefore, due to the social nature of such an agreement, it is immune from Union competition law under certain circumstances, namely:

- if the parties are representatives of both sides of industry, not of one side only;
- the agreement is "concluded in good faith" (i.e. is not a hardcore cartel in disguise);
- the agreement deals with "core" collective bargaining matters; and
- the agreement has no direct effect on third parties (i.e. it does not affect employers' relations with suppliers, competing employers, customers or consumers).[49]

1.19 The Court is somewhat broader in its respect for collective autonomy, even where some restriction of competition is involved:[50]

"It is beyond question that certain restrictions of competition are inherent in collective agreements between organisations representing employers and workers.

---

[48]   Case C-67/96 *Albany Int. BV v Stichting Bedrijfspensioenfonds Textielindustrie* [1999] ECR I-5751.
[49]   Ibid., opinion of AG Jacobs of 28 January 1999, paras 169 and 186–194.
[50]   Ibid., judgment of 21 September 1999, paras 59–60.

However, the social policy objectives pursued by such agreements would be seriously undermined if management and labour were subject to Article [101(1)] when seeking jointly to adopt measures to improve conditions of work and employment [...] It therefore follows from an interpretation of the provisions of the Treaty as a whole which is both effective and consistent that agreements concluded in the context of collective negotiations between management and labour in pursuit of such (i.e. social policy) objectives must, by virtue of their nature and purpose, be regarded as falling outside the scope of Article 101 TFEU (ex-Article 81 EC)."

The Court implicitly recognised the priority of collective autonomy in the field of labour relations over competition rules, albeit within certain limits.[51] The later *Pavlov* case[52] makes it clear that this immunity relates only to collective bargaining in the traditional sense, not to rules of professional associations that have anti-competitive effects.

5. CONCLUSION: FRAMING OF AUTONOMY UNDER WELFARISM ASPECTS – GOING BEYOND THE TRADITIONAL APPROACH?

1.20 In order to allow some conclusions on the role, function and limitations of "framed autonomy" in EU civil law, I will make reference to a seminal paper by Thomas Wilhelmsson which appeared in 2004.[53] In his paper Wilhelmsson discusses a set of different "social justice" concepts and "welfare state" values "intruding" into traditional, market-oriented contract law based on autonomy as part of a general EU principle. These concepts and values are usually described using the traditional dichotomies of "liberal" vs. "social",[54] "individual autonomy" vs. "collective organisation",[55] "market complementary" vs. "market compensatory"[56] or "formal" vs. "substantive" elements[57] in European private law. In Wilhelmsson's view, each of the dichotomies refers to different aspect of a "socialisation" of contract law and is thus independent, but also overlaps with others. To take account of the somewhat unclear relationships between these dichotomies, Wilhelmsson distinguishes six main types ("schemes") of

---

51   For a discussion cf. M. Kiikeri, *Comparative legal reasoning*, 2001, 222–241.

52   Joined Cases C-180–185/98 *Pavel Pavlov et al v Stichting Pensioenfonds Medische Specialisten* [2000] ECR I-6451.

53   T. Wilhelmsson, 'Varieties of Welfarism in European Contract Law', ELJ 2004, 712; see C. Mak, *Fundamental Rights in European Contact Law*, 2008, at 286–289; N. Reich in: R. Schulze/H Schulte-Nölke, *European Private Law*, 2011, 57.

54   T. Wilhelmsson, 'Social Justice in European Contract Law: a Manifesto', ELJ 2004, 653.

55   D. Schiek, 'Is There a Social Ideal of the ECJ?', in: U. Neergard et al. (eds.), *The Role of Courts in Developing a European Social Model*, 2009, 63 at 96.

56   N. Reich, *Markt und Recht*, 1977, 198 and 217.

57   D. Kennedy, 'Form and Substance in Private Law Adjudication', Harvard Law Rev 1976, 561, at 616.

"welfarism in contract law" that correlate with different aims and instruments and are used to frame autonomy, allowing us to go beyond the traditional conception of autonomy.

Scheme	Objectives/Instruments
1. Market-rational welfarism	Regulation aimed at improving party autonomy and the function of the market mechanisms (e.g. information rules)
2. Market-correcting welfarism	Regulation aimed at rectifying outcomes of the market mechanism in order to promote acceptable contractual behaviour (e.g. substantive fairness rules)
3. Internally redistributive welfarism	Regulation aimed at redistributing benefits in favour of a group of weaker parties in a contractual relationship (e.g. rules affecting main subject matter of contract)
4. Externally redistributive welfarism	Regulation aimed at redistributing benefits in favour of the disadvantaged within a group of contract parties in similar situations (e.g. equality rules)
5. Need-rational welfarism	Regulation aimed at giving benefits to parties with special needs in comparison with other parties in similar situations (e.g. rules on social *force majeure*)
6. Public values welfarism	Regulation aimed at giving contract law protection to interests and values not related to the parties (e.g. protection of environmental values and human rights)

1.21   I will use the schemes (1) to (5) (scheme (6) will be omitted from our context because EU law so far has not dealt with this topic) in this and in the following chapters as analytical tools to find out, as set out in the introduction, the different dimensions of EU civil law. The book mostly looks at EU contract law and the provisions of civil liability. The areas covered will include *consumer law, non-discrimination law,* and the newly emerging contract law of *services of general economic interest* (SGEI), namely electronic communication and energy. *Employment law* will be covered, but not in detail, because we are told that it is a useful source for understanding the specifics of EU civil law.[58]

There will however be one important addition to the use of Wilhelmsson's scheme on in the areas of consumer, employment, non-discrimination and SGEI contract law. I will insist in particular on how far EU law – mostly secondary law in the form of directives – *intends to confer rights on individuals,* for example with regard to its (however limited) "horizontal direct effect" or to the interrelation between "rights and duties".[59]

---

[58]   For an excellent overview see N. Countouris, 'European Social Law as an Autonomous Legal Discipline', YEL 2009, 95.

[59]   N. Reich, 'The public/private divide in European law', in: H.-W. Micklitz/F. Cafaggi, *European Private Law after the Common Frame of Reference*, 2010, 56; id., 'Rights without Duties? The interrelation between rights and duties in EU law', YEL 2010, 112.

I suggest the following correlation between what I will call the "Wilhelmsson scheme" and my own rights approach based on *mandatory* civil law and followed in this study:

–   Scheme (1): right to information (2.6);
–   Scheme (2): right to substantive and procedural fairness (2.3, 2.8, 4.15, 7.4);
–   Scheme (3): right to fairness of core terms (price) (5.3);
–   Scheme (4): right to non-discrimination (3.1);
–   Scheme (5): (exceptional) right to help in need (*social force majeure*) (3.19).

This scheme – which is meant to be an analytical one and will be followed up in the coming chapters – allows us to examine the degree of involvement of EU civil law in traditional areas of autonomy as the basic concept of Member State private law.[60] The scheme should be extended by the principle of effective legal protection (Chapter 4), and by certain methodological imperatives characteristic of EU civil law like balancing, proportionality and an emerging principle of good faith (Chapters 5, 6, 7). It should also allow a critical evaluation of the present state of general principles in EU law, as developed by the case law of the ECJ and (although in a rather piecemeal way) EU legislation under the impact of its "constitutionalisation" required by Articles 51 and 52 of the Charter.

---

[60]   A comprehensive approach has now been presented in D. Leczykiewicz/S. Weatherill (eds.), *The Involvement of EU Law in Private Law Relationships*, 2012.

CHAPTER 2

THE PRINCIPLE OF PROTECTION
OF THE WEAKER PARTY

Contents

Bibliography 37
1. Elements of protection of the weaker party. 38
2. Minimum standards of working hours and paid annual leave 41
    2.1. Objectives of the Working Time Directive 41
    2.2. What is "working time" and who determines it? 42
    2.3. Right to paid annual leave: a fundamental right in the EU? 44
3. EU consumer law: information vs. protection 47
    3.1. EU consumer contract law: paternalism or protection? 47
    3.2. Prevalence of consumer information 48
    3.3. Mandatory content-related rules as an exception 50
    3.4. Who is a consumer in need of information and protection? 51
    3.5. The "vulnerable" consumer standard. 54
4. Conclusion: generalising the protection of weaker parties and its limits. . . . 56

Bibliography

C. Barnard, *EU Employment Law*, 4th ed. 2012; A.L. Bogg, 'The Right to Paid Annual Leave in the Court of Justice: the Eclipse of Functionalism', ELRev 2006, 892; F. Benyon (ed.), *Services and the EU Citizen*, 2013; D. Caruso, 'The Baby and the Bath Water – A Critique of European Contract Law', American JCompL 2013, 475; O. Cherednyshenko, *Fundamental Rights, Contract Law, and the Protection of the Weaker Party*, 2008; H. Collins, 'The constitutionalisation of European private law as a path to social justice?', in: H.-W. Micklitz (ed.), *Social Justice in EU Private Law*, 2011; H. Collins, 'Social Dumping, Multi-level Governance and Private Law Employment Relationships', in: D. Leczykiewicz/S. Weatherill (eds.), *The Involvement of EU Law in Private Law Relationships*, 2013, 223; W. Däubler, 'Auf dem Weg zu einem europäischen Arbeitsrecht', in: L. Krämer et al., (eds.) *Law and diffuse interests – Liber amicorum N. Reich*, 1997, 441; S. Grundmann/W. Kerber/S. Weatherill (eds.), *Party Autonomy and the Role of Information in the Internal Market*, 2001; N. Helberger et al., *Digital Consumers and the Law*, 2013; M. Karanikic/H.-W. Micklitz/N. Reich (eds.), *Modernising Consumer Law – The Experience of the Western Balkan*, 2012; S. O'Leary, *Employment Law and the ECJ*, 2002; B. Lurger, *Grundfragen der Vereinheitlichung des Vertragsrechts in der EU*, 2002; B. Lurger, 'The Common Frame of Reference/Optional Code and the Various Understandings of Social Justice in Europe', in: T. Wilhelmsson et al. (eds.), *Private Law and the Many Cultures of Europe*, 2007; H.-W. Micklitz (ed.), *Social Justice in EU Private Law*, 2011;

H.-W. Micklitz, *Brauchen Unternehmen und Verbraucher eine neue Architektur des Verbraucherrechts, Gutachten 69. Dt.- Juristentag*, 2012; H.-W. Micklitz, 'The future of consumer law – plea for a movable system', EUVR 2013, 5; H.-W. Micklitz/N. Reich/P. Rott, *Understanding EU Consumer Law*, 2009; H.-W. Micklitz/N. Reich, 'Cronica de una muerte anunciada – The Commission Proposal on a Directive of Consumer Rights', CMLRev 2009 471; L. Nogler, 'Why do Labour Lawyers Ignore the Question of Social Justice in European Contract Law?', ELJ 2008, 483; N. Reich, 'Crisis or Future of European Consumer Law?', in: *Yearbook of Consumer Law 2009*, 2010, 3; N. Reich, 'The Social, Political and Cultural Dimension of EU Private Law', in: R. Schulze, *European Private Law – Current Status and Perspectives*, 2011, 57; K. Riesenhuber, *European Employment Law*, 2012; V. Roppo, 'From Consumer Contracts to Asymmetric Contracts', ERCL 2009, 304; H. Roesler, 'Protection of the Weaker Party in European Contract Law – Standardised and Individual Inferiority in Multi-Level Private Law', ERPrL 2010, 729; D. Schiek, *Economic and Social Integration*, 2012; A. Somma, 'At the roots of European private law: social justice, solidarity, and conflict in the proprietary order', in: H.-W. Micklitz (ed.), *Social Justice in EU Private Law*, 2011, 187; R. Sefton-Green (ed.), *Mistake, Fraud and Duties to Information*, 2005; Study Group on Social Justice in European Private Law. Social Justice in European Contract Law: A Manifesto, ECJ 2004, 653; K. Tonner/K. Fangerow, 'Directive 2011/83 on consumer rights: a new approach to European consumer law?', EUVR 2012, 67; H. Unberath/A. Johnston, 'The double headed approach of the ECJ concerning consumer protection', CMLRev 2007, 1237; S. Weatherill, *EU Consumer Law and Policy*, 2005, 2nd ed. 2013; T. Wilhelmsson et al. (eds.), *Private Law and the Many Cultures of Europe*, 2007; T. Wilhelmsson, 'Varieties of Welfarism in European Contract Law', ELJ 2004, 712.

1. ELEMENTS OF PROTECTION OF THE WEAKER PARTY

2.1   EU civil law has emerged not so much as a body of rules with an objective of enabling citizens to use their autonomy for purposes, whether economic or not, to be determined by themselves, but rather as a body of provisions that tries to protect the weaker party and to combat discrimination (Chapter 3). To put it simply, at least three areas can be distinguished and have found their way into the Charter, frequently based on prior extensions of citizens' rights by EU law amendments that will not be documented here, in particular in the field of social and consumer policy:[1]

(1) An important element of EU social policy has been the protection of persons in dependent employment situations by guaranteeing fair and just working conditions, Article 31 of the Charter, including the "right (of every worker) to limitation of maximum working hours, to daily and weekly rest periods and to an annual period of paid leave".[2] This conforms to Article 3(3) TEU

---

[1]   See the overview in N. Reich, *Bürgerrechte*, 1999.

[2]   AG Tizzano referred to it even before its official enactment by the Lisbon Treaty, opinion of 18 February 2001 in case C-173/99 *BECTU v Secretary of State for Trade and Industry* [2001] ECR I-4881, paras 26–28, not taken up by the Court at that time.

on establishing a "social market economy".[3] Article 8 of the Community Charter of Fundamental Social Rights of 1989 which is referred to in Article 151(1) TFEU, has similar provisions;[4] the ECJ has on several occasions made reference to it.[5] A prominent example to be studied here is the Working Time Directive (WTD) 2003/88/EC of 4 November 2003 (recast),[6] and its predecessor Directive 93/104/EC of 23 November 1993 concerning certain aspects of the organisation of working time.[7] Their controversial interpretation by the ECJ will be taken as an example (2.3–2.4).

(2) Another area where EU law has been active is the protection of consumers as typically weaker parties to contracts with business partners (B2C). This principle is now enshrined in Article 38 of the Charter,[8] although in rather general terms. It was already contained in the old Article 129a EEC under the Maastricht Treaty of 1992, which became Article 153(2) EC of the Amsterdam Treaty and has now been transferred to Article 12 TFEU.[9] Its key point is that it guarantees the consumer a "right to information", while the other elements of consumer law like protection of safety and health, fairness in bargaining situations, and access to law had been left to secondary legislation and have evolved into a genuine principle of *effective legal protection* to be examined in Chapter 4. The protection of the consumer as the weaker party will be demonstrated by reference to the recent Consumer Rights Directive 2011/83/EU of 25 October 2011 (CRD)[10] as a follow up to abundant, but not necessarily coherent, consumer protection legislation by the EU. As a new element, the protection of so-called "vulnerable" consumers emerged without having a clear scope of application (2.11).

(3) The protection of private parties to network services has been a more recent element of EU civil law as a result of the ongoing privatisation of essential services like transportation, energy and telecommunications in the EU. Civil law, in particular contract law, had to take over functions of public law

---

[3] Overview by C. Barnard, *EU Employment Law*, 4th ed. 2012, 534; H. Collins, 'Social Dumping, Multi-level Governance and Private Law Employment Relationships', in: D. Leczykiewicz/ S. Weatherill (eds.), *The Involvement of EU Law in Private Law Relationships*, 2013, 223 at 241; K. Riesenhuber, *European Employment Law*, 2012, p. 13.

[4] K. Riesenhuber, *supra* note 3, at 19 and 48; the Social Policy Protocol of 1992 which was first rejected by the UK became part of the Amsterdam Treaty of 1997.

[5] Case C-151/02 *Kiel v Jaeger* [2003] ECR I-8389, para 47.

[6] [2003] OJ L 299/9.

[7] [1993] OJ L 307/18.

[8] See now case C-12/11 *D. McDonagh v Ryanair* [2013] ECR I-(31.01.2013), para 63, justifying restrictions of the contractual autonomy of airlines under Articles 16 and 17 of the Charter.

[9] Overview by N. Reich, in: H.-W. Micklitz/N. Reich/P. Rott, *Understanding EU Consumer Law*, 2009, 13.

[10] [2011] OJ L 304/64; overview of preceding EU legislation in the work by H.-W. Micklitz/ N. Reich/P. Rott, *Understanding EU Consumer Law*, 2009.

and thereby limit traditional concepts of autonomy. This process has been reflected in Article 36 of the Charter whereby the "Union recognises and respects access to services of general economic interest [...] in order to promote the social and territorial cohesion of the Union". It can also be found in Article 14 TFEU; this will be discussed in connection with the concept of the "vulnerable consumers" (2.11), and in the context of the "non-discrimination" principle, since the focus is on access rights (3.15).

(4) EU law has not developed any particular countervailing principle of protecting small and medium undertakings (SMU) as weaker parties in a system of "open and competitive markets", even though the Union and Member States shall encourage "an environment favourable to initiative and to the development of undertakings throughout the Union, particularly SMUs" as part of EU industrial policy (Article 173(1) TFEU).[11]

The rights and principles enshrined in the Charter will usually give general guidelines only and therefore do not enjoy direct effect.[12] Their impact on private law through mandatory rules framing freedom of contract will differ according to the specific problem area considered; each area needs to be studied separately. It is still an open question as to what extent general principles of EU civil law can be derived from the rights and principles of the Charter. If one takes as a starting point the assumption that these rights and principles are not meant to be a source of directly applicable provisions but rather as a guide for interpretation and gap filling, as well as to some extent for reviewing the legality of EU and implementing national law, it is suggested here that such a *general principle of the protection of the weaker party in civil law relations* can be said to exist within the applicable secondary law.

The following examples from EU legislation and ECJ case law are only meant to illustrate the complexities of such a principle, one which is subject to doubt and criticism by many but which, in my opinion, has been pushed forward quite substantially by a more or less coherent ECJ case law.

---

[11] See the remarks in H.-W. Micklitz, *Brauchen Konsumenten und Unternehmen eine neu Architektur des Verbraucherrechts – Gutachten zum 69 DJT*, 2012, A 32; short English version in EUVR 2013, 5.

[12] AG Trstenjak, opinion of 8 September 2011, in case C-282/10 *Dominguez v CICOA* [2012] ECR I-(24.01.2012), para 83, denying any horizontal direct effect of fundamental rights of the Charter; the same is even more true with fundamental principles.

2. MINIMUM STANDARDS OF WORKING HOURS AND PAID ANNUAL LEAVE

2.1. OBJECTIVES OF THE WORKING TIME DIRECTIVE

2.2 The Working Time Directive (WTD) goes back to a 1975 Council Recommendation which wanted to limit weekly work to 40 hours and allow four weeks of paid annual leave. These rather generous entitlements had to be reduced to a more realistic threshold by the 1993 WTD, Directive 93/104/EEC, based on the new majority voting under the concept of "working environment" of Article 118a EEC (now Article 153 TFEU). The UK, which was ultimately out-voted, challenged the legal basis of the Directive but lost because the Court interpreted broadly the competence basis as "embracing all factors, physical or otherwise, capable of affecting the health and safety of workers in his working environment, including in particular certain aspects of the organisation of working time".[13] It stressed the social policy objective of EC legislation in this field by having as its "principal aim the protection of the health and safety of workers".[14] Therefore, contractual issues were not the centre of attention for the legislator. This changed only later in the interpretation of the central concepts of the Directive in the case law of the Court, which took a specific individual protective view of the worker as the weaker party.

Directive 93/104, followed by Directive 2003/88, was subject to a number of important ECJ judgments. As a result, this case law substantially limited the freedom of contract by the employer in relation to working hours and paid annual leave and extended this protection also against collective agreements between employer and employee organisations or institutions. Member State law was limited to improving worker protection under the minimum harmonisation concept of Article 153(4) TFEU (ex-Article 118a(4) EEC), but not to restrict it or to make it subject to conditions that were not expressly recognised in the Directive. This ECJ case law shows – despite strong protests by Member State governments and employers' associations – a remarkable protective spirit with a strong *individualistic "Vorverständnis"* ("pre-understanding": 0.2). The worker is seen as the typically weaker party in employment contracts who needs to be protected against a unilateral use of the contractual freedom of the employer even though this may be supported by the Member States themselves. This is justified by the concept of the worker, which, in an autonomous EU interpretation, is regarded as "a person who, for a certain period of time, performs services for and under the direction of another person in return for which he receives remuneration".[15] This creates a

---

13   Case C-84/94 *UK v Council* [1996] ECR I-5755, paras 14–15.
14   Ibid., para 22.
15   Case C-428/09 *Union Syndicale Solidaires Isère* [2010] ECR I-9961, para 28, referring to a similar concept in the Treaty provisions on free movement of workers (Article 45 TFEU).

situation of *dependency* justifying legal intervention, including fixed-term contracts and education commitment contracts. Some ECJ cases may support this argument.

2.2. WHAT IS "WORKING TIME" AND WHO DETERMINES IT?

2.3 Article 6 of the WTD 2003/83 contains a definition of "working time":

"Maximum weekly working time
Member States shall take the measures necessary to ensure that, in keeping with the need to protect the safety and health of workers:
(a) the period of weekly working time is limited by means of laws, regulations or administrative provisions or by collective agreements or agreements between the two sides of industry;
(b) the average working time for each seven-day period, including overtime, does not exceed 48 hours."

This is quite a formal definition of working time that does not seem to leave much room of modification either by Member States or by employers. Its minimum protective scope, which cannot be lowered by Member States, has been affirmed in Article 23 which had a similar predecessor in Directive 93/104. According to Article 22, an extension is possible under certain circumstances on "agreement of the worker to perform such work" (with longer working hours). The individual worker may to a limited extent therefore waive his protection, but this waiver is subject to strict conditions and limitations. The protective ambit of Article 6 WTD has been stressed by the Court in its judgment in *Fuß*:[16]

"[That] provision constitutes a particularly important rule of European Union social law which requires the Member States to fix an upper limit of 48 hours for the maximum average weekly working time, including overtime, as is expressly laid down in that provision and from which, in the absence of implementation in national law of the first subparagraph of Article 22(1) of the directive, no derogation may be made in respect of activities such as those of fire fighters at issue in the main proceedings."

Is this waiver also possible by collective agreement, as was the case with German fire fighters? In the *Pfeiffer* case,[17] concerning the extension of the working time by collective agreement beyond the 48-hour limit of Article 6(2) of Directive 93/104 (now Article 6(b) of Directive 2003/88), the Court denied such a possibility and maintained a strictly individualistic approach to the objectives of the Directive:

---

[16]   Case C- 243/09 *Günter Fuß v Stadt Halle* [2010] ECR I-9849, para 47.
[17]   Case C-397–403/01 *Pfeiffer et al v DRK* [2004] ECR I-8835, para 82; see also the discussion on opting out by C. Barnard, *supra* note 3, at 550; for a criticism of the individual approach by the ECJ, see H. Collins *supra* note 3, at 239.

"That interpretation derives from the objective of Directive 93/104, which seeks to guarantee the effective protection of the safety and health of workers by ensuring that they actually have the benefit of, inter alia, an upper limit on weekly working time and minimum rest periods. Any derogation from those minimum requirements must therefore be accompanied by all the safeguards necessary to ensure that, if the worker concerned is encouraged to relinquish a social right which has been directly conferred on him by the directive, he must do so freely and with full knowledge of all the facts. Those requirements are all the more important given that the worker must be regarded as the weaker party to the employment contract and it is therefore necessary to prevent the employer being in a position to disregard the intentions of the other party to the contract or to impose on that party a restriction of his rights without him having expressly given his consent in that regard."

A number of cases concerned the controversial question of whether time on call could be regarded as "working time" and therefore fall under the 48 hours regime, unless an express derogation was provided by the Directive, particularly concerning doctors on call at their hospital, mostly at night, but not actually performing medical work. Starting with *SIMAP*,[18] this case law was continued concerning German law on health care services in *Jaeger*[19] on whether to count hospital service on call as working time or rest time. Even where the doctor is not working, he is still at his employer's disposal. This is justified by teleological considerations based, I would add, on the Court's understanding of the regulation of working time in the interest of the employee as a "general principle protecting the weaker party" in EU civil (employment) law. The Court in *SIMAP* justified its case law with the following teleological observations:[20]

"that interpretation [is] in conformity with the objective of Directive 93/104, which is to ensure the safety and health of workers by granting them minimum periods of rest and adequate breaks, whereas to exclude duty on call from working time within the meaning of the directive if physical presence is required would seriously undermine that objective."

In *Jaeger* it made the following distinction concerning on-call duties not performed in the hospital:[21]

"It should be added that, as the Court already held at paragraph 50 of the judgment in *Simap*, in contrast to a doctor on stand-by, where the doctor is required to be

---

18   Case C-303/98 *Simap* [2000] ECR I-7963.
19   Case C-151/02 *Kiel v Jaeger* [2003] ECR I-8389, para 70; confirmed in case C-14/04 *Dellas* [2005] ECR I-10253; rejecting the French system of calculation of hours of presence differentiated according to the intensity of the activity. On the consequences of a broad definition of working time see the overview by C. Barnard, *supra* note 3, at 548. See also the critical analysis of H. Collins, *supra* note 3, at 247. K. Riesenhuber, *supra* note 3, at 391, criticises the failed attempt at flexibility of the Court's approach by creating different types of "duties on call". The EU legislator has not been able to remedy this inconsistency.
20   Case C-303/98 *Simap* [2000] ECR I-7963, para 50.
21   Case C-151/02 *Kiel v Jaeger* [2003] ECR I-8389, para 65.

permanently accessible but not present in the health centre, a doctor who is required to keep himself available to his employer at the place determined by him for the whole duration of periods of on-call duty is subject to appreciably greater constraints since he has to remain apart from his family and social environment and has less freedom to manage the time during which his professional services are not required. Under those conditions an employee available at the place determined by the employer cannot be regarded as being at rest during the periods of his on-call duty when he is not actually carrying on any professional activity."

This differentiation between "full duties on call" in the hospital which count as working time, and periods where the worker is "merely contactable", and which therefore count as rest time, is in practice hard to implement. Riesenhuber therefore pleads for a "middle category" which would allow more flexibility to employers.[22] Attempts at a legislative solution however have failed. Article 22 as mentioned above allows some flexibility, but must respect the need for an agreement with the worker which cannot be presumed nor be put into the general terms of the employment contract, even if agreed with the worker's representatives. Individual autonomy beats collective autonomy!

Collins,[23] expressing no surprise, insists on the rather conflicting and paradoxical results of the case law of the ECJ:

"It is hardly surprising therefore, that as a consequence of decisions like the one found in *Jaeger,* employers have sought routes around the legislative constraints, and governments have been willing to create flexible opt-out mechanisms."

2.3. RIGHT TO PAID ANNUAL LEAVE: A FUNDAMENTAL RIGHT IN THE EU?

2.4 Article 7 gives the worker a right to paid annual leave. It reads:

"Annual leave
1. Member States shall take the measures necessary to ensure that every worker is entitled to paid annual leave of at least four weeks in accordance with the conditions for entitlement to, and granting of, such leave laid down by national legislation and/or practice.
2. The minimum period of paid annual leave may not be replaced by an allowance in lieu, except where the employment relationship is terminated."

The importance of this right – but also its limitation – was recently underlined by the ECJ in *KHS* which concerned limits of carry-over regulations on lapse of

---

22   K. Riesenhuber, *supra* note 3, at 392.
23   Ibid., at 248.

right to paid annual leave due but not taken because of illness on the expiry of a period:[24]

> "The right to paid annual leave is, as a principle of European Union social law, not only particularly important, as noted in paragraph 23 above, but is also expressly laid down in Article 31(2) of the Charter of Fundamental Rights of the European Union, which Article 6(1) TEU recognises as having the same legal value as the Treaties. It follows that, in order to uphold that right, the objective of which is the protection of workers, any carry-over period must take into account the specific circumstances of a worker who is unfit for work for several consecutive reference periods. Thus, the carry-over period must inter alia ensure that the worker can have, if need be, rest periods that may be staggered, planned in advance and available in the longer term. Any carry-over period must be substantially longer than the reference period in respect of which it is granted. That carry-over period must also protect the employer from the risk that a worker will accumulate periods of absence of too great a length, and from the difficulties for the organisation of work which such periods might entail."

The carry-over period may be limited to 15 months in a collective agreement. On the expiry of the carry-over period, the right to paid annual leave lapses where this period limited the accumulation of entitlements to paid leave of a worker who is unfit for work for several consecutive reference periods.[25]

The *Dominguez* case was concerned with the question of whether the period of annual leave in Article 7 of Directive 2003/88 could be calculated only on the basis of actual work done, or would include also periods of absence from work due to an accident. The Court answered in the second sense:[26]

> "In that regard it should be noted that, according to settled case-law, the entitlement of every worker to paid annual leave must be regarded as a particularly important principle of European Union social law from which there can be no derogations and whose implementation by the competent national authorities must be confined within the limits expressly laid down by Council Directive 93/104/EC."

Another controversial question concerned the practice in the UK in particular to "roll-over" holiday pay as an additional sum added to regular pay and paid out in small instalments. In the *Robinson-Steele* judgment,[27] the ECJ condemned such practice as being incompatible with the worker's right to annual leave which does not allow any "derogation from that entitlement by contractual

---

24 Case C-214/10 *KHS v Winfrid Schulte* [2011] ECR I-(22.11.2011) paras 37–39; "qualifying" the judgment in joined cases C-350 + 520/06 *Schulze-Hoff et al v DRB* [2009] ECR I-179, para 28; comment K. Riesenhuber, *supra* note 3, at 403.

25 K. Riesenhuber, *supra* note 3, at 403.

26 Case C- 282/10 *M. Dominguez v CICOA* [2012] ECR I-(24.01.2012), para 16.

27 Joined Cases C-131 + C-257/04 *Robinson-Steele et al v Retail Services et al* [2006] ECR I-2531; comment C. Barnard, *supra* note 3, at 543 ff., concerning the possibility of a transit regime for already over-subscribed holiday pay.

arrangement" (para 52). This allowance cannot be replaced by an allowance in lieu.[28]

> "That prohibition is intended to ensure that a worker is normally entitled to actual rest, with a view to ensuring effective protection of his health and safety."

The case law of the ECJ has been criticised as being overtly worker-friendly in a purely individualistic and paternalistic sense,[29] by undermining principles of national labour law, and by not respecting collective autonomy that also exists in employment relations.[30] In referring to Article 31 of the Charter as an interpretative principle (as was done by AG Tizzano in his opinion of 18 February 2001 in *BECTU*,[31] an approach that was surprisingly rejected by AG Trstenjak in her opinion in *Dominguez*,)[32] the Court could have given its interpretation more "flesh and juice" and a more convincing argument even before the entering into force of the Charter on 1 December 2009 (Article 6 TEU). Shortly after *Robinson-Steele* the Court, in its judgment of 27 June 2006[33] concerning the constitutionality of derogations from the right to family reunion as established by Directive 2003/86[34] "upgraded" the Charter with the following words:[35]

> "The Charter was solemnly proclaimed by the Parliament, the Council and the Commission in Nice on 7 December 2000. While the Charter is not a legally binding instrument, the Community legislature did, however, acknowledge its importance by stating, in the second recital in the preamble to the Directive, that the Directive observes the principles recognised not only by Article 8 of the ECHR but also in the Charter. Furthermore, the principal aim of the Charter, as is apparent from its preamble, is to reaffirm 'rights as they result, in particular, from the constitutional traditions and international obligations common to the Member States, the Treaty on European Union, the Community Treaties, the [ECHR], the Social Charters adopted by the Community and by the Council of Europe and the case-law of the Court [...] and of the European Court of Human Rights."

This judgment was the first to recognise the legal importance of the Charter, even though it was not formally part of EC law at the time of the judgment. This was an important interpretative guideline on protecting weaker parties.

On the other hand, reform of the WTD was attempted at several stages but did not advance due to different conceptions of how to allow derogations from

---

28   Ibid., para 60.
29   A.L. Bogg, ELRev 2006, 892.
30   H. Collins, *supra* note 3, at 251.
31   *Supra* note 2.
32   Case C-282/10 *M. Dominguez v CICOA* [2012] ECR I-(24.01.2012), para 99, because "[i]t is questionable that the right to paid annual leave meets the requirements established in case-law for a general principle" which however could be derived from Article 31(2) of the Charter.
33   Case C-540/03 *EP v Council* [2006] ECR I-5769.
34   [2003] OJ L 251/12.
35   Case C-540/03 *EP v Council* [2006] ECR I-5769, para 38.

its other strict obligations of worker protection. More "flexible" working arrangements were however invented to avoid the rigidities of the WTD.[36]

3. EU CONSUMER LAW: INFORMATION VS. PROTECTION

3.1. EU CONSUMER CONTRACT LAW: PATERNALISM OR PROTECTION?

2.5   Another area of contract law where the EU has been particularly active has been consumer law. Its scope and justification are still quite controversial: for some it is an aspect of EU "social law", for others it is a corollary to market regulation, and for some of its critics it amounts to a form of "paternalism". These controversies will not be taken up in this overview. In order to understand its protective ambit, at least in the words of the ECJ in interpreting the Unfair Terms Directive 93/13/EEC[37] (adopted in the same year as the Working Time Directive 93/104), I will cite a quotation from the *Penzügij Lizing* case[38] that has been repeated over time where the concept of the "consumer as the weaker party" has been used to justify a specific type of interpretation (4.15–4.17):

> "[A]ccording to settled case-law, the system of protection introduced by the Directive is based on the idea that the consumer is in a weak position vis-à-vis the seller or supplier, as regards both his bargaining power and his level of knowledge. This leads to the consumer agreeing to terms drawn up in advance by the seller or supplier without being able to influence the content of those terms [...] The Court of Justice has also held that, on account of that weaker position, Article 6(1) of the Directive provides that unfair terms are not binding on the consumer. As is apparent from case-law, that is a mandatory provision which aims to replace the formal balance which the contract establishes between the rights and obligations of the parties with an effective balance which re-establishes equality between them [...] In order to guarantee the protection intended by the Directive, the Court has also stated that the imbalance which exists between the consumer and the seller or supplier may be corrected only by positive action unconnected with the actual parties to the contract."

This case law is seemingly concerned only with Directive 93/13 but can also be seen as the ECJ's general approach to the objectives of EU consumer law. The ECJ frames party autonomy in B2C transactions in favour of the consumer as the

---

36   C. Barnard, *supra* note 3, at 558.
37   [1993] OJ L 95/29.
38   C-137/08 *VB Penzügji Lizing v Schneider* [2010] ECR I-10847, para 46; for a critical overview see H. Unberath/A. Johnston, CMLRev 2007, 127 at 1281 noting the ECJ's "pro-consumer bias".

typically weaker party in relation to the business or professional partner who is seen to be regularly in a stronger bargaining position (consequences at 4.15). This is confirmed by a quotation from the ECJ's *Putz-Weber* judgement[39] concerned with consumer protection sales contracts according to Directive 99/44 (4.18):

> "In that context, it must be pointed out that Article 3 [of Directive 99/44] aims to establish a fair balance between the interests of the consumer and the seller, by guaranteeing the consumer, as the weak party to the contract, complete and effective protection from faulty performance by the seller of his contractual obligations, while enabling account to be taken of economic considerations advanced by the seller."

The corrective instruments used by EU consumer law directives, most recently Directive 2011/83 (CRD),[40] are twofold:

- imposition of information and transparency requirements; and
- mandatory provisions which function one-sidedly in favour of the consumer without any contracting-out being possible.

The instruments for their enforcement will be discussed in Chapter 4 on the principle of effectiveness.

3.2. PREVALENCE OF CONSUMER INFORMATION

2.6 The CRD contains two important general provisions on information, namely Article 5 "for contracts other than distance or off-premise contracts", and Article 6 on "consumer information and right of withdrawal for distance and off-premises contracts". The consumer right of information has already been part of Article 169(1) TFEU (ex-Article 153(1) EC), can be found in great detail in many consumer law directives, and must be regarded as a "general principle" of EU consumer law, to be balanced with the other principle of autonomy of business in consumer contracting.[41] Article 5 of the CRD has codified this general right as a condition to a binding contract:

---

[39] Joined Cases C-65 + 89/09 *Weber + Putz v Wittmer + Medianess El.* [2011] ECR I-5257, para 75; critical comment by A. Johnston/H. Unberath, CMLRev 2012, 793 at 806 concerning the costs of higher consumer protection.

[40] For a critical analysis see S. Weatherill, 'The CRD: How and why a quest for "coherence" has (largely) failed', CMLRev 2012, 1279; more a positive view, O. Unger, 'Die Richtlinie über Rechte der Verbraucher', ZEuP 2012, 270; E. Hall/G. Howells/J. Watson, 'The Consumer Rights Directive', ERCL 2012, 139; for a different approach see S. Grundmann, 'Die EU-Verbraucherrechte-Richtlinie', JZ 2013, 53; K. Tonner/K. Fangerow, 'Directive 2011/83 on consumer rights: a new approach to European consumer law?', EUVR 2012, 67.

[41] See N. Reich in H.-W. Micklitz/N. Reich/P. Rott, *Understanding EU Consumer Law*, 2009, §1.11.

"Before the consumer is bound by a contract other than a distance or off-premises contract, or any corresponding offer, the trader shall provide the consumer with the following information in a clear and comprehensible manner, if that information is not already apparent from the context."

Article 5(1)(a) to (h) lists in detail what that information consists of, for example the main characteristics of the goods or services, the total price of the goods or services inclusive of taxes (VAT), the duration of the contract and as a novelty, and "where applicable, the functionality, including applicable technical protection measures, of digital content and any interoperability of digital content with hardware and software that the trader is aware of or can reasonably be expected to have been aware of" (6.23 for recent developments).[42] Paragraph 3 contains an exception for day-to-day transactions that are to be performed immediately, while paragraph 4 allows Member States to adopt or maintain additional pre-contractual requirements.

Article 6 contains similar requirements for off-premises and distance contracts, with some specificities concerning additional information about the right of withdrawal and the consequences in case of withdrawal.

2.7 EU consumer contract law has certainly been from the very beginning, as is well known, the most detailed and at the same time most debated body of EU civil law; nevertheless, Directive 2011/83/EC at least to some extent consolidates earlier initiatives. The various Directives, in particular the recent ones on Consumer Credit 2008/48/EC and Time-Share 2008/122/EC, but also earlier ones on Distance Selling 97/7/EC in general (now repealed by Directive 2011/83) and Distance Selling of Financial Products 2002/65/EC, are examples of this approach.[43] The obligations as to what information must be provided are quite detailed, usually put into the form of an annex couched in highly technical language to be attached to the contract.

These information requirements have been extended by a right of withdrawal, a so-called "cooling-off period" in certain areas of contracting, to allow the consumer who has been caught in situations of restrictive decision-making (off-premises contracts), or who may be entering into a transaction where he does not know enough about the good or service to be provided (distance selling), or

---

[42] For details see N. Helberger et al., 'Digital Content Contracts for Consumers', JCP 2013, 37 at 46.

[43] Directive 2008/48/EC of the EP and the Council of 23 April 2008 on credit agreements for consumers and repealing Council Directive 87/102/EEC [2008] OJ 122/66; Directive 2008/122/EC of the EP and the Council of 14 January 2009 on the protection of consumers in respect of certain aspects of timeshare, long-term holiday products, resale and exchange contracts [2009] OJ L 33/10; Directive 97/7/EC of the EP and of the Council of 20 May 1997 on the protection of consumers in respect of distance contracts [1997] OJ L 14/ 19; Directive 2002/65/EC of the EP and of the Council of 23September 2002 concerning the distance marketing of consumer financial services and amending Council Directive 90/619/EEC and Directives 97/7/EC and 98/27/EC [2002] OJ L 271/16.

where he may not immediately understand the service because of its complexity and inherent risks (for example insurance, timeshare or consumer credit).

The usefulness and effectiveness of these information requirements has been subject to a controversial debate which ranges, on the one extreme, from criticism of the merely symbolic character of these regulations that are based on a model of the "rational informed consumer" contradicted by behavioural studies, to a more traditional critique fearing an erosion of the *pacta sunt servanda* principle, "protecting" the irresponsible consumer and putting unnecessary costs on business. I will not go into this discussion, even though it is true that EU law tends to provide for a certain – and highly selective and specific – "overkill of information duties".[44] These duties do not contain "personalised information" even if necessary.[45] Instead of an "information excess", information must be framed so as to meet consumer demands. Not more but better information is necessary.[46] The current requirements are at best a mere minimum of protection. As *information rights* they should correspond to the pronouncement of Article 169(1) TFEU (ex-Article 153 EC) and to a specific understanding of EU fundamental freedoms from the perspective of proportionality.[47] Four main questions remain:[48]

- Are information rules sufficient to give the consumer a fair chance to participate in consumer markets as a "passive market citizen"?
- Are information rules efficient in achieving their objective of strengthening party autonomy and consumer choice?
- Are information provisions effectively implemented?
- Are information provisions used as an element in limiting liability of the business party?[49]

3.3. MANDATORY CONTENT-RELATED RULES AS AN EXCEPTION

2.8 Mandatory consumer contract law is the other, more "interventionist", element of EU consumer law. It can be found in many directives which expressly preclude the parties to a B2C contract to contract out of mandatory protective

---

[44]   G. Howells/T. Wilhelmsson, 'EC Consumer Law – Has it Come of Age', ELR 2003, 370; R. Sefton-Green (ed.). *Mistake, Fraud and Duties to Information*, 2005, 396; P. Giliker, 'Pre-contractual good faith and CESL', ERPL 2013, 79 at 98; N. Reich, 'The Social, Political, and Cultural Dimension of EU Private Law', in: R. Schulze/H. Schulte-Nölke, *European Private Law – Current Status and Perspectives*, 2011, 80.
[45]   E. Hall/G. Howells/J. Watson, *supra* note 40, at 141.
[46]   N. Helberger et al., *Digital Consumers and the Law*, 2012, 68.
[47]   H.-W. Micklitz/N. Reich/P. Rott, *Understanding EU Consumer Law*, 2009, paras 1.11–1.14.
[48]   N. Reich, *Yearbook of Consumer Law 2009*, 2010, 8.
[49]   N. Helberger et al., *supra* note 46, at 95.

provisions (see latest Article 25 CRD). But the extent of substantive rules is much more limited in EU contract law, although it does exist, however selectively. In areas like sales law under Directive 99/44/EC,[50] the EU legislator certainly wants to give the consumer a set of minimum rights that cannot be waived by contract. In academic writing there is no agreement as to how far EU law should go with regard to substantive fairness rules: some fear unwanted "paternalism" (Grundmann/Ogus/Wagner),[51] while other authors, on the contrary, in line with the "Manifesto" group,[52] want to extend these rules as basis for a "social justice agenda for European contract law", namely to "fairness", "constitutionalisation of private law", and "legitimacy modes of governance".

The CRD as the most recent example contains some additional consumer rights in Chapter 4, like those on delivery, passing of risk, and additional payments.[53] The CRD has however not really extended the scope and extent of mandatory provisions of consumer contracting, even though that was originally foreseen in the 2008 proposal, which, however, did not succeed due to its "full harmonisation approach".[54] One of the "last minute" amendments to the proposal for a CRD now found in the final text is the concept of "fees that exceed the cost borne by the trader for the use of such means" (of payment) in Article 19. How is this to be calculated in a simple and cost-effective way? The ECJ will have to give its answers at a later date.

3.4. WHO IS A CONSUMER IN NEED OF INFORMATION AND PROTECTION?

2.9   Perhaps the central problem of EU consumer law had been the *concept of the consumer* itself. Usually the relevant Directives have taken a rather formal and abstract approach:

> "'Consumer' means any natural person who, in contracts covered by this directive, is acting for purposes which are outside his trade or business."[55]

---

[50]   Directive 1999/44/EC of the EP and of the Council of 25 May 1999 on certain aspects of the sale of consumer goods and associated guarantees [1994] OJ L 171/12.

[51]   S. Grundmann/W. Kerber, 'Information Intermediaries', in: S. Grundmann/W. Kerber/ S. Weatherill (eds.), *Party Autonomy and the Role of Information in the Internal Market*, 2001, 264, preferring information-type rules over mandatory standards; A. Ogus, 'The paradoxes of legal paternalism and how to resolve them', Legal Studies 2010, 61; G. Wagner, 'Zwingendes Privatrecht', ZEuP 2010, 243, pleading for a restrictive use of mandatory rules in contract law.

[52]   Study Group on Social Justice, ELJ 2004, 653 at 664; B. Lurger, 'The Common Frame of Reference/Optional Code and the Various Understandings of Social Justice in Europe', in: T. Wilhelmsson et al. (eds.), *Private Law and the Many Cultures of Europe*, 2007, 177.

[53]   For an analysis S. Weatherill, *supra* note 40, at 1305; S. Grundmann, *supra* note 40, at 60.

[54]   For a critique H.-W. Micklitz/N. Reich, CMLRev 2009, 471 at 507 (consumer sales), and 510 (unfair terms).

[55]   Article 2(1) of Directive 2011/83/EU.

In the case law of the ECJ, this definition has been interpreted as not covering non-profit legal persons, commercial persons acting outside their normal business, and assignees of consumer contracts.[56] The private guarantor of doorstep lenders is – due to the ancillary nature of the guarantee – only protected by Directive 85/577/EEC[57] if "a consumer assumes obligations towards the trader with a view to obtaining goods or services from him". If the personal and non-profit guarantee is given for a commercial credit negotiated at the doorstep, then the right to withdraw under Directive 85/577/EEC is not applicable – a somewhat paradoxical result because of the increased risk of such credit guarantees.[58] The guarantor of a consumer credit under the old Directive 87/102/EEC[59] is even worse off because he is completely excluded from its protective ambit; the Court justifies this with the limited extent of protection offered by Directive 87/102/EEC itself which mostly relates to information and "is almost devoid of provisions that might afford an effective safeguard to the guarantor".[60] The legislative definition of the consumer, followed by the ECJ's restrictive case law, creates a number of arbitrary delimitations and excludes in particular persons who are also in need of protection.

Mixed contracts depend on what element is most prominent – there is a presumption that the contract has been concluded for business or professional purposes which must be refuted by the consumer, "unless the trade or professional purpose is so limited as to be negligible in the overall context of the supply, the fact that the private element is predominant being irrelevant in that respect".[61] It should not be forgotten that this narrow definition was first developed in matters of jurisdiction where, according to the Court, not only questions of consumer protection, but also of legal and procedural certainty concerning the place where a case is to be heard, must be taken into account. Since in jurisdiction matters the Brussels Convention,[62] respectively Regulation (EC) 44/2001,[63] takes as a starting point the rule *actor sequitur forum rei*, meaning that usually the domicile of the defendant is relevant for determining jurisdiction within the EU, any rule departing from this principle, for example

---

[56] Joined Cases C-541 + 542/99 *Idealservice* [2001] ECR I-9049; C-361/89 *di Pinto* [1991] ECR I-1189; C-89/91 *Shearson Lehmann Hutton v TVB Treuhandgesellschaft* [1993] ECR I-139; for details see H.-W. Micklitz, *Münchner Kommentar vor §§13/14 BGB*, para 34; M. Tamm, *Verbraucherschutzrecht*, 2011, 325.

[57] [1985] OJ L 372/31.

[58] Case C-45/96 *Bay, Hypotheken und Wechselbank v Dietzinger* [1998] ECR I-1199, para 22.

[59] [1987] OJ L 42/48.

[60] Case C-208/98 *Berliner Kindl Brauerei v A. Siepert* [2000] ECR I-1741, para 25.

[61] Case C-464/01 *Johann Gruber v Bay Wa AG* [2005] ECR I-439.

[62] [1998] OJ C 27/1 (consolidated version).

[63] Council Regulation (EC) No 44/2001 of 22 December 2000 on jurisdiction and the recognition and enforcement of judgments in civil and commercial matters [2001] OJ L 12/1, 1, now superseded by Regulation (EU) No. 1215/2012 of 12 December 2012 on jurisdiction and the recognition and enforcement of judgments in civil and commercial matters [2012] OJ L 351/1.

in the area of consumer litigation, is an exception and must be interpreted narrowly in the interest of legal certainty.[64] This argument, however, is not true for consumer transactions where only the position of the "non-professional market participant" outside the courtroom is at stake, like in all transactions that are pre-determined by the marketing strategies of a business (including use of pre-formulated terms) where the receiving party (the consumer or individual customer) is usually in a "take it or leave it" situation.

It seems that the EU legislator itself is trying to take a more flexible concept of the consumer as a starting point where a double purpose transaction is concerned. Even though Article 2(f) of the recently adopted CRD repeats the now classic "narrow definition" of consumer, its recital 17 contains a kind of an opening clause to be used for interpretation purposes and confirms the importance of the principle of protection of the weaker party:

> "The definition of consumer should cover natural persons who are acting outside their trade, business, craft or profession. However, in the case of dual purpose contracts, if the contract is concluded for purposes partly within and partly outside the person's trade and the trade purpose is so limited as not to be predominant in the overall context of the supply, that person should also be considered as a consumer."

2.10 The traditional narrow concept of consumer in the context of the multi-governance system of EU legislation and legal practice has a number of disadvantages which lead Micklitz to plead for a "movable system" of consumer law:[65]

–   This narrow concept creates rather arbitrary delimitations between the sphere of consumer law where mandatory provisions prevail, and general contract law which is subject to freedom of contract within rather fluid limitations differing among Member States. This fault line will become even deeper once the Commission proposal of 11 October 2011 for a Common European Sales Law (6.12)[66] has been adopted as a directly effective EU Regulation. If chosen by the parties to a cross-border transaction, this Regulation contains mostly mandatory rules for consumer sales and connected service contracts (B2C) under the narrow definition of the consumer as mentioned above, while provisions relating to B2B/SMU contracts contain only default rules with very few mandatory provisions.[67]
–   This concept allows Member States to arbitrarily extend the personal scope of their implementing consumer legislation and thereby creates additional

---

[64]   Case C-269/95 *Benincasa* [1997] ECR I-3767, paras 14–17.
[65]   H.-W. Micklitz, EUVR 2013, 5, with comments by C. Twigg-Flesner, EUVR 2013, 12.
[66]   COM (2011) 635 of 11.10.2011.
[67]   For criticism, see H.-W. Micklitz/N. Reich, 'The Commission Proposal for a "Regulation on a Common European Sales Law (CESL)" – too broad or not broad enough?', EUI Working Paper Law 2012/04, Part I, para 20.

distortions within the internal market, despite the promise to contribute to harmonisation of law under Article 114 TFEU.

– The narrow concept of consumer is not flexible enough to cover varying needs for protection, in particular in the area of services and in other situations of permanent inferiority of one party, for instance personal guarantees given to banks by family members of the consumer-debtor.[68]

– Since the concept of consumer depends on the purpose of an individual's activity, this subjective factor may not be known to the other party and may thereby cause legal uncertainty as to what type of rules will apply to their contract.

– The rather formal concept of "consumer" leads at the same time to "over-protection" and "under-protection". For the first, take the *Mietz* case[69] as an example, where the owner of a luxury yacht claimed protection under the Brussels Convention for consumer litigation. The Court implicitly accorded this protection to him; however, this would not be the case with a small business (SMU) ship-owner using the vessel for catching fish as part of his income. The luxury yacht owner is better protected than the SMU even though the latter needs his vessel to make a living. Conversely, in *Dietzinger/ Berliner Kindl*,[70] the ECJ refused to grant protection of a consumer who was guaranteeing consumer credit to family members.

3.5. THE "VULNERABLE" CONSUMER STANDARD

2.11   Vulnerable consumers are those who cannot, or can no longer, cope with the requirements of the modern consumer society. These consumers run the risk of being isolated from social and economic life, be it by over-indebtedness, illness or a lack of ability to communicate. This also includes the growing problem of "social deprivation". This group of consumers was once the focus of the national consumer policies of the 1960s and 1970s. It was exactly this political movement that concentrated on the right to protect the weaker party to a contract. Consumer policy and consumer law policy will always try to integrate this group of vulnerable consumers. In the Lisbon Strategy, the EU explicitly mentioned for the first time the existence of different types of consumers. It speaks of humans 'living below the poverty line and in social exclusion'.[71]

---

[68]   See the unclear case law of the ECJ in *Dietzinger* and *Berliner Kindl, supra* notes 58 and 60; for an overview see C. Mak, *Fundamental Rights in European Contract Law*, 2008, 282 ff., referring to the somewhat differing case law of the Member States.

[69]   Case C-99/06 *Mietz v Intership Yachting* [1999] ECR I-2277, para 32.

[70]   *Supra* notes 58 and 60.

[71]   COM (2010) 2020 03.03.2010 <www.europarl.europa.eu/summits/lis1_en.htm> last accessed 31.07.12; for an overall assessment see H.-W. Micklitz, *supra* note 11, at A 40.

Improved provision of information and market transparency are of little help to vulnerable consumers when it comes to leading a self-determined life. It is rather the targeted promotion of infrastructure and intelligent, realistic schemes for providing advice that enable such consumers to participate independently in economic and social life. If inclusion and social participation are the objectives, then one also has to take care of vulnerable consumers.[72] Amazingly enough, the vulnerable consumer has entered the European consumer policy agenda. Recital 34 of the CRD insists:

> "In providing that information, the trader should take into account the specific needs of consumers who are vulnerable because of their mental, physical or psychological infirmity, age or credulity in a way which the trader could reasonably be expected to foresee. However, taking into account such specific needs should not lead to different levels of consumer protection."

However, the recital did not make it into the specific information requirements of the CRD!

The legalisation of this new type of consumer is closely linked to the liberalisation of the energy and telecommunications markets, which was so strongly promoted by the European Commission after the adoption of the Single European Act entailed the creation of new structures based on civil law, not as before on administrative law. The guarantee of supply for everybody was added to the concept of universal services. This obligation not only refers to vulnerable consumers, but includes them under its protection. For the first time the concept appears in Directive 2002/22/EC on universal services and users' rights relating to electronic communications networks and services (Universal Service Directive,[73] see 3.19).

Article 1(1) of the Universal Service Directive aims at ensuring the availability throughout the Community/Union of good quality and publicly available services through effective competition and choice; further, it aims to deal with circumstances *in which the needs of end-users are not satisfactorily met by the market*. According to recital 7, the Directive's focus is to ensure the "same conditions [of] access, in particular for the elderly, the disabled and for people with special social needs". Directive 2009/140/EC has not changed the terms defined in Directive 2002/21/EC Article 2. For the first time disabled persons are granted special rights under Article 7 of the amended Universal Service Directive 2009/136/EC of 25 November 2009.[74]

---

[72] <www.bmelv.de/SharedDocs/Downloads/EN/Ministry/Trusting-Vulnerable-Responsible-Consumer.pdf>.

[73] [2002] OJ L 108/51.

[74] [2009] OJ L 337/11.

In the Internal Market in Electricity Directive 2003/54/EC[75] and the Internal Market in Natural Gas Directive 2003/55/EC,[76] the so-called second generation of the liberalisation of the energy markets, the European Commission coined the notion of the "vulnerable customer".[77] In view of the increasing problems of social exclusion as a consequence of the liberalisation of the Single European Market, the EU has even tightened its approach in the new Electricity Directive 2009/72/EC of 13 July 2009.[78] However, the EU leaves it to the Member States to substantiate the term "vulnerable consumer", under Article 3(7) of Directive 2009/72/EC.

The conceptual differentiation in Directive 2005/29/EC on Unfair Commercial Practices[79] can also be considered to belong to the grey areas of traditional civil law understanding. Interestingly the Directive does not speak of the "vulnerable consumer", but of "consumers whose characteristics make them particularly vulnerable" to unfair commercial practices. This term is taken to include consumers with characteristics such as "age, physical or mental infirmity or credulity that render them susceptible".[80] The law does not define the "normal addressee of advertisement", who in the Directive is spoken of as an "average consumer".

The practical impact of the vulnerable consumer standard is not yet easy to evaluate. However, it is clear that European consumer law has again changed its outlook. Today it is fair to assume that the vulnerable consumer concept stands side-by-side with the informed consumer concept.

4. CONCLUSION: GENERALISING THE PROTECTION OF WEAKER PARTIES AND ITS LIMITS

2.12   Can the rather heterogeneous examples of protecting the weaker party in employment and consumer law relations be "upgraded" to a "general principle" of EU civil law? Despite some uncertainty in the literature and despite the somewhat inchoate approaches of the ECJ, I think such a principle can indeed be developed. I remind the reader that these principles are not meant to extend the scope of EU law: they will be applicable only within existing EU law. This is particularly true both in employment and in consumer law, which regulate only certain types of relations between employer and employee or business and consumer. Within this limited scope of application, an autonomous, EU-specific

---

[75]   [2003] OJ L 176/37.
[76]   [2003] OJ L 176/57.
[77]   Compare Article 3(5) of Directive 2003/54/EC and Article 3(3) of Directive 2003/55/EC: "vulnerable consumer respectively vulnerable customer".
[78]   [2009] OJ L 211/55.
[79]   [2005] OJ L 149/29.
[80]   Compare Article 5(3) of Directive 2005/29/EC: "particularly vulnerable".

definition of the weaker party has emerged in the meantime and been guided by the ECJ's interpretation. The weaker party is defined as either *the worker* or *the consumer* (notwithstanding differentiations within this concept: informed vs. vulnerable consumer).

These definitions have become the basis for "typifying" a set of persons that EU law regards as being in need of protection, despite the general recognition of contractual autonomy for themselves and their counterparts. Autonomy that is merely a formality is substituted for a more substantive one and reflects the input of fundamental rights and principles of the Charter. This circular relation between legal entitlements on the one hand – the WTD and the CRD were given as examples – and the general principle of protection of weaker parties on the other provides guidelines for their interpretation. It should not come as a surprise that the Court, in its interpretative work legitimised by Article 19 TEU, takes these principles seriously and in fact did extend protection beyond a mere formal understanding of the relevant EU acts. Much of the criticism voiced against this "worker"- or "consumer"-friendly interpretation by the ECJ is therefore not justified because it simply reflects the mandate given to it under primary EU law. Of course that does not shield the ECJ from methodological criticism. On the other hand, and as will be shown later, the ECJ has tried to limit certain elements of a perceived "over-protection" (5.9) by adopting a "balancing" approach.

The approach in this study to the protection of weaker parties will leave certain observers dissatisfied because it seemingly does not challenge the overtly individualistic *Vorverständnis* (pre-conception) of the ECJ (2.2). It is however one thing to raise methodological criticism of this *Vorverständnis*, as has and will be done throughout this study, and another to deny the legitimacy of the ECJ to apply its own *Vorverständnis* in filling gaps in the relevant EU acts. A paradigm change of such *Vorverständnisse* requires a coherent political process within the EU, something which seems difficult to attain due to the different traditions of social and consumer policy in the Member States.

On the other hand, the focus on individuals' rights both in the WTD and the CRD does not seem to allow an extension to other persons in a similar need. This is the "flip-side" of the concept of "autonomous" interpretation of EU law. Concerning, for example, the protection given by the WTD to persons who do not qualify as *workers* because they do not receive "remuneration" even if they are in a dependent situation, for example franchisees,[81] this will not be possible under the conceptual restraints of the aforementioned general principles. Member States may extend protection to those persons under the minimum protection principle, but the Court does not feel itself to be authorised to do so.

In a similar spirit, according to recital 13 of the Consumer Rights Directive 2011/83/EC the concept of *consumer* can be broadened by Member States to the following persons:

---

[81]   C. Barnard, *supra* note 3, at 537.

"Member States should remain competent, in accordance with Union law, to apply the provisions of this Directive to areas not falling within its scope. Member States may therefore maintain or introduce national legislation corresponding to the provisions of this Directive or certain of its provisions in relation to transactions that fall outside the scope of this Directive. For instance, Member States may decide to extend the application of the rules of this Directive to legal persons or to natural persons who are not "consumers" within the meaning of this Directive, such as non-governmental organisations, start-ups or small and medium-sized enterprises."

But Member States have to do so and are thereby acting outside the scope of the CRD. Even if all Member States were to do so, this would not necessarily be "upgraded" to a general principle of EU law.

This reservation leaves ample room for the relevance of the general principle of protecting the weaker party in EU civil law. Its gap-filling function was demonstrated in the WTD concerning "on call work" (2.3). A similar broadening of the scope of application of the CRD seems possible and is authorised by recital 17 with regard to double purpose contracts (2.8). It seems that this use of the principle is exactly what the Court is doing, despite criticism from Member States and academia. In addition, the importance of general principles can be shown as regards remedies, a topic that will be explored more in depth in the discussion of the principle of effectiveness in Chapter 4.

CHAPTER 3

THE PRINCIPLE
OF NON-DISCRIMINATION

Contents

Bibliography 60
1. "Spill-over" effects of non-discrimination on civil law? 60
2. Non-discrimination in employment law relations: overview. 64
    2.1. EU nationality as a factor 64
    2.2. Sex-based discrimination 66
    2.3. Racial discrimination 67
    2.4. Age discrimination 67
    2.5. Discrimination based on sexual orientation. 70
    2.6. Discrimination against disabled persons. 71
3. Citizenship: extending the scope of the principle of non-discrimination
    by primary law. 72
4. Extension of the non-discrimination principle to business-consumer
    relations by EU secondary law. 74
5. A controversy: unisex tariffs in insurance and conflicts with private
    autonomy 76
    5.1. A "monist" reading of the non-discrimination principle by the
        ECJ? 76
    5.2. A possible criticism of the judgment: too much "equal
        treatment", too little autonomy left? 80
6. Non-discrimination in access to and treatment in services of general
    economic interest and in network services: framed autonomy 81
7. Equal treatment beyond non-discrimination? 84
    7.1. Access to information in broadcasting services 84
    7.2. No equal treatment of minority shareholders in public
        companies. 86
8. Conclusion: the varied impact of the non-discrimination principle
    on civil law relations 87

Bibliography

A. Arnull et al. (eds.), *A Constitutional Order of States – Essays in Honour of A. Dashwood*, 2011; C. Barnard, *EU Employment Law*, 4th ed. 2012; J. Basedow, 'Grundsatz der Nichtdiskriminierung', ZEuP 2008, 230; R. Brownsword et al. (eds.), *The Foundations of European Private Law*, 2011; V. Kosta, 'Internal Market Legislation and the Civil Law of the Member States – The Impact of Fundamental Rights', ERCL 2010, 409; A.V. Lauber, *Paritätische Vertragsfreiheit und Gerechtigkeit im Vertragsrecht Englands, Deutschlands und der EU*, 2010; S. Leible/D. Schlachter, *Diskriminierungsschutz durch Privatrecht*, 2007; D. Leczykiewicz/S. Weatherill (eds.), *The Involvement of EU Law in Private Law Relationships*, 2013; K. Lenaerts/J. Gutiérrez-Fons, 'The Constitutional Allocation of Powers and General Principles of EU Law', CMLRev 2010, 1629; P. Mazière, *Le principe d'égalité en droit privé*, 2003; A. Metzger, *Extra legem, intra ius: Allgemeine Rechtsgrundsätze im Europäischen Privatrecht*, 2009; H.-W. Micklitz, *The Politics of Judicial Co-operation in the EU*, 2005; H.-W. Micklitz (ed.), *The Many Concepts of Social Justice in European Civil Law*, 2011; L. Niglia (ed.), *Pluralism and European Private Law*, 2012; N. Reich, 'The public/private divide in European law', in: F. Cafaggi/H.-W. Micklitz (ed.), *After the Common Frame of Reference*, 2010, 56; N. Reich, 'The Impact of the Non-Discrimination Principle on Private Autonomy', in: D. Leczykiewicz/S. Weatherill (eds.), *The Involvement of EU Law in Private Law Relationships*, 2013, 253; N. Reich et al., *Understanding EU Internal Market Law*, 3rd ed. forthcoming, §12; K. Riesenhuber, *European Employment Law*, 2012; D. Schiek, *Differenzierte Gerechtigkeit*, 2000; D. Schiek et al. (eds.), *Non-discrimination law*, 2007; R. Schulze (ed.), *Non-Discrimination in European Private Law*, 2011; R. Schulze/H. Schulte-Nölke (eds.), *European Private Law – Current Status and Perspectives*, 2011; T. Tridimas, *The General Principles of EU Law*, 2nd ed. 2006, 59–64; T. Wilhelmsson, 'Varieties of Welfarism of in European Contract Law', ELJ 2004, 173.

1. "SPILL-OVER" EFFECTS OF NON-DISCRIMINATION ON CIVIL LAW?

3.1 The concept of non-discrimination, also called "equal treatment", plays an important role in Union law, and has in many cases decided by the Court of Justice of the EU been understood as a general constitutional principle.[1] As regards the economic law of the Union, market subjects should be treated as equals if they are in a comparable situation, or conversely, law should not impose equal treatment on them if they are in different situations, unless such this difference is objectively justified.[2] The *Codorniú* case provides us with an example.[3] The Court invalidated a Community regulation forbidding Spanish producers from using the traditional term *crémant* by reserving it to French and

---

[1] Overview by T. Tridimas, *The General Principles of EU Law*, 2nd ed. 2006, 59–64; N. Reich et al., *Understanding EU Internal Market Law*, 3rd ed. forthcoming, para 13.2; J. Basedow, 'Grundsatz der Nichtdiskriminierung', Zeitschrift für Europäisches Privatrecht (ZEuP) 2008, 230 at 238; P. Mazière, *Le principe d'égalité en droit privé*, 2003, 429.

[2] Cases 117/76 + 16/77 *Ruckdeschel* [1977] ECR 1753, para 7; C-15/95 *EARL de Kerlast v Union régionale de coopératives agricoles (Unicopa) and Coopérative du Trieux* [1997] ECR I-1961, para 35; C-127/07 *Arcelor Atlantique and Lorraine and Others* [2008] ECR I-9835, para 23.

[3] Case C-309/89 *Codorniú Sa v Council* [1994] ECR I-1853.

Luxembourg producers of sparkling wine. The measure was held to violate the principle of non-discrimination because Spanish producers were without justification put on an unequal basis relative to other producers.

Over time EU non-discrimination law, apart from the distinctly market-orientated approach, has also taken on a social dimension by including within its ambit the struggle against discrimination based on gender, race, ethnic origin, age, disability or sexual orientation. This development is part of a more general trend in fundamental rights in the EU.

3.2   Article 21 on "non-discrimination" of the Charter of Fundamental Rights, which became formally part of EU law after the Lisbon Treaty was ratified, but which had guided the ECJ in its interpretation and application of Community law beforehand,[4] reads:

> "1. Any discrimination based on any ground such as sex, race, colour, ethnic or social origin, genetic features, language, religion or belief, political or any other opinion, membership of a national minority, property, birth, disability, age or sexual orientation shall be prohibited.
> 2. Within the scope of application of the Treaty [...] and without prejudice to the special provisions [...] any discrimination on grounds of nationality shall be prohibited."

Article 23 of the Charter contains a specific provision on "equality between men and women", including but not limited to employment relations:

> "Equality between men and women must be ensured in all areas, including employment, work and pay. The principle of equality shall not prevent the maintenance or adoption of measures providing for specific advantages in favour of the under-represented sex."

These are obviously broad formulations and are to some extent a mixture between "rights" and "principles" (0.6) without direct effect; they need to be transformed into subjective "rights" by EU legislation and Court practice. They are addressed to the Union itself and, according to the general clause of Article 51 of the Charter, to the Member States "only when they are implementing Union law", which must be read as meaning "acting within the scope of EU law". The more extensive understanding of the Charter's scope of application corresponds to the existing case law of the ECJ on the application of general

---

[4]   For the general approach of the ECJ in applying the Charter even before its formal enactment, see case C-540/03 *EP v Council* [2006] ECR I-5769; for a specific example see case C-272/06 *Productores de Música de Espana (Promusicae) v Telefónica de Espana SAU* [2008] ECR I-271, paras 62–63, on the need to balance between the right to effective protection of property (copyright) and the right of protection of personal data and hence of civil life in civil litigation between a rights management society and internet providers concerning disclosure of user data of copyrighted music; see also 4.1.

principles and of fundamental rights.[5] As can be seen both in the pre-existing case law of the ECJ on the principle of non-discrimination, and in its Charter manifestation, the rights that this principle gives rise to have first a "vertical direction" – in relations of the citizens to the Union or the Member States, the latter including anybody or institution governed by public law.

In this chapter I will discuss another dimension of the principle of non-discrimination in EU law. I will focus my analysis on civil law relations, which in all Member States[6] and in Union law itself are subject to the principle of "framed autonomy" (see 1.3). However, an inevitable clash exists between the rationale behind the principle of non-discrimination and the logic of civil law fuelled by the concern for economic efficiency and free choice of business partners. This entitlement to free choice is protected by the fundamentals of civil law relations, namely freedom of contract and party autonomy, which the application of the principle of non-discrimination would contradict. This has been expressed in an article authored by a prominent German scholar, Jürgen Basedow:[7]

> "The principles of equality or the prohibition of discrimination are not part of the traditional principles of civil law. He who concludes a contract does this in his own interest and not in order to do justice to others. She who has to choose a contract partner among several candidates has according to a German saying the 'pain of choice' because there usually exist several selection criteria, the relative value of which can only be assessed with reference to subjective preferences."

In his article Basedow undertakes a detailed and critical analysis of primary and secondary EU law, as well as of the practice of the ECJ, and comes to the conclusion that "there are only limited and selective prohibitions of discrimination, usually aimed at creating balance in situations of power, and not a general prohibition of discrimination in the conclusion of contracts."[8]

The purpose of this chapter is to challenge the traditional conception of civil law whereby non-discrimination is not one of its constitutive principles. Drawing

---

[5]   See case 5/88 *Wachauf v Bundesamt für Ernährung* [1989] ECR I-2609, para 19, and now case C-279/09 *DEB Deutsche Energiehandels- und Beratungsgesellschaft mbH v Bundesrepublik Deutschland* [2010] ECR I-13849; C-617/10 *Aklagaren v H.A. Fransson* [2013] ECR I-(26.03.2013), para 19. K. Lenaerts/J. Gutiérrez-Fons, CMLRev 2010, 1649 at 1660; a more restrictive opinion has been taken by M. Borowsky, in: J. Meyer, *Kommentar zur Charta*, 3rd e-book ed. 2011, Article 51 para 14; a narrower reading has been suggested by W. Cremer, 'Grundrechtsverpflichtete und Grundrechtsdimensionen nach der Charta der Grundrechte in der EU', EuGRZ 2011, 545, strictly distinguishing between *Durchführung* (implementation) and *Anwendungsbereich* (scope of application) of Union law by Member States.

[6]   See the overview of the development of contract law under aspects of "social justice" in England, France and Germany by H.-W. Micklitz (ed.), *The Many Concepts of Social Justice in European Civil Law*, 2011, 8.

[7]   *Supra* note 1, at 230. Translated by the author.

[8]   Ibid., at 250.

---

on an argument that I have presented elsewhere,[9] I will show that the traditional distinction between public and private law that is so dear to continental lawyers does not exist with similar rigour in EU law. For this reason, it cannot be used to "shield" civil law against provisions and concepts of non-discrimination. This does not imply that party autonomy should not be recognised as one of the "fundamental pillars" of EU law.[10] It is after all finding its place in the "freedom to conduct a business" under Article 16 and the "right to property" under Article 17 of the Charter (1.13). My view is, however, that civil autonomy should balanced against other "constitutional principles", such as the protection of the weaker party (2.12) and the *ordre public* of the European Union, as recognised by Article 52(1).[11]

It will be shown in this chapter that this "balancing" between the seemingly conflicting principles of autonomy and non-discrimination is relative in terms of two factors. First, the location of balance will depend on the *area of law* in the context of which the non-discrimination principle is invoked. There will be different rules in employment law, consumer law and services in the general public interest on the one hand, and in genuine commercial relations that are only subject to competition rules (and perhaps some scant rules protecting SMUs (6.22)) on the other. Secondly, certain characteristics on the basis of which discrimination occurs can usually only be taken into account in EU law (the "legally incriminated grounds of discrimination").[12] The EU prohibition on discrimination is typically based on such personal characteristics as gender, ethnic origin, nationality, age and sexual orientation, which are part of the identity of a person (*askriptive Perönlichkeitsmerkmale*), as explained by Schiek,[13] but not so much on economic grounds like income, social or family status and similar characteristics. The question of "equal treatment" implies *a value judgment* based on a "limited list of characteristics that are considered to be so delicate as to lead to every differentiation which is made on the basis of such characteristic to be considered discriminatory".[14] Articles 21 and 23 of the Charter contain just such (long) lists of "incriminated" characteristics that had

---

[9]   For details see N. Reich, 'The public/private divide in European law', in: F. Cafaggi/ H.-W. Micklitz (ed.), *After the Common Frame of Reference*, 2010, 56.

[10]   For a discussion see M. Hesselink, 'If You Don't Like Our Principles We Have Others', in: R. Brownsword et al. (eds.), *The Foundations of European Civil Law*, 2011, 59, with critical reference to the so-called "underlying principles" of the Outline Edition of the DCFR of 2009; see 5.10.

[11]   N. Reich, 'Balancing in Civil Law and the Imperatives of the Public Interest', in: R. Brownsword et al. (eds.), *The Foundations of European Civil Law*, 2011, 221.

[12]   H. Cousy, 'Discrimination in Insurance Laws', in: R. Schulze (ed.), *Non-Discrimination in European Private Law*, 2011, 81 at 83.

[13]   For a broader discussion see D. Schiek, *Differenzierte Gerechtigkeit*, 2000, 27 ff.

[14]   H. Cousy, *supra* note 12, at 84.

already been specified by Directives 2000/43,[15] 2000/78[16] and 2004/113.[17] In exceptional cases equal treatment will apply beyond the concept of non-discrimination (3.21).

The following sections will discuss the non-discrimination law in the EU with regard to both the area concerned and the characteristic applied. It will be shown that a *differentiated answer* is necessary to adequately understand the impact of the non-discrimination principle on civil law in the Union. It will be impossible to analyse in depth the sometimes very detailed case law of the ECJ; therefore, an overview must suffice.

2. NON-DISCRIMINATION IN EMPLOYMENT LAW RELATIONS: OVERVIEW

2.1. EU NATIONALITY AS A FACTOR

3.3   Recent ECJ case law extends the protection of fundamental freedoms, and as a corollary principle of non-discrimination based on EU nationality (Article 18 TFEU and Article 21(2) of the Charter) beyond state rules also against collective regulations by private actors. In the *Wouters* case,[18] the Court summarised and confirmed its practice as regards *collective regulation by private entities*:

> "[T]he abolition, as between Member States, of obstacles to freedom of movement for persons would be compromised if the abolition of State barriers could be neutralised by obstacles resulting from the exercise of their legal autonomy by associations or organisations not governed by public law."

That this "intrusion" of the Union freedoms into civil law relations is most relevant in labour relations became evident in later ECJ judgments concerning collective action by trade unions against the use of the fundamental freedoms by businesses. The *Viking* and *Laval*[19] cases of 2007 must be cited as the

---

[15]   Council Directive 2000/43/EC of 29 June 2000 implementing the principle of equal treatment between persons irrespective of racial or ethnic origin [2000] OJ L 180/22.

[16]   Council Directive 2000/78/EC of 27 November 2000 establishing a general framework for equal treatment in employment and occupation [2000] OJ L 303/16.

[17]   Council Directive 2004/113/EC of 13 December 2004 implementing the principle of equal treatment between women and men in the access to and supply of goods and services [2004] OJ L 373/37.

[18]   Case C-309/99 *J.C.J. Wouters et al v Algemene Raad von de Nederlandse Ordre van Advocaaten* [2002] ECR I-1577, para 120.

[19]   Case C-438/05 *International Transport Workers Federation (ITW) and Finnish Seamans Union (FSU) v Viking Line* [2007] ECR I-10779; C-341/05 *Laval & partneri v Bygnadds* [2007] ECR I-11767, referring to the earlier cases C-415/93 *ASBL v Bosman* [1995] ECR I-4921, paras 83–85, and C-281/98 *R. Angonese v Casa di Risparmio de Bolzano* [2000] ECR I-4139, paras 31–36.

outstanding and controversial examples of this approach (5.12). In *Raccanelli*,[20] which concerned a complaint of discrimination by a doctoral student from Italy against the German Max Planck-Gesellschaft (an association under civil law but funded by government), the Court took a somewhat broader approach[21]

> "with regard to Article 39 EC (now Art. 45 TFEU), which lays down a fundamental freedom and which constitutes a specific application of the general prohibition of discrimination contained in Article 12 EC (Art. 18 TFEU), that the prohibition of discrimination applies equally to all agreements intended to regulate paid labour collectively, *as well as to contracts between individuals*."

Article 18 TFEU, when strictly applied according to its wording, opposes direct discriminations. States may however also shape their rules on access to and termination of employment in such a way that not nationality, but seemingly neutral criteria such as residence, type of work and so on, are taken as the basis for a rule on different treatment. However, these may have the same effect as openly discriminatory rules. Examples from Court practice concern provisions on contracting teachers of a foreign language who may enjoy less protected standards on termination than teachers of other subjects, and who in the end are hit more severely as nationals of another EU country than those from the host country.[22] Certain wage or pension privileges may be limited to those residing in a certain territory identical with a Member State, thereby conferring an undue reward by regularly excluding nationals from other EU states.

The concept of *indirect discrimination* is not easily verifiable. According to the Court in *Raccanelli*:[23]

> "discrimination consists in the application of different rules to comparable situations or in the application of the same rule to different situations; (it is a matter of the national court) to establish whether, by reason of the application of different rules to comparable situations [...] the potential withholding of that choice resulted in inequality in the treatment of domestic and foreign doctoral students."

Intention to discriminate is not necessary, because it would be difficult to prove in any event. An *effects test* has to be used in order to verify whether indirect discrimination of a certain group of people, to be distinguished by their nationality, exists vis-à-vis another group. Statistical data may suffice to establish such a pattern of discriminatory effects of a certain ruling. Indirect discrimination will therefore be assessed by objective, typical factual constellations showing that other EU nationals are treated less favourably than a Member State's own nationals.

---

[20] Case C-94/07 *Raccanelli v MPG* [2008] ECR I-5939.
[21] Ibid., para 45 (emphasis added).
[22] Joined Cases C-259/91 + 331/91 + 332/91 *Pilar Allué and Carmel Mary Coonan et al v Unviersitá degli studi di Venezia and Università degli studi di Parma* [1993] ECR I-4309; Case C-272/92 *Maria Chiara Spotti v Freistaat Bayern* [1993] ECR I-5185.
[23] *Supra* note 20, para 47.

While direct discrimination cannot usually be justified because it runs counter to the very principles of Union law,[24] a more flexible test is used with regard to indirect discrimination. If it can be shown that differentiation between persons is based on other factors than nationality, or if this meets a certain societal need, then indirect discrimination is justified. The best examples are again language tests as a basis for access to employment. Knowledge of a certain regional language for teachers may be required to maintain the cultural identity of a nation. But even in this case such requirements must meet the *proportionality* criteria. That is, language tests should be easily accessible to every candidate, and requirements should not be unreasonable.[25] They should also be limited to teachers of subjects where the local language is really needed; this will not be the case for teaching sciences or foreign languages.

Under general principles, the party invoking a justification of indirect discrimination will need to prove that it serves a recognised societal need, and that its application meets the standard of proportionality (4.17). On the other hand, the discriminatory effect of a measure must be proven by the plaintiff. This may be difficult as far as access to statistical data is concerned.

2.2. SEX-BASED DISCRIMINATION

3.4 The first context in which the principle of non-discrimination was pronounced in EU law was that of employment. The principle of equal treatment between men and women with regard to pay for work of the same value had been part of the original EEC Treaty. The well known *Defrenne II* judgment[26] insisted on the horizontal direct effect of the principle of equal pay in what was then Article 119 EEC (now Article 157 TFEU). Equal access to employment and equality in working conditions were not part of primary Community law, as was firmly established by the Court in its *Defrenne III* judgment,[27] and therefore had to be introduced by secondary law, namely Directive 76/207[28] – a Directive which through extensive ECJ case law has acquired a *constitutional status.*[29] It has now been supplemented by Directive 2006/74, which will not be discussed

---

[24] Cf. Case C-415/93 *ASBL v Bosman* [1995] ECR I-4921.

[25] Case 379/87 *Groener v Minister for Education and City of Dublin Vocational Committee* [1989] ECR 3967; comment H.-W. Micklitz, ZEuP 2003, 635.

[26] Case 43/75 *G. Defrenne v SABENA* [1976] ECR 455; for details see N. Reich, in R. Schulze (ed.), *Non-Discrimination in European Private Law*, 2011, 58.

[27] Case 149/77 *G. Defrenne v SABENA* [1978] ECR 1365.

[28] Council Directive 76/207/EEC of 9 February 1976 on the implementation of the principle of equal treatment for men and women as regards access to employment, vocational training and promotion, and working conditions [1976] OJ L039/40.

[29] The ECJ had recognised the extension of the general principle of non-discrimination based on sex as a fundamental right of the then Community in its seminal case C-25/02 *Katharina Rinke v Ärztekammer Hamburg* [2003] ECR I-8349.

here.[30] The case law on sex-based discrimination – both direct and indirect – and its justification is abundant and will not be followed up here.[31] Particularly important has been its impact on the shaping of effective remedies (4.12, referring to *Von Colson*).[32]

2.3. RACIAL DISCRIMINATION

3.5   The first case referring to Directive 2000/43, *Feryn*,[33] concerned a charge brought against a Belgian producer of external door fitters who announced publicly that he would not employ "immigrants" as a result of his clients' fear that their work might endanger the safety of their property. There was no proof that any foreign applicant was actually rejected because of his or her ethnic origin. The ECJ, in a somewhat more cautious formulation than AG Poiares Maduro, agreed that – subject to factual findings by the national court – the concept of discrimination in Directive 2000/43 does not depend "on the identification of a complainant who claims to have been the victim".[34] In other words, the Directive wants to prevent discriminatory recruitment practices as such and will step in even before a specific victim has been identified, although the wording is somewhat unclear and ambiguous. Member States, under the minimum protection rule, may empower NGOs to bring a preventative action against discriminatory practices by potential employers. The employer has the burden of proof that his actual recruitment practice is not discriminatory (4.36).

2.4. AGE DISCRIMINATION

3.6   A bold new "constitutional approach" was taken by the ECJ in the context of age discrimination in employment law in the *Mangold* litigation.[35] The main question in that case was whether Germany, though not yet formally bound by the Framework Directive 2000/78/EC that prohibits under certain circumstances any discrimination based on age, violated a general principle of discrimination in lowering the age limit for fixed term contacts. In his opinion of 30 June 2005, AG Tizzano wrote:[36]

---

30   Recast Directive 2006/54/EC of the EP and the Council of 5 July 2006 on the implementation of the principle of equal opportunities and equal treatment of men and women in matters of employment [2006] OJ L 204/23.
31   N. Reich et al., *Understanding EU Internal Market Law*, 3rd ed. forthcoming, §12; C. Barnard, *EU Employment Law*, 4th ed. 2012, 253; K. Riesenhuber, *European Employment Law*, 2012, 277.
32   Case 14/83 *Von Colson and Kamann v Land Nordrhein-Westfalen* [1984] ECR 1891.
33   Case C-54/07 *Centrum voor gelijkheid van kansen en voor racismebestrijding (CGKR) v Firma Feryn NV* [2008] ECR I-5187.
34   Ibid., para 25.
35   Case C-144/04 *Werner Mangold v Rüdiger Helm* [2005] ECR I-9981.
36   Ibid., para 82.

"It may also be recalled that, even before the adoption of Directive 2000/78 and the specific provisions it contains, the Court had recognised the existence of a general principle of equality which is binding on Member States 'when they implement Community rules' and which can therefore be used by the Court to review national rules which 'fall within the scope of Community law'. That principle requires that 'comparable situations must not be treated differently and different situations must not be treated in the same way unless such *treatment* is *objectively justified*' by the pursuit of a legitimate aim and provided that it 'is *appropriate and necessary* in order to achieve' that aim."

The Court largely adopted this argument, thereby *de facto* eliminating the special *délai de grace* afforded to Germany for implementation:[37]

"The principle of non-discrimination on grounds of age must thus be regarded as a general principle of Community law. Where national rules fall within the scope of Community law, [...] and reference is made to the Court for a preliminary ruling, the Court must provide all the criteria of interpretation needed by the national court to determine whether those rules are compatible with such a principle."

This proclamation of a general principle of non-discrimination on grounds of age has given rise to an intense and mostly critical discussion amongst legal scholars.[38] It was also criticised in a subsequent opinion of AG Mazak in *Palacios de la Villa*,[39] which noted that the international instruments and constitutional traditions referred to in *Mangold* did enshrine the general principle of equal treatment, but it had been a bold proposition and a significant step to infer from that the existence of a specific principle prohibiting age discrimination. The AG also referred to the *Grant* case,[40] in which the Court held that Community law, as it stood, did not cover discrimination based on sexual orientation. The Court remained unimpressed by the criticism that its

---

[37] Ibid., para 75.

[38] For an overall discussion see A. Metzger, *Extra legem, intra ius: Allgemeine Rechtsgrundsätze im Europäischen Privatrecht*, 2009, 344–346; for criticism, N. Reich, EuZW 2006, 21, and 2007, 198; J. Basedow, 'The Court of Justice and Civil Law', ERevPrL 2010, 443 at 463; E. Spaventa, 'The Horizontal Application of Fundamental Rights as General Principles of Union Law', in: A. Arnull et al. (eds.), *A Constitutional Order of States – Essays in Honour of A. Dashwood*, 2011, 199 ff.; an interesting methodological argument combining primary EU law, general principles and secondary law has been advanced by M. Dougan, 'In Defence of *Mangold*?', in: A. Arnull et al., ibid., 219 ff.; further references can be found in the opinion of AG Sharpston in case C-427/06 *B. Bartsch v Bosch and Siemens (BSH) Altersfürsorge* [2008] ECR I-7245 which concerned the compatibility of a so-called "age-gap" clause in a pension scheme with primary (Article 13 EC) or secondary (Directive 2000/78) Community law.

[39] Case C-411/05 *Palacios de la Villa* [2007] ECR I-8531.

[40] Case C-249/96 *Lisa Jacqueline Grant v South-West Trains* [1998] ECR I-621; the EU legislator reacted by implementing Directive 2000/78; it is however not clear whether *Grant* would have been decided differently after this Directive.

---

judgment in *Mangold* received. In *Kücükdevici*[41] it repeated its broad approach concerning remedies against violations of the non-discrimination principle with respect to age in employment relations (details 3.14).

3.7 To the surprise of many observers, who read the *Lisbon* judgment of the Bundesverfassungsgericht (the German Constitutional Court) of 30 June 2009, and the earlier *Maastricht* judgment of the same court of 12 October 1993[42] as a challenge to the supremacy doctrine of the ECJ, the so-called *Honeywell* order of 6 July 2010[43] basically endorsed the *Mangold* case law. Strict limits were put on the *ultra vires* control of ECJ judgments under German constitutional law. The Bundesverfassungsgericht held that it would use its powers only in cases of a "sufficiently serious" (*hinreichend qualifiziert*) violation of competences:[44]

> "This requires that the action of a Union authority be regarded as manifest and that the attacked act leads to a structurally important modification of competences to the detriment of Member states in the EU."

In *Honeywell* the Bundesverfassungsgericht expressly recognised the power of the Court of Justice of the EU to create law *(Rechtsfortbildung)* by "methodologically constrained case law [*methodisch gebundene Rechtsprechung*] based on primary and secondary law as well as on unwritten general principles of the constitutional traditions of the Member States". It also put strict procedural restrictions on any *ultra vires* control; only the Bundesverfassungsgericht was held to have the power to declare Union acts inapplicable in Germany, and the ECJ was recognised as having the privilege of a possibility to clarify its position before such the decision of non-applicability is taken. This meant that in order for the plea to set aside the Union act (including the judgment of the ECJ) to be successful, a German court other than the Bundesverfassungsgericht had first to refer the case to the ECJ. The practical result of this ruling was a recognition by the German Constitutional Court of the precedence of ECJ judgments insofar as they concern interpretation of EU law and fall within the Court's mandate under Article 19(1) TEU to "ensure that [...] *the* law is observed"[45] (0.1), which includes the further development and application of general constitutional principles, such as the principle of non-discrimination.[46]

---

[41]   Case C-555/07 *Seda Kücükdevici v Swedex GmbH* [2010] ECR I-365, recently confirmed in case C-447/09 *R. Prigge et al v Lufthansa* [2011] ECR I-(13.09.2011), para 38; the broad approach of the Court has been criticised by M. Dougan, *supra* note 38, at 238 ff.

[42]   BVerfG(E) 89, 155 (English translation [1994] 1 CMLR 57; 123, 267; [2010] 3 CMLR 13).

[43]   BVerfG(E) 126, 286, with dissenting opinion of Judge Landau referring to the Lisbon judgment and criticising the ECJ's *Mangold* judgment, 318, 324.

[44]   BVerfG(E) 126, 286, headnote 1.

[45]   Emphasis added.

[46]   For a discussion on the importance of the *Honeywell* order of the BVerfG, see M. Payandeh, CMLRev 2011, 9.

2.5. DISCRIMINATION BASED ON SEXUAL ORIENTATION

3.8 A debate similar to *Mangold* also followed in another case decided by the ECJ. *Römer*[47] concerned an alleged discrimination against an *Eingetragene Lebenspartnerschaft* (registered same-sex couple), in comparison to persons in an heterosexual marriage, in the German system of supplementary retirement pensions for former employees of local authorities. In a strong but controversial opinion of 15 July 2010, AG Jääskinen, referring to *Mangold* and *Kücükdevici*, found that acts of discrimination over tax and related benefits had already been committed from 2001 onwards, the time of the registration of the partnership, and not from 2003, when the Member States were to implement Directive 2000/78/EC. This finding was supported by the view that the principle of non-discrimination on grounds of sexual orientation was in operation even before the transposition deadline for the Directive had expired. Its status as a "general principle" was evidenced by Article 21 of the Charter and the ECHR law. In its judgment of 10 May 2011, the ECJ decided not to follow the same approach to discrimination as in *Mangold*. It followed the AG only insofar as it condemned discrimination against registered same-sex couples through their exclusion from the pension scheme. However, Germany was not held to have been bound by the principle of non-discrimination on grounds of sexual orientation before the date of implementation of the Directive. Discrimination suffered by the couple after their partnership was registered but before the Directive's transposition deadline remained outside the scope of EU law. The ECJ thereby, without expressly distinguishing *Mangold*, implicitly denied the existence in EU law of a general principle of non-discrimination against same-sex partners that pre-dated the coming into effect of the Charter of Fundamental Rights.

The *ACCEPT* case[48] concerned discrimination on the grounds of sexual orientation by Mr Becali, a leading figure of the Romanian football club FC Steaua, on the transfer of a professional football player of alleged homosexual orientation. Mr Becali in strong words to the public had stated:

> "Not even if I had to close [FC Steaua] down would I accept a homosexual on the team. Maybe he's not a homosexual. But what if he is? There's no room for gays in my family, and [FC Steaua] is my family. Rather than having a homosexual on the side it would be better to have a junior player. This isn't discrimination: no one can force me to work with anyone. I have rights just as they do and I have the right to work with whoever I choose. Even if God told me in a dream that it was 100 percent certain that X wasn't a homosexual I still wouldn't take him. Too much has been written in the papers about his being a homosexual. Even if [player X's current club] gave him to me

---

47   Case C-147/08 *Jürgen Römer v Freie und Hansestadt Hamburg* [2011] ECR I-3591; for a criticism of the opinion of AG Jääskinen, N. Reich, EuZW 2010, 685.
48   Case C-81/12 *Asociatia ACCEPT v CNPCD* [2013] ECR I-(25.04.2013).

for free I wouldn't have him! He could be the biggest troublemaker, the biggest drinker [...] but if he's a homosexual I don't want to know about him."

The question before the ECJ did not turn so much on the discriminatory aspects of the statement of Mr Becali, but rather above of all on whether this could be attributed to the club, in which he owned shares but did not hold any formal management position. The Court answered as follows,[49] referring to its earlier *AGM-COSMET* judgment:[50]

> "It follows that a defendant employer cannot deny the existence of facts from which it may be inferred that it has a discriminatory recruitment policy merely by asserting that statements suggestive of the existence of a homophobic recruitment policy come from a person who, while claiming and appearing to play an important role in the management of that employer, is not legally capable of binding it in recruitment matters. In a situation such as that at the origin of the dispute in the main proceedings, the fact that such an employer might not have clearly distanced itself from the statements concerned is a factor which the court hearing the case may take into account in the context of an overall appraisal of the facts."

From this argument it follows that the club cannot hide behind the formal allocation of competences and has an obligation to distance itself from homophobic statements made in its name.

2.6. DISCRIMINATION AGAINST DISABLED PERSONS

3.9 In the *Navas* case[51] the Court was cautious in interpreting the concept of "disability" and insisted "that a person who has been dismissed by his employer solely on account of sickness does not fall within the general framework laid down for combating discrimination on grounds of disability by Directive 2000/78".[52] This follows from the need for a uniform and autonomous interpretation of the Directive, taking into account its objectives without referring to Member State law. The general Community/Union law principle of non-discrimination did not allow the prohibition on discrimination because of disability to be extended to sickness.[53]

Disability discrimination by "association" was the issue before the Court in *Coleman*.[54] It had to decide the question of whether in a dismissal case direct

---

[49] Ibid., paras 49–50.
[50] Case C-470/03 *AGM-COSMET* [2007] ECR I-2749, paras 55–58.
[51] Case C-13/05 *Sonja Chacón Navas v Eurest Colectividades* [2006] ECR I-6467; for criticism, E. Howard, ELJ 2011, 785 at 793, referring to the UN Convention on the Rights of Persons with Disabilities which includes persons with chronic diseases.
[52] Ibid., para 47.
[53] Ibid., para 56.
[54] Case C-303/06 *S. Coleman v Attridge Law et al* [2008] ECR I-5603.

discrimination on the grounds of disability, in the sense of Article 2(1) of Directive 2000/78, is also present where the employee herself is not disabled but whose newborn child is. The Court responded in the affirmative, insisting that the purpose of the Directive was to "combat all forms of discrimination on grounds of disability",[55] and to establish "a level playing field as regards equality in employment and occupation" in the EU,[56] regardless of whether the employee herself is disabled or, as in the situation before the Court, her newborn child. The Court did not concretely define what sort of relationship must exist between the employee and the disabled person; it is limited to the facts of the case, which concerned a mother and child. This interpretation is also relevant for the issue of harassment. As regards burden of proof, the applicant must establish "facts from which it may be presumed that there has been direct discrimination on grounds of disability contrary to the directive". It is then for the employer to prove that "the employee's treatment was justified by objective facts unrelated to any discrimination on grounds of disability and to any association which that employee has with a disabled person".[57]

3. CITIZENSHIP: EXTENDING THE SCOPE OF THE PRINCIPLE OF NON-DISCRIMINATION BY PRIMARY LAW

3.10 Primary EU law has extended the principle of non-discrimination to civil law situations, under specific circumstances, beyond employment. An example of this trend is the use of the concept of *citizenship* in Article 20 TFEU (ex-Article 17 EC) to expand the scope of the prohibition on discrimination based on nationality, which applies only "within the scope of application of the Treaty" (Article 18 TFEU, ex-Article 12 EC, see above 3.3). The application of the non-discrimination principle is seen as a step towards guaranteeing the autonomy of persons as EU citizens to enjoy a bundle of rights, in particular the right to free movement. In the exercise of their free movement rights EU citizens should not be unduly restricted by provisions normally coming under the regime of civil law, for example unfair contract terms (1.7).

Although there has not yet been a case concerning discrimination in civil law relations, the arguments developed by the Court with regard to fundamental freedoms, namely the existence of a "collective regulation" (or an employment contract in the sense used by the Court in *Raccanelli*),[58] can also be used to attack – directly or indirectly – nationality clauses in standard contract forms,

---

[55] Ibid., para 38.
[56] Ibid., para 47.
[57] Ibid., para 55.
[58] Case C-94/07 *Raccanelli v MPG* [2008] ECR I-5939.

or in by-laws of civil associations like boarding schools or private universities concerning admission, tuition or employment.

3.11 This "constitutional approach" to non-discrimination, which perceives equality as a necessary attribute of the position of individuals as EU citizens, has also been used by the Court in cases involving challenges to national legislation on surnames, usually a matter of (non-harmonised) private international law. In *Garcia Avello*[59] the Court had to decide whether the Belgian law on names of children, which, unlike Spanish law, excluded the use of both parents' surnames, could be applied to children of Belgian citizens who also held Spanish citizenship. The Court relied on the "second limb" of the non-discrimination principle, namely *that* "different situations should not be treated alike, unless this is objectively justified" to rule that:[60]

> "In contrast to persons having only Belgian nationality, Belgian nationals who also hold Spanish nationality have different surnames under the two legal systems concerned. More specifically, in a situation such as that in issue in the main proceedings, the children concerned are refused the right to bear the surname which results from application of the legislation of the Member State which determined the surname of their father."

The Court did not find any justification for applying the strict Belgian law on names to the Avello children to the effect that they were unable to use their double-barrelled surnames.

In a later case, *Grunkin and Paul*,[61] the Court of Justice adopted different reasoning from that in *Garcia Avello*, although the case also concerned the autonomy in the choice of the surname format. The *Grunkin and Paul* case was brought by a German citizen born in Denmark, where his name was determined according to the *ius soli*, which allowed him to take the last name of both of his father and mother, while under the German *ius sanguinis* and *lex nationalitis* his parents were forced to choose between the last name of the father or that of the mother. When he settled in Germany he applied to maintain his Danish double-barrelled name, but the request was refused by the competent German authority.

---

[59] Case C-148/02 *Garcia Avello* [2003] ECR I-11613; for its importance to fundamental rights protection of economically inactive citizens, see M. Elsmore/P. Starup, 'Union Citizenship – Background, Jurisprudence, and Perspective', YEL 2007, 57 at 93.

[60] Ibid., para 35.

[61] Case C-353/06 *Grunkin and Paul* [2008] ECR I-7639; see already the opinion of AG Jacobs of 30 June 2005 in the preceding case C-96/04 [2006] ECR I-3561 where the ECJ however regarded the reference as inadmissible. In his earlier opinion of 13 September 1992 in case C-168/01 *Konstantinidi*s [1993] ECR I-1191, argued before the enactment of the citizenship concept in EU law, AG Jacobs pointed to the fundamental right of a person to his name as part of European citizenship: "*civis Europeus sum*", para 46; the Court agreed with the argument against the somewhat artificial market aspects of distorting the spelling of a name which may create confusion with potential clients of Mr Konstantinidis and therefore disproportionately restrict his right to establishment.

In its judgment of 13 October 2008 the Court regarded German legislation on names as an unjustified, disproportionate interference with the free movement rights of a Union citizen, rather than with the principle of non-discrimination, as was the case in *Garcia Avello*.

Interestingly, in both *Garcia Avello* and *Grunkin and Paul* the litigation concerned a "vertical" conflict between an EU citizen and a Member State, namely a national agency or a court that determined the question of name. However, the substance of the cases concerned a *civil law question*, that of a name of a citizen, which in cross-border situations is determined by the rules of *private international law*.[62] This particular aspect of international civil law is not harmonised by primary or secondary EU law. However, Member States are still asked to avoid discrimination of citizens of other Member States, as in *Garcia Avello*, or refrain from creating unjustified restrictions on free movement, as in *Grunkin and Paul*.

4. EXTENSION OF THE NON-DISCRIMINATION PRINCIPLE TO BUSINESS-CONSUMER RELATIONS BY EU SECONDARY LAW

3.12   Secondary law has extended the prohibition on discrimination to civil law relationships beyond employment[63] with reference to grounds such as ethnic and racial origin (Article 3(1)(h) of Directive 2000/43/EC), gender (Article 5(1) of Directive 2004/113/EC), and legal residence (Article 11(1)(f) of the Long-term Resident Directive 2003/109/EC).[64] The situations in which individuals are protected by EU law encompass the "access to and supply of goods and services available to the public". The term "including housing" is mentioned only in Directive 2000/43, not in Directive 2004/113; Directive 2003/109 is limited to "procedures for obtaining housing". Therefore, not every differentiation in the selection of contract partners is a violation of EU law; there must already be an initial availability of certain goods and services to the public, for example via advertising or marketing.[65] Article 3(2) and recital 14 of Directive 2004/113

---

62   P. Lagarde, 'Droit international privé', in: R. Schulze/H. Schulte-Nölke (eds.), *European Private Law – Current Status and Perspectives*, 2011, 249 at 257.

63   For an overview see D. Schiek et al. (eds.), *Non-discrimination law*, 2007, 11–14; N. Reich, *supra* note 1, at para 13.19. J. Basedow, *supra* note 1, at 238, differentiates between a genuine "prohibition of discrimination", which is not the formulation of the directives, and the need to "combat discrimination", for example according to Article 1 of Directive 2000/43; Article 2(1) of that Directive states that "there shall be no direct or indirect discrimination based on race or ethnic origin." Is the latter formula really a different from a "prohibition" *strictu sensu*? Otherwise the need for effective sanctions would not be understandable. Obviously, the Member States have a (limited) discretion on how to implement this obligation, 3.13.

64   [2004] OJ L 16/44.

65   N. Reich, *supra* note 1, at para 13.29; M. Schreier, 'Das Allgemeine Gleichbehandlungsgesetz – wirklich ein Eingriff in die Vertragsfreiheit?', KritJ 2007, 278 at 285, referring to the

expressly guarantee the freedom to choose a contractual partner (1.13), so long as that choice is not based on the person's gender. Special rules apply to insurance contracts (see below 3.15). Both intentional and indirect discrimination is prohibited, the latter situation being where seemingly neutral provisions create unjustified negative effects.[66]

3.13 The *Belov* case[67] concerned an alleged indirect race discrimination case against the Roma minority in Montana, Bulgaria. The Bulgarian Center against Discrimination (KZD) brought an injunction against the Bulgarian power supplier who had put electricity meters at a height of 7m to prevent frequent power manipulations in a district mostly populated by the Roma people, where the complainant Mr Belov lived. In her very careful opinion AG Kokott – first affirming that the KZD was a "court or tribunal" in the sense of Article 267 TFEU – found an indirect discrimination based up the traditional formula of the ECJ that was forbidden under Directive 2000/43; the supply of electricity and the provision of meters concern "access to and supply of goods and services available to the public" without it being necessarily the case that a "right" of Mr Belov had been violated. The AG then turned to possible justifications for the supplier's actions, namely to combat fraud and abuse under the proportionality principle. She found that the measure was possibly suitable and necessary and did not have undue adverse effects of the inhabitants of the districts concerned, if supported by the facts to be established by KZD under the EU rules of a presumption of discrimination (Article 8(1) of Directive 2000/43). She concluded:

> "In summary, a measure like the one at issue in the present case may be justified if it prevents fraud and abuse and contributes to ensuring the quality of the electricity supply in the interest of all consumers, provided
> – no other, equally suitable measures can be taken to achieve those aims, at financially reasonable cost, which would have less detrimental effects on the population in the districts concerned,
> – the measure taken does not produce undue adverse effects on the inhabitants of the districts concerned, due account being taken of the risk of an ethnic group being stigmatized and of the consumer's interest in monitoring their individual electricity consumption by means of a regular visual, check of their electricity meters."

---

somewhat misleading term in the implementing German legislation (AGG – Allgemeines Gleichbehandlungsgesetz von 2006) *"Massengeschäft"* in contrast to "individual transactions" where personal characteristics of the partner are important; analysis by K. Riesenhuber, 'Das Verbot der Diskriminierung aufgrund der Rasse und der ethnischen Herkunft sowie aufgrund des Geschlechts beim Zugang zu und der Versorgung mit Gütern und Dienstleistungen', in: S. Leible/M. Schlachter, *Diskriminierungsschutz durch Privatrecht*, 2007, 124 at 129, insisting on "objective criteria".

[66]   K. Riesenhuber, *supra* note 65, at 133; H. Cousy, *supra* note 12, at 85.
[67]   C-394/11.

The conclusion of the opinion may be questioned. The ECJ, in its judgment of 31 January 2013, however, dismissed the case on formal grounds because it did not regard KZD as a "court" in the sense of Article 267 TFEU; regrettably it did not make any statement on the discrimination issue. In any case, the opinion of AG Kokott gives a very useful analysis of the legal and consumer issues in a case to which there is not an easy answer.

3.14   On 2 July 2008 the Commission proposed extending the principle of equal treatment between persons irrespective of religion or belief, disability, age or sexual orientation to also include civil law relations outside the labour market, in particular to consumer markets where "access to and supply of goods and services available to the public, including housing" are concerned. The proposal has been met with a strong resistance from the Member States.[68] While allowing some exceptions, the German *Allgemeine Gleichbehandlungsgesetz* (AGG) of 14 August 2006 already contains a similar provision in §19.

5.   A CONTROVERSY: UNISEX TARIFFS IN INSURANCE AND CONFLICTS WITH PRIVATE AUTONOMY

5.1. A "MONIST" READING OF THE NON-DISCRIMINATION PRINCIPLE BY THE ECJ?

3.15   A more recent debate concerns the problem of whether the EU legislator may restrict the non-discrimination principle in a Directive aimed at combating discrimination. This question arose in an action brought by the Belgian consumer association *Test-Achats* before its Constitutional Court, which then referred the matter to the ECJ, the sole competent judicial authority to invalidate EU acts.[69] The Belgian Constitutional Court's question concerned the validity of Article 5(2) of the above-mentioned non-discrimination directive (Directive 2004/113/EC), which reads:

> "Notwithstanding paragraph 1, Member States may decide before 21 December 2007 to permit proportionate differences in individuals' premiums and benefits where the use of sex is a determining factor in the assessment of risk based on relevant and accurate actuarial and statistical data. The Member States concerned shall inform the Commission and ensure that accurate data relevant to the use of sex as a determining actuarial factor are compiled, published and regularly updated. These Member States

---

[68]   COM (2008) 426 final; for discussion see A.-S. Vandenberghe, 'Proposal for a new Directive on non-discrimination', ZEuP 2011, 235.
[69]   Case C-236/09 *Ass. Belge Test-Achats et al* [2011] ECR I-773; see the detailed comments on the Belgian legislation by H. Cousy, *supra* note 12, at 99.

shall review their decision five years after 21 December 2007, taking into account the Commission report referred to in Article 16, and shall forward the results of this review to the Commission."

Could this exception relating to an autonomous rate of insurers' calculation (even if it was somewhat camouflaged by reference to statistics) be upheld against the general principle of non-discrimination on the basis of gender which is enshrined in Articles 21(1) and 23 of the Charter, which has become binding from 1 December 2009 on all EU institutions? The opinion of AG Kokott of 30 September 2010[70] condemns in very strong words this exception in secondary law as violating the higher ranking EU non-discrimination principle. She writes:[71]

"[W]ith Directive 2004/113, particularly with Article 5, the Council made a conscious decision to adopt anti-discrimination legislation in the field of insurance. Such provisions must, without restriction, withstand examination against the yardstick of higher-ranking European Union law, in particular against the yardstick of the fundamental rights recognised by the Union. They must, to use the words of Article 13(1) EC (now Article 19(1) TFEU), be 'appropriate' for combating discrimination; they may not themselves lead to discrimination. The Council cannot evade that examination by simply arguing that it could also have taken no action."

She has also rejected the argument that gender is one of the actuarial factors that can be taken into account for risk assessment in life, health and car insurance:[72]

"In view of social change and the accompanying loss of meaning of traditional role models, the effects of behavioural factors on a person's health and life expectancy can no longer clearly be linked with his sex. To refer once again to a few of the examples just mentioned: both women and men nowadays engage in demanding and sometimes extremely stressful professional activities, members of both sexes consume a not inconsiderable amount of stimulants and even the kind and extent of sporting activities practised by people cannot from the outset be linked to one or other of the sexes."

3.16 On 1 March 2011 the ECJ condemned the exemption from the non-discrimination principle in insurance contracts by ruling in the *dispositif* of its judgment:

"Article 5(2) of Council Directive 2004/113/EC of 13 December 2004 implementing the principle of equal treatment between men and women in the access to and supply of goods and services is invalid with effect from 21 December 2013."

---

[70]   For criticism, U. Karpenstein, 'Harmonie durch die Hintertür? Geschlechtsspezifisch kalkulierte Versicherungstarife und das Diskriminierungsverbot', EuZW 2010, 885.

[71]   Case C-236/09 *Ass. Belge Test-Achats et al* [2011] ECR I-773, para 35.

[72]   Ibid., para 63.

The judgment is surprisingly short,[73] quite in contrast to the lengthy opinion of AG Kokott. The ECJ shows its willingness to control strictly the conformity of EU provisions with the human rights regime to which the EU subscribed in a number of documents, the latest one being the "elevated" Charter of Fundamental Rights, which from 1 December 2009 has had the same value as the EU Treaties. The Court's ruling is based on several arguments. First, the Charter cannot be directly used to assess the conformity of Article 5(2) of Directive 2004/113 because the Charter was not yet a binding document at the time when the Non-Discrimination Directive was adopted (13 December 2004) or became binding upon the Member States (21 December 2007). Instead, the Charter had relevance only by the Directive's "auto-reference" to Articles 21 and 23 of the Charter as a document expressing the political will of the Union (then the Community) to protect and promote fundamental rights, including equality of the sexes.[74] The Court also refers to the fact that "the right to equal treatment for men and women is the subject of (several) provisions of the FEU Treaty".[75]

Secondly, the Court recognises that such equality cannot be simply produced by "legal *fiat*", but contains an evolutionary element which must be "progressively achieved".[76] The EU non-discrimination directives do not immediately forbid discrimination but contain a *mandatory* political programme to be elaborated and implemented over time. The Union itself, via legislation and the Member States, as well as civil actors (insurance companies doing business in the EU according to the relevant legislation), to which the equality regime is addressed in the end, must cooperate in this task, for example, by offering "unisex" tariffs from a date to be determined by legislation. In order to fulfil this dynamic element of non-discrimination, legislative action "must contribute, in a *coherent manner*, to the achievement of the intended objective, without prejudice of providing for transitional periods or derogations of limited scope".[77] This "inner-legislative" coherence requires that such periods be limited in time. They cannot last "eternally" or give Member States or companies unfettered discretion as to how to achieve this objective. Since such a time limit was missing from the Directive, the Court invalidated it, but only with *ex nunc* consequences, beginning five years after the Directive's entry into force. This is a courageous step, but well known of the case law of the German Constitutional Court, which

---

[73] Comment N. Reich, 'Some Thoughts after the "Test Achats" Judgment', EJRR 2011, 283; K. Purnhagen, EuR 2011, 690; D. Effer-Uhe, 'Gleichbehandlung in Versicherungsverträgen', in: R. Schulze (ed.), Non-Discrimination in European Private Law, 2011, 109 ff.; C. Tobler, 'Case note', CMLRev 2011, 2041; P. Watson, 'Equality, fundamental rights and the limits of legislative discretion', ELRev 2011, 896.

[74] Case C-236/09 *Ass. Belge Test-Achats et al* [2011] ECR I-773, para 17. See V. Kosta, 'Internal Market Legislation and the Civil Law of the Member States – The Impact of Fundamental Rights', ERCL 2010, 409.

[75] Case C-236/09 *Ass. Belge Test-Achats et al* [2011] ECR I-773, para 18.

[76] Ibid., at para 20.

[77] Ibid., at para 21 (emphasis added).

has frequently invalidated a legislative measure held to violate fundamental rights only with *ex nunc* effect, in order to give the legislator time to remedy the complex political, economic or legal circumstances.

3.17   The ECJ expressly condemned the exemption in Article 5(2) as a violation of the equality principle, which was (and still is) the basis for legislative action under Article 13 EC (now Article 19 TFEU). In consistent case law, the ECJ defines the principle of equal treatment as requiring that "comparable situations must not be treated differently, and that different situations must not be treated in the same way, unless such treatment is objectively justified".[78] Despite the different risk profiles of the sexes in certain types of insurance, for example third party liability of car drivers, where men seem to take more risks and are responsible for more accidents, on the one hand, and life and health insurance, where women have a higher and more costly risk profile according to relevant statistics, these differences were expressly ruled not to be relevant by Article 5(1) of Directive 2004/113. Men and women, despite the difference in life expectancy, have to be treated as "normatively comparable" even though "empirically different".[79] The ECJ did not find any justification for this differentiation to continue without a time limit. It amounted to a "pure and simple" discrimination to persist indefinitely.[80] In order to remedy this situation, the Court took upon itself the position of legislator and imposed a time limit of its own accord, without invalidating the entire legislative act. As a consequence, existing insurance contracts with different premiums, tariffs and benefits for men and women that are not overtly inconsistent with Article 5(2) (for example §20(2) of the German *Allgemeine Gleichbehandlungsgesetz* (AGG))[81] can be maintained until 20 December 2012, but may not be offered from 21 December 2012 onwards, when "unisex" tariffs will become mandatory. This means that premiums for "new contracts" concluded after this date will have to be recalculated compared to those charged before 20 December 2012, which may result in general premium increases.[82] The new premium tariffs will only be legal under EU law if they do not (overtly or indirectly) discriminate but only differentiate on the basis of accepted actuarial techniques.

The ECJ does not seem to require, contrary to what was suggested by AG Kokott,[83] that existing tariffs, premiums and benefits, even contracts of long

---

[78]   Ibid., at para 28.

[79]   See ibid., at para 30.

[80]   Ibid., at para 33.

[81]   Concerning the constitutionality of the exception under German law see F. Rödl, in U. Rust/ J. Falke (eds.), *Kommentar zum AGG*, §20 para 37, arguing that differentiation concerning insurance tariffs is justified for objective reasons (*sachlicher Grund*). This argument can no longer be maintained due to the priority of EU law.

[82]   This was rightly feared by many observers: see the article in Süddeutsche Zeitung of 19.03.2011, 33.

[83]   Case C-236/09 *Ass. Belge Test-Achats et al* [2011] ECR I-773, para 81 of the opinion of AG Kokott.

duration that violated the principle of non-discrimination, be altered. The "dynamic" reasoning of the Court clearly suggests that, despite doubts, the Member State exemption of Article 5(2) was perfectly legal for five years, and would only lose its justifying force for tariffs that discrimination based on gender agreed after 21 December 2013. Therefore, there is *no retroactive effect* of the Court's judgment on the existing tariffs used before that date.[84] Insurers will appreciate this solution, while clients may regret that they will not profit from the judgment, neither for the past, nor in all probability for the future. Non-discrimination comes at a price and is unlikely to be a "consumer-friendly" measure because, for example, cautious women drivers will have to subsidise more risk-taking male drivers, and insured men will have to pay for the additional costs of women's medical treatment and their longer life expectancy.

5.2. A POSSIBLE CRITICISM OF THE JUDGMENT: TOO MUCH "EQUAL TREATMENT", TOO LITTLE AUTONOMY LEFT?

3.18 The judgment has obviously been subject to the fundamental criticism that the Court has sacrificed civil autonomy (including calculation of premiums by insurers according to their business models) on the "altar of non-discrimination", despite the assurance in Article 3(2) of Directive 2004/113 that the measure will not prejudice the freedom to choose a contractual partner, with a somewhat obscure exception "so long as an individual's choice is not based on that person's sex".[85] Indeed, there seem to be three fundamental weaknesses to the Court's argument. First, the yardstick for measuring "equal treatment" is a *formal* one as written into Directive 2004/113, not a substantive one, based on a value judgment inherent in the concept of "discrimination" itself. Following this argument through to its ultimate consequences, the EU legislator should not even be entitled to impose a transition period, in contrast to the grace period of five years allowed by the Court to the EU legislator. Secondly, as pointed out by Effer-Uhe,[86] the Court invalidated the optional provision of Article 5(2) of Directive 2004/113 even though it was that very point that enabled a unanimous adoption of the Directive, as required by Article 19 TFEU (then Article 13 EC). It could be argued that by invalidating the provision the Court rendered the requirement of "unanimity" nugatory. Personally, I find this argument

---

[84]   Against C. Tobler, *supra* note 73, at 2057. For a restrictive interpretation of the concept of "new contracts" in Article 5(1) of Directive 2004/114, see the Commission guidelines of 13 January 2012 [2012] OJ C 11/1, excluding automatic extensions, unilateral premium adjustments, follow-on policies pre-agreed before 21 December 2012 (no. 13).

[85]   J. Lüttringhaus, 'Europaweit Unisex-Tarife für Versicherungen', EuZW 2011, 296.

[86]   D. Effer-Uhe, *supra* note 73, at 113. Concerning the compromise version of Article 5(2) see H. Cousy, *supra* note 12, at 99.

unconvincing because there can be no exemption from the fundamental rights control by the Court for optional EU-law provisions, the application of which would allow Member States to maintain "unconstitutional" provisions.

Thirdly, while according to Article 23 of the Charter "equality between men and women must be ensured in *all areas*",[87] equality is also subject to proportionate limitations by law under Article 52(1) of the Charter. As Lüttringhaus observed,[88] the Court did not seriously consider possible justifications for "discriminations" – or rather differentiations – between men and women in calculating insurance tariffs. Following the detailed socio-legal argumentation of AG Kokott, such a strict proportionality test could have resulted in condemning higher tariffs for men in third party liability car insurance and for women in health insurance, because of fragmented and inconclusive statistical evidence not taking into account different risk profiles and lifestyles of insured persons, making gender no longer a determining factor. But *bonus/malus* schemes could have been found to be a more flexible and therefore a more proportionate instrument to avoid the "moral hazard" on part of the insured persons. Under these circumstances, gender was a rather "crude" and therefore discriminatory method of risk determination. On the other hand, it is arguable that premiums for life insurance should be allowed to be calculated differently for the simple fact that in the EU the average life expectancy for women is still longer than that for men, and therefore women pay more and for a longer time before they start enjoying the benefits. Reference to publicly available statistics determining different risk profiles of men and women has nothing to do with "discrimination" or "unequal treatment", but simply takes differences in life expectancies at their face value in order to avoid men with an on-average shorter life expectancy having to subsidise longer-lived women. It follows that it is possible to argue that the ECJ failed to carry out the necessary balancing between "party autonomy" and "equal treatment" in the insurance market, which is a basic pillar of pluralism in civil law as understood in this context.

6. NON-DISCRIMINATION IN ACCESS TO AND TREATMENT IN SERVICES OF GENERAL ECONOMIC INTEREST AND IN NETWORK SERVICES: FRAMED AUTONOMY

3.19   Services of general economic interest, like communications, energy and transport, have only recently come within the scope of Union law, in line with deregulation and privatisation trends affecting these sectors. In the "old days" these services were highly regulated by public law, where the principles of non-

---

[87]   Emphasis added.
[88]   J. Lüttringhaus, *supra* note 85, at 298.

discrimination could be applied without dogmatic problems relating to party autonomy. The new regime is, by contrast, more concerned with competition and choice. Accordingly, it has had to develop standards of its own, in particular by transposing (somewhat hesitantly) the idea of *solidarity* alongside the more economic and competition-orientated understanding of public services, and thus including questions of consumer (or rather user) access and equality.[89] The EU Commission has proposed including these services in its work on consumer protection.[90] Because the provision of these services requires conclusion of a contract, EU law that regulates services of general economic interest could be seen as also belonging to "civil law" and as concerning horizontal situations, albeit ones extensively regulated by economic law.

The most important elements of EU regulation of services of general economic interest have been, on the one hand, the internal market approach, and on the other, the so-called "universal service obligation" of providers.[91] This is to some extent required by the principle of "access to services of general economic interest" as written into Article 36 of the Charter, which has to be "provided for in national laws and practices, in accordance with the TEU, in order to promote the social and territorial cohesion of the Union." Its impact on free choice in access to services and on obligations of non-discriminatory treatment without distinguishing between consumers in the traditional sense and other users remains to be clarified by legislation. For example, under the Universal Services Directive 2002/22/EC[92] and the revised Electricity/Gas Directives 2003/54/EC and 2003/55/EC,[93] "household customers" should not be prevented from switching to another provider through direct or indirect impediments.[94] On 17 July 2009 the European Parliament and the Council adopted Directives 2009/72/EC and 2009/73/EC concerning common rules for the internal market

---

[89]   M. Ross, 'Promoting Solidarity: From Public Service to a European Model of Competition?', CMLRev 2007, 1057 at 1070, insisting on the applicability of the general norm of Article 16 EC (now Article 14 TFEU).

[90]   Consumer Policy Strategy, COM (2002) para 3.1.5; also COM (2007) 99 at 12: EU Consumer Policy Strategy 2007–2013.

[91]   P. Rott, 'Consumers and Services of General Interest: Is EC Consumer Law the Future?', JCP 2007, 53; N. Reich, 'Crisis of Future of European Consumer Law?', in: *Yearbook of Consumer Law 2008*, 2009, 3 at 20; H.-W. Micklitz, 'The Visible Hand of European Regulatory Civil Law', YEL 2009, 3 at 22 ff.

[92]   Directive 2002/22/EC of the EP and the Council of 2002 on universal service and user's rights relating to electronic communications, networks and services (Universal Services Directive) [2002] OJ L 108/51, amended by Directive 2009/136/EC of 19 December 2009 [2009] OJ L 337.

[93]   Directive 2003/54/EC of the European Parliament and the Council of 26 June 2003 concerning Common Rules for the Internal Market for Electricity [2003] OJ L 176/37; for Gas [2003] OJ L 176/57.

[94]   P. Rott, *supra* note 91, at 56; H.-W. Micklitz, 'The Concept of Competitive Contract Law', PennStateLJ 2005, 549 at 576; C. Willet, 'General Clauses on Fairness and the Promotion of Values important in Services of General Interest', in C. Twigg-Flesner et al. (eds.), *Yearbook of Consumer Law 2007*, 2008, 67 at 95–100.

of electricity and gas and repealing Directives 2003/54/EC and 2003/55/EC.[95] Article 3(7) of Directive 2009/72 contains general obligations on Member States to protect final, in particular *vulnerable* (2.11), consumers in markets through universal service obligations:

> "In this context, each Member State shall define the concept of vulnerable customer which may refer to energy poverty and, inter alia, to the prohibition of disconnection of electricity to such customer in critical times."

These provisions try to improve the position of consumers, in particular vulnerable ones, as compared to their situation in the old Directive 2003/54 mentioned above, although only half-heartedly. They are too non-specific to take direct effect. Much more specific are the transparency requirements of Annex I of Directive 2009/72 concerning the (right to) contract with the universal service supplier.

3.19a These principles should be extended to other network services like banking. Article 28 of Directive 2007/64/EC on payment services[96] contains rather unspecific provisions protecting the "recipient of services" against discrimination. This proposed right of "access" to payment services without discrimination may have the effect of transforming payment systems in the EU, despite their heterogeneity, into a "service of general economic interest" based on civil law (without, however, a "universal service obligation" and "direct effect") and subject to special rules that go beyond the traditional concepts of civil autonomy and freedom of contract.

In the meantime, the Commission has published on 8 May 2013 a "Proposal for a Directive on the comparability of fees related to payment accounts, payment account switching, and access to payment account with basic features".[97]

Article 14 (Non-discrimination) requires Member States to ensure that consumers are not discriminated against on the basis of their nationality or residence when applying for a payment account or in their use of a payment account.

Article 15 (Right of access to a payment account with basic features) establishes a right of access to a basic payment account for consumers in any Member State. It also establishes an obligation on Member States to designate at least one payment service provider to offer a basic payment account.

Article 16 (Characteristics of a payment account with basic features) specifies the list of payment services that a payment account with basic features should include.

Without going into details of the proposal, its political, economic and legislative aspects are not yet clear at the time of writing. Much depends of

---

[95]   [2009] OJ L 211/55; for Gas [2009] OJ L 211/94.
[96]   [2007] OJ L 319/36.
[97]   COM (2013) 266.

course on the willingness of the Member States to designate one or several "universal" payment service provider(s).

3.20 Quite surprisingly, the impact of this encroachment of regulation on civil law has hardly been discussed in the scholarship so far. The non-discrimination principle has a special role to play in this context and yet the area seems to be, as Micklitz correctly observes,[98] a blind spot in the eyes of civil law scholars, who believe that this highly regulated sector still follows the principle of party autonomy. As Micklitz writes:

> "The network law develops, within the boundaries of universal services, concepts and devices whose reach must be tested with regard to their potential for general application beyond the narrow subject matter. Just one example may be mentioned: despite privatisation, network industries have to guarantee the accessibility and the affordability of their services. What is at stake here is the obligation to contract (*Kontrahierungszwang*) and the duty to continue delivery even in cases of late payment."

As a result of these developments, the principle of non-discrimination is "creeping" into European contract law. It has the potential to expand its scope of application beyond the areas and grounds recognised so far in EU law, and briefly mentioned in this paper. Its impact on citizens and consumers may however be double-headed, as the recent *Test-Achats* case shows. Equal treatment comes at a cost. Somebody has to bear the financial consequences of the expansion of this principle.

7. EQUAL TREATMENT BEYOND NON-DISCRIMINATION?

7.1. ACCESS TO INFORMATION IN BROADCASTING SERVICES

3.21 Access rights similar to those under the regime of services in the general economic interest have also been granted by EU law with regard to broadcasting services, although in a more limited and indirect way. The basis of this is Article 15(1) and (6) of the Audiovisual Media Services Directive 2010/13/EU (AMSD)[99] which reads:

---

[98] H.-W. Micklitz, *supra* note 91, at 23.
[99] Directive 2010/13/EU of the European Parliament and the Council of 10 March 2010 (Audiovisual Media Service Directive) [2010] OJ L 95/1.

"1. Member States shall ensure that for the purpose of short news reports, any broadcaster established in the [European] Union has access on a fair, reasonable and non-discriminatory basis to events of high interest to the public which are transmitted on an exclusive basis by a broadcaster under their jurisdiction. [...]

6. Without prejudice to paragraphs 1 to 5, Member States shall ensure, in accordance with their legal systems and practices, that the modalities and conditions regarding the provision of such short extracts are defined, in particular, any compensation arrangements, the maximum length of short extracts and time limits regarding their transmission. Where compensation is provided for, it shall not exceed the additional costs directly incurred in providing access."

The constitutionality of this provision was before the ECJ in the *Sky/ORF* case.[100] The Court examined this case under the fundamental right of freedom to conduct a business found in Article 16 of the Charter (1.13). It held this provision to be applicable to the duty of the holder of an exclusive license to allow another broadcaster to use a short news report on the condition that it paid compensation linked to the transmission costs but that it could not, as a condition of acquiring the right to transmission, recover some of the considerable license fees due to it. This restriction was however justified by a proportionate public interest. The Court stated:[101]

"In the light, first, of the importance of safeguarding the fundamental freedom to receive information and the freedom and pluralism of the media guaranteed by Article 11 of the Charter and, second, of the protection of the freedom to conduct a business as guaranteed by Article 16 of the Charter, the European Union legislature was entitled to adopt rules such as those laid down in Article 15 of Directive 2010/13, which limit the freedom to conduct a business, and to give priority, in the necessary balancing of the rights and interests at issue, to public access to information over contractual freedom."

At first sight, the litigation was concerned with the opposing rights of broadcasters in relation to public events under an exclusive licence to one of them, and does not directly relate to the access of the consumer to news services. One could argue that it is sufficient and economically more efficient that the consumer of such events has to access to them by paying for participation in the broadcast of such events. But this would force upon the consumer a contract s/he may not want or need. S/he may just be interested in being informed visually about the results of the event; therefore, the right to information becomes a consumer right to participate in market-governed events of public interest. They become part of the package the broadcaster can acquire under the exclusive licence. The very public nature of the interest for which the broadcaster pays

---

[100]   Case C-283/11 *Sky Österreich v ORF* [2013] ECR I-(23.01.2013).
[101]   Ibid., para 66.

dearly makes it subject to a corresponding restriction in the public interest. It excludes a market-centred approach and requires a regulatory measure. There is no market for short news reports of these events – they belong to the public domain due to their very nature and cannot be totally privatised. In putting a cap on the compensation,[102]

> "any broadcaster [is guaranteed] access to the event, which is to be provided [...] in compliance with the principle of equal treatment [...] thereby providing any broadcaster with the opportunity to make short news reports."

The principle of equal treatment as imposed by the legislature is justified for guaranteeing effective access to basic broadcasting services in the interest of the end-user and consumer whose right to receive information is also protected under Article 10 ECHR and Article 11(1) of the Charter.

7.2. NO EQUAL TREATMENT OF MINORITY SHAREHOLDERS IN PUBLIC COMPANIES

3.22   As mentioned above (0.3), the ECJ, following a detailed opinion of AG Trstenjak of 30 June 2009, denied the existence of a general principle of equal treatment of minority shareholders.[103] The Court wrote:

> "A principle such as that proposed by Audiolux [equal treatment of minority shareholders] presupposes legislative choices, based on a weighing of the interests at issue and the fixing in advance of precise and detailed rules [...] and cannot be inferred from the general principle of equal treatment. The general principles of Community law have constitutional status while the principle proposed by Audiolux is characterised by a degree of detail requiring legislation to be drafted and enacted at Community level by a measure of secondary Community law. Therefore, the principle proposed by Audiolux cannot be regarded as an independent general principle of Community law."

This judgment makes clear that not every variation in treatment of persons in similar situations can be regarded as discrimination violating *per se* the general EU principle of equal treatment and giving rise to legal consequences. A value judgment is required in any case, either by the legislator or – absent such determination – by the Court as part of its mission to interpret and apply *the law* (0.1.).

---

[102]   Ibid., para 56.
[103]   Case C-101/08 *Audiolux* [2010] ECR I-9823, paras 62–63.

8. CONCLUSION: THE VARIED IMPACT OF THE NON-DISCRIMINATION PRINCIPLE ON CIVIL LAW RELATIONS

3.23 The general EU principle of non-discrimination, now part of the Charter (Articles 21 and 23) has an impact on civil law relations, thereby framing autonomy by limiting the choice of contractual partners and the imposition of varying terms on them. However, this is not a free-standing principle but must be implemented by EU legislation defining the area concerned (namely employment and to a lesser extent, consumer law and services of general economic interest, therefore excluding commercial relations), and the incriminated ground of differentiation (nationality, gender, ethnic origin, sexual orientation, disability, age or religion or belief). ECJ case law and academic literature has usually distinguished between direct and indirect discrimination; only the latter may be justified by objective reasons that meet a societal need, that have nothing to do with the incriminated ground of differentiation, that must respect the proportionality criteria, and that must be proven by the defendant. The case law of the ECJ is characterized by setting rather "bold" precedents (*Mangold, Kücükdevici, Feryn* and *Test-Achats*) that are subject to criticism but are in general supported by this author.

CHAPTER 4

THE PRINCIPLE
OF EFFECTIVENESS

Contents

Bibliography 90
1. Article 47 of the Charter and Article 19 TEU: anything new? 90
2. The "eliminatory" function of the effectiveness principle. 91
3. Effectiveness as a "hermeneutical" principle 95
4. Effectiveness as a "remedial" principle: "upgrading" national remedies . . . 97
5. Some examples applying the effectiveness test in EU civil law 99
    5.1. *Von Colson* and *Kaman*: from a conditional to a direct remedy 99
    5.2. An open constitutional dimension: *Kücükdevici* 101
    5.3. Effective protection against unfair terms in consumer contracts:
          Invitel/Camino/Aziz 102
    5.4. The extent of strict liability in sales law: *Weber-Putz*. 106
    5.5. A missed opportunity: the *Heininger* saga 108
    5.6. Summary of the case studies 111
6. Primary Union law: rules on competition. 112
    6.1. Direct effect of the competition rules. 112
    6.2. New trends in competition law: the *Courage* doctrine and its
          follow-up by *Manfredi* 114
    6.3. The consequences of *Courage/Manfredi*: extent and limits
          of compensation. 115
7. Compensation for violations of directly applicable provisions
    of primary Union law 117
8. The importance of Article 47 of the Charter and Article 19(1) TEU
    for EU civil law revisited. 120
    8.1. A substantive understanding of the Article 47 Charter/19 TEU
          tandem. 120
    8.2. "Full" effectiveness: too "full", too "empty", or "just right"? The
          need for a balancing approach. 124
    8.3. Relevance of the effectiveness principle for collective remedies? 125
9. Conclusion: how effective is the effectiveness principle? 129

Bibliography

F. Benyon (ed.), *Services and the EU Citizen*, 2013; U. Bernitz et al. (eds.), *General Principles of Community Law as a Process of Development*, 2008; U. Bernitz et al. (eds.), *General Principles of EU law and Private Law*, 2013; U. Bernitz/N. Reich, 'Comment to the judgment of the Swedish Arbetsdomstolen of 2.12.2009 in Laval', CMLRev 2011, 603; R. Brownsword et al. (eds), *The Foundations of European Private Law*, 2011; T. Eilmannsberger, *Rechtsfolgen und subjektives Recht im Gemeinschaftsrecht*, 1997; T. Eilmannsberger, 'The relationship between rights and remedies in EC-Law: In search of the missing link', CMLRev 2004, 1198; W. van Gerven, 'Of Rights, Remedies, and Procedures', CMLRev 2000, 501; A. Hartkamp, *European Law and National Private Law*, 2012; H. Koziol/R. Schulze (eds.), *Tort Law of the European Community*, 2008; J. Lindholm, *State Procedure and Unions Rights*, 2007; D. Leczykiewicz, 'The Constitutional Dimension of Private Liability Rules in the EU', in: D. Leczykiewicz/S. Weatherill (eds.), *The Involvement of EU Law in Private Law Relationships*, 2013, 199; C. Mak, 'Rights and Remedies. Article 47 EUCFR and Effective Judicial Protection in European Private Law Matters', in: H.-W. Micklitz (ed.), Collected Courses EUI Summer School 'The Constitutionalization of European Private Law', 2013 (forthcoming); H.-W. Micklitz/N. Reich/P. Rott, *Understanding EU Consumer Law*, 2009; H.-W. Micklitz/B. de Witte (eds.), *The ECJ and the Autonomy of Member States*, 2012; D. Poelzig, *Normsetzung durch Privatrecht*, 2013; N. Reich, *Individueller und kollektiver Rechtsschutz im EU-Verbraucherrecht – Von der „Nationalisierung" zur „Konstitutionalisierung" von Rechtsbehelfen*, Schriftenreihe der Juristischen Studiengesellschaft Hannover Bd. 51, 2012; N. Reich, 'The interrelation between rights and duties in EU Law: Reflections on the state of liability law in the multilevel governance system of the Union – Is there a need for a more coherent approach in European private law?', YEL, 2010, 112; N. Reich, 'The Principle of Effectiveness and EU Private Law', in: U. Bernitz et al., *General Principles of EU Law and European Private Law*, 2013, 301; O. Remien (ed.), *Schaden-ersatz im Europäischen Privat- und Wirtschaftsrecht*, 2012; K. Riesenhuber (ed.), *Europäische Methodenlehre*, 2010; H. Rösler, *Europäische Gerichtsbarkeit auf dem Gebiet des Zivilrechts*, 2012; P. Rott, 'The ECJ's Principle of Effectiveness and its Unforeseeable Impact on Private Relationships', in: D. Leczykiewicz/S. Weatherill (eds.), *The Involvement of EU Law in Private Law Relationships*, 2013, 181; R. Schulze (ed.), *Compensation of Private Losses*, 2011: R. Schulze, *European Private Law – Current Status and Perspectives*, 2011; V. Trstenjak/E. Beysen, 'European Consumer Protection Law: *Curia semper dabit remedium*?', CMLRev 2011, 95.

1. ARTICLE 47 OF THE CHARTER AND ARTICLE 19 TEU: ANYTHING NEW?

4.1 This chapter will be concerned with a specific aspect of the *constitutionalisation of civil law*, namely the principle of effectiveness now written into Article 47(1) of the Charter, which reads:

> "Everyone whose rights and freedoms guaranteed by the law of the Union are violated has the right to an effective remedy before a tribunal in compliance with the conditions laid down in this Article."

Article 19(1) TEU puts the responsibility for "providing remedies sufficient to ensure effective legal protection in the fields covered by Union law" on Member States through the status of their courts of law as "Union courts". A similar provision was contained in Article I-29(1) of the Draft EU Constitution, which was rejected in the Dutch and French referenda, but which later formed the basis of the TEU.[1]

On a traditional reading, the constitutional "tandem" of Article 47 of the Charter and Article 19 TEU does not seem to contain anything new. It simply restates the existing EU *acquis* based on the so-called "procedural autonomy" of Member States to enforce Union rights, with some specific limitations developed under the so-called *REWE/Comet* case law to be discussed below (4.3). Its importance for civil law still remains to be discovered.

4.2 This chapter will take a different approach. The three strands of the argument examine the different ways in which the principle of effectiveness can be understood as a "constitutional principle" (0.7) in the case law of the ECJ:

- the first, rather more traditional reading understands effectiveness as an "*elimination rule*" (4.3);
- the second uses it as a "*hermeneutical*", i.e. interpretative, principle (4.7); and
- the third is concerned with its "*remedial*" *function* (4.10).

The argument will be limited to ECJ case law related to civil law and is illustrated by case studies. This is a relatively new area of EU law, which goes some way to explaining some of its difficulties and inconsistencies. But it seems that a new, more useful and aggressive approach to the "tandem" Articles 47 of the Charter and 19 TEU can be discovered. Later in this chapter we will be concerned with the development of EU-specific remedies for breaches of primary law, namely the competition (4.30) and free movement (4.34) provisions. The last section will draw some general conclusions, including the importance and limits of the effectiveness principle with regard to collective remedies (4.35–4.37).

2. THE "ELIMINATORY" FUNCTION OF THE EFFECTIVENESS PRINCIPLE

4.3 The effectiveness principle was, as is well known, first developed in the *Comet/REWE* cases dating from 1976 and basically means that national remedies and procedural rules must not render the exercise of Union rights *practically*

---

[1]   T. Tridimas, *The General Principles of EU Law*, 2nd ed. 2006, 419; the more recent study by D. Poelzig, *Normsetzung durch Privatrecht*, 2013, 270, analyses the principle of effectiveness as starting point for individual enforcement of Union law, but does not even mention Article 47 of the Charter.

impossible[2] or – as was later added[3] – *excessively difficult.* In parallel to this, the ECJ developed the principle of "equivalence" based on non-discrimination considerations: rights should not be treated less favourably under EU law than in domestic actions.[4] However, these principles only allow a "minimum", not an "adequate", protection, as AG van Gerven had observed;[5] they have a mostly "negative" content, as the intense case law shows. I therefore call this the "eliminatory function" of the effectiveness principle (in parallel with the equivalence principle): these two principles eliminate restrictions *to* protection, but do not create remedies *for* protection. As a consequence it can be said that once the ECJ (or a national court) has established that a national rule makes the implementation of EU rights excessively difficult, or that it does not put national and EU law rights on an equal footing, the competent national court must either disapply the incriminated national provision, or interpret it in conformity with EU law under the principle of (limited) horizontal direct effect.

4.4   The explanation for this limited effect of the effectiveness principle – in contrast to what its name seems to suggest – is the so-called "procedural autonomy" of Member States. The standard formulation of procedural autonomy reads:

> "[I]n the absence of Community rules on this subject, it is for the domestic legal system of each Member State to designate the courts having jurisdiction and to determine the procedural conditions governing actions at law intended to ensure the protection of the rights which citizens have from the direct effect of Community law."[6]

Later litigation tried to clarify the scope and limits of the principle of procedural autonomy, which has remained a controversial principle in the scholarship in terms of how to balance with the seemingly opposing principles of effectiveness and equivalence. Therefore, some authors criticise or even deny the existence of such a principle of "procedural autonomy", or find that it has been applied by the Court in a more or less contradictory, sometimes only symbolic, way.[7] In my

---

2   Case 33/76 *REWE Central Finanz* [1976] ECR 1989, para 5; Case 45/76 *Comet* [1976] ECR 2043, paras 13–16.

3   Case 199/82 *San Georgio* [1983] ECR 3595, para 14.

4   Case law on defining equivalence in practice has been quite complex and cannot be adequately discussed here; the Court prefers a broad teleological, not a narrow formal, approach; see T. Tridimas, *supra* note 1, at 418.

5   W. van Gerven, 'Of Rights, Remedies, and Procedures', CMLRev 2000, 501 at 504 and 529.

6   See the above mentioned *REWE* and *Comet* cases.

7   A. Adinolphi, 'The "Procedural Autonomy" of Member States and the Constraints Stemming from the ECJ's Case Law: Is Judicial Activism Still Necessary?', in: H.-W. Micklitz/B. de Witte (eds.), *The ECJ and the Autonomy of Member States*, 2012, 281; M. Bobek, 'Why There is No Principle of "Procedural Autonomy" of the Member States', in: H.-W. Micklitz/B. de Witte (eds.), ibid., 305; D.-U. Galetta, Procedural Autonomy of EU Member States: Paradise Lost?, 2011, 34, referring to the principle of consistent interpretation as a limitation of procedural autonomy, in particular in sex discrimination cases, at 41.

opinion, it seems that this controversy is to some extent rendered superfluous by a closer look at the more recent case law of the ECJ, to which I will turn later in this chapter.

4.5 The main area of application of the effectiveness principle – together with the principle of equivalence – has indeed been administrative law and procedure, for instance in scrutinising time limits for recovery of overcharged duties, tariffs or taxes, or limitation periods for compensation in EU or state liability cases.[8] I have found only a limited number of genuine civil law cases where the Court referred to those principles, but this will increase over time.

Levez[9] concerned prescription periods for claims of compensation in discrimination cases. The referring English court stated that Ms Levez was caught by a two year prescription period – which as such did not violate the effectiveness principle – because of incorrect information on her case by her employer. The Court found:[10]

> "In short, to allow an employer to rely on a national rule such as the rule at issue would, in the circumstances of the case before the national court, be manifestly incompatible with the principle of effectiveness referred to above. Application of the rule at issue is likely, in the circumstances of the present case, to make it virtually impossible or excessively difficult to obtain arrears of remuneration in respect of sex discrimination. It is plain that the ultimate effect of this rule would be to facilitate the breach of Community law by an employer whose deceit caused the employee's delay in bringing proceedings for enforcement of the principle of equal pay."

In *Manfredi*[11] as a follow up of *Courage*[12] concerning compensation for breaches of competition rules (4.26) the Court wrote that:[13]

> "the full effectiveness of Article 81 EC and, in particular, the practical effect of the prohibition laid down in Article 81(1) EC would be put at risk if it were not open to any individual to claim damages for loss caused to him by a contract or by conduct liable to restrict or distort competition [...] As to the award of damages and the possibility of an award of punitive damages [...] it is for the domestic legal system of each Member State to set the criteria for determining the extent of the damages, provided that the principles of equivalence and effectiveness are observed [...] it

---

8   For a recent restatement see cases C-445/06 *Danske-Slagterier* [2009] ECR I-2119, para 32, and C-533/10 *CIVS v Receveur des Douanes de Roubaix* [2012] ECR I-(14.06.2012), para 22; for an overall discussion see T. Tridimas, *supra* note 1, at 427.

9   Case C-326/96 *Levez v Harlow Pools* [1998] ECR I-7835; for a somewhat different analysis of the effectiveness principle see case C-249/09 *S. Bulicke v DBS* [2010] ECR I-7003, para 41.

10   Case C-326/96 *Levez v Harlow Pools* [1998] ECR I-7835, para 32.

11   Joined Cases C-295–298/04 *Vicenzo Manfredi et al v Lloyd Adriatico Asssicurazioni SpA et al* [2006] ECR I-6619.

12   C-453/99 *Courage Ltd v Crehan* [2001] ECR I-6297.

13   Joined Cases C-295–298/04 *Vicenzo Manfredi et al v Lloyd Adriatico Asssicurazioni SpA et al* [2006] ECR I-6619, paras 90–95.

follows from the principle of effectiveness and the right of any individual to seek compensation for loss caused by a contract or by conduct liable to restrict or distort competition that injured persons must be able to seek compensation not only for actual loss (*damnum emergens*) but also for loss of profit (*lucrum cessans*) plus interest."

A third case, *Alassini*,[14] concerned an Italian requirement for consumer complaints against telecommunication operators to first make use of ADR/ODR proceedings, as foreseen in Directive 2002/22,[15] before going to court. The Court discussed this requirement, considering both the equivalence and the effectiveness principle, but did not find a violation. It wrote:[16]

> "In those circumstances, it must be held that the national legislation at issue in the present case complies with the principle of effectiveness in so far as electronic means is not the only means by which the settlement procedure may be accessed and in so far as interim measures are possible in exceptional cases where the urgency of the situation so requires."

In *Aziz*[17] the Court was confronted with issue of the protection of debtors defaulting on an outstanding mortgage who, under existing Spanish law, cannot oppose the claim of the creditor against execution even if clauses in the contract on acceleration, default interests and unilateral determination of the amount of unpaid debt may be found to be unfair under Article 3 of the Unfair Terms Directive 93/13. In her opinion of 8 November 2012, AG Kokott referred to the principle of effective legal protection of the debtor which must give the judge the possibility to stay execution proceedings in order to find out whether the disputed clause is abusive or not (para 57). The Court in its judgment of 14 April 2013 followed suit, stating that the principle of effectiveness must be assessed "by reference to the role of that provision in the procedure, its progress and its features, viewed as a whole, before the various national bodies" (para 53).

4.6 The cases are somewhat specific inasmuch as *Levez*, *Alassini* and more recently *Aziz* are closely linked to a procedural enforcement of Union rights, specifically non-discrimination, and consumer rights of effective complaint handling respectively of defences against unfair terms. In *Alassini*, the Court expressly refers to the importance of Article 47 of the Charter even though it does not extract any "extra legal value" from it; its use as an argument looks rather superficial and not well developed from a legal perspective. *Manfredi* seems to be somewhat broader as it defines minimum substantive requirements

---

14 Case C-317/08 *Rosalba Alassini et al v Telecom Italia* [2010] ECR I-2214.
15 Directive 2002/22/EC of 7 March 2002 of the EP and of the Council on Universal Services in Electronic Communications [2002] OJ L108/ 51.
16 Case C-317/08 *Rosalba Alassini et al v Telecom Italia* [2010] ECR I-2214, para 60.
17 Case C-415/11 *Aziz v Catalunyacaixa* [2013] ECR I-(14.04.2013).

of effectiveness (for details see 4.26). On the other hand, there is also a strong procedural element in *Manfredi*: a damage claim is seen as a corollary to effective enforcement of competition law (4.25, referring to the ECJ *Courage* case). This link between substantive and procedural remedies seems to be particularly important and will be taken up later on (4.30).[18]

3. EFFECTIVENESS AS A "HERMENEUTICAL" PRINCIPLE

4.7 There are many cases where the Court went beyond the merely "eliminatory" approach of the classical *REWE/Comet* formula and developed a positive *effet utile* or "full effectiveness" test[19] as mentioned in *Manfredi*. This requires the Court to take a two step approach to EU law:

It must first find out the *Union right* which must be protected by an adequate remedy (*ubi ius, ibi remedium*).[20] This is basically a matter of interpretation of Union law, which is the prime (but not exclusive) responsibility of the Court itself. These Union rights, whether based on primary or secondary law:

– should be sufficiently precise and unconditional with regard to their legal content, and
– need no further implementing measures by the Union.

4.8 With regard to *secondary law*, the Court will have to find out the remedies provided by regulations or directives themselves. As an example one could refer to the case law concerning compensation under the Air-Passenger Regulation 261/2004,[21] not only for cancellation but also for "long delays" in excess of three hours. In its controversial *Sturgeon* case[22] the Court, despite a legislative decision to the contrary, allowed such an extension of compensation for reasons of equality: the passenger experiencing a long delay was said to be in a comparable situation to the one whose flight had been cancelled, and hence there was no justification for treating these two similar situations differently. The principle of "equal treatment" justified an analogy despite, as was in particular criticised in German scholarship,[23] the absence of a legislative "gap".

---

[18] C. Mak, 'Rights and Remedies – Article 47 EUCFR and Effective Judicial Protection in European Private Law Matters', unpublished paper on file with the author.

[19] For a critique see J. Lindholm, *State Procedure and Union Rights*, 2007, 126; for a differing view, N. Reich, 'Federalism and Effective Legal Protection', in: A. Colombi Ciacchi et al. (eds.), *Liability in the Third Millennium: FS für Gert Brüggemeier*, 2009, 381.

[20] T. Tridimas, *supra* note 1, at 422; W. van Gerven, *supra* note 5, at 511.

[21] [2004] OJ L 46/1.

[22] Case C-402 + 432/07 [2009] ECR I-10923, para 54.

[23] K. Riesenhuber, 'Interpretation and Judicial Development of EU Private Law – The Example of the Sturgeon Case', ERCL 2010, 384; a more nuanced appraisal has been put forward by

Many national courts criticised the ECJ's approach in extending liability as being against the intention of the EU legislator, and therefore referred the question to the Court again. In its recent *Nelson* judgment[24] the Grand Chamber of the ECJ implicitly rejected any criticism against the *Sturgeon* judgment of its Fourth Chamber without adding anything new. It simply referred to the comparable situation of passengers with long delays and those with cancellations:[25]

> "In addition, passengers in either group are in practice denied the opportunity to reorganise their travel arrangements freely, since they are faced either with a serious incident in the operation of their flight which is about to depart or already underway, or with the cancellation of their flight giving rise, as the case may be, to an offer to re-route. Consequently, if, for one reason or another, they are absolutely required to reach their final destination at a particular time, they cannot avoid the loss of time inherent in the new situation, having no leeway in that regard."

The Court however did not address the more fundamental question of its competence to simply extend the scope of an EU act beyond its clear wording without finding a "legislative gap", which in legal methodology[26] seems to be the prerequisite of an analogy. Instead the Court will apparently stick to its jurisdiction under Article 267 TFEU and be concerned only with the "*interpretation*" of acts of the Union. As far as the question of "effective application" of Regulation 261/2004 according to recital 7 is concerned, the Court did not refer to it, but implicitly seems to take the view that without also extending liability of air-carriers to long delays, the protection of passengers remains insufficient and must therefore be regarded as ineffective.[27]

As far as interpreting remedies provided in directives is concerned, the ECJ has not hesitated to extend them under an implicit recognition of the effectiveness principle as will be shown in the following case studies, for example with regard to non-discrimination and consumer protection law. Under

---

S. Garben, 'Sky-high controversy and high-flying claims? The Sturgeon case in the light of judicial activism, euroscepticism, and eurolegalism', CMLRev 2013, 15; J. Karsten, in: F. Benyon (ed.), *Services and the EU Citizen*, 2013, 42.

[24] Joined Cases C-582 + 629/10 *Nelson et al v Deutsche Lufthansa et al* [2012] ECR I-(24.10.2012).

[25] Ibid., para 35.

[26] For a general methodological discussion, see the contributions in K. Riesenhuber (ed.), *Europäische Methodenlehre*, 2nd ed. 2010, particularly that of C. Baldus, 'Auslegung und Analogie im 19. Jh.', 6; R. Stotz, 'Die Rechtsprechung des EuGH', 653; on *Rechtsfortbildung* (continuous development of EU law) see M. Pechstein/C. Drechsler, 'Die Ausbildung und Fortbildung ders Primärrechts', 224; on a rather restrictive use of the argument of analogy in secondary law, see J. Köndgen, 'Die Rechtsquellen des Europäischen Privatrechts', 189. For a broader discussion based on "general principles of EU law" see M. Herdegen, 'General Principles of EU Law – the Methodological Challenge', in: U. Bernitz et al. (eds.), *General Principles of Community Law as a Process of Development*, 2008, 343; T. Tridimas, *supra* note 1, at 17 (gap-filling function of general principles) and 51 (rules of Treaty interpretation).

[27] S. Garben, *supra* note 23, at 43, insisting that the judgment is an expression of increased consumer rights in a time of deregulation.

Article 19(1) TEU it is the task of Member State courts to provide remedies "sufficient" to ensure the protection of EU-granted rights.

4.9 Much more difficult and controversial are the steps to be taken in the interpretation of national law concerning implementation of EU law rights. Under the principle of division of competences, it is not up to the ECJ to interpret national law; this must be left to the competent courts of the Member States.[28] On the other hand, in reference proceedings, the Court has frequently given guidelines on how to understand national law in the light of Union law. There is an indirect spill-over of EU law to national law, at least insofar as an inconsistent application can be stated, and the Court will rule that a certain application or interpretation of national law is "precluded" by EU law, a formula used in many controversial cases. The mechanism of "preclusion" is in the end nothing more than the imposition on national law of an interpretation given to EU law by the ECJ with consequences for available remedies to be discussed in the next section.

4. EFFECTIVENESS AS A "REMEDIAL" PRINCIPLE: "UPGRADING" NATIONAL REMEDIES

4.10 The remedial function of the effectiveness principle requires Member State courts to create or improve remedies of their own that are "sufficient" for the effective protection of Union rights, of which I will give some examples below. Article 19(1) TEU posits a clear link between "effective protection" and "sufficient remedies". Both concepts are those of Union, not Member State, law and are therefore subject to autonomous interpretation by the ECJ. They are not limited to administrative and procedural effectiveness,[29] but include as prerequisite remedies under substantive civil law as well, for example compensation, restitution or annulment of contracts to be implemented before courts of law,[30] as has already be shown with respect to the "eliminatory function" of the effectiveness test (4.3). It will of course not be easy to measure in a particular case whether this relationship between "rights" and "remedies" – whether substantive or procedural – in the spirit of the *ubi ius, ibi remedium* paradigm, has been fulfilled in a positive or

---

[28] W. van Gerven, *supra* note 5, at 502, suggesting that the concept of "procedural autonomy" should be seen as a question of "procedural competence"; see also R. Stotz, in: K. Riesenhuber, *supra* note 26, at 663, referring to Article 267 TFEU.

[29] In this sense, A. Eser, comment Art. 47 para 19, in: J. Meyer (ed.), *Charta der Menschenrechte in der EU Kommentar*, 3rd ed. 2011: "ernsthafte und unparteiliche Prüfung durch ein Gericht" ("a serious and impartial examination by a court"); H.J. Blanke, comment on Art. 47 Charta para 2, in: C. Calliess/M. Ruffert, *Kommentar zum EUV/AEUV*, 4th ed. 2011.

[30] W. van Gerven, *supra* note 5, at 509 and 516; V. Trstenjak/E. Beysen, 'European Consumer Protection Law: Curia semper dabit remedium?', CMLRev 2011, 95, 109; A. Hartkamp, *The Impact of EU Law on National Private Laws*, 2012, para 111; D. Poelzig, *supra* note 1, at 306.

instead a negative sense. In the latter case, the Commission may bring infringement proceedings against non-compliant Member States under Article 260 TFEU which it only rarely does.[31] In the end it will be the task of Member State courts as "EU courts" themselves to guarantee this equilibrium between rights and remedies.

4.11 This EU law process of linking rights to remedies (and ultimately to procedures before courts of law) should be done using what I have called a "hybridisation approach".[32] This approach combines Member State autonomy – whether remedial or procedural – with the need to enforce EU-granted rights. In short it requires a three-step test:

-   The first step is concerned with finding appropriate national remedies in case of violations of EU-granted rights (whether primary or secondary law); therefore, the applicable Member State law has to be clarified, ultimately by the competent national court of law.
-   Second, this "national remedy" has to be measured
    -   against the yardstick of the "negative, eliminatory" EU principles of effectiveness and equivalence, and
    -   if the result is unsatisfactory from an EU law point of view, in that it is interpreted as providing "insufficient remedies", it has to be "upgraded" to meet EU standards.
-   This remedy thus found is a "hybrid" insofar as it takes up elements of national law in the limits of the principle of procedural autonomy, as well as effectiveness in its different functions. It should be "sufficient" to ensure effective protection in the words of Article 19(1) TEU, that is to meet the "adequacy" standard set by AG van Gerven.[33]

The circular relationship between

-   remedies under national law ("procedural autonomy"),
-   the effectiveness principle (Article 47 Charter) in a broad, remedy-oriented reading, and
-   their "upgrading", via the principle of consistent interpretation, to "hybrids" (Article 19(1) TEU)

---

[31]   See case C-144/99 *Commission v Netherlands* [2001] ECR I-3541, para 21, insisting that an interpretation of national (Dutch) law that conforms to Directive 93/13 on unfair terms in consumer contracts "cannot achieve the clarity and precision needed to meet the requirement of legal certainty. That, moreover, is particularly true in the field of consumer protection".

[32]   N. Reich '"Horizontal liability" in EC Law – "Hybridisation" of remedies for compensation in case of breaches of EC rights', CMLRev 2007, 705 at ' 708; U. Bernitz/N. Reich, CMLRev 2011, 615.

[33]   *Supra* note 5 at 529.

can be demonstrated in the following way:

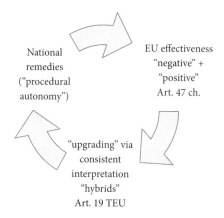

5. SOME EXAMPLES APPLYING THE EFFECTIVENESS TEST IN EU CIVIL LAW

5.1. *VON COLSON* AND *KAMAN*: FROM A CONDITIONAL TO A DIRECT REMEDY

4.12 *Von Colson*[34] concerned the refusal to employ a woman as a warden in a male prison. This was clearly regarded as discrimination based on the sex of the candidate which could not be justified under the restrictive regime of justifications under the then applicable Directive 76/206/EEC, now Directive 2006/54.[35] Whether this refusal could be qualified as a contract or a tort case depends on the national law, which is not a matter of the ECJ to decide. Under German law, this case came under the principle of *culpa in contrahendo* as a matter of (pre-)contractual liability[36] which allows only compensation of the so-called "negative interest", that is the damage which would not have occurred had the defendant acted legally. In this specific situation, this would have to be limited to the costs of making the unsuccessful application, for example postage costs and the costs of transportation to the interview and the like.

---

[34] Case 14/83 *Von Colson and Kamann v Land Nordrhein-Westfalen* [1984] ECR 1891.
[35] Recast Directive 2006/54/EC of the EP and the Council of 5 July 2006 on the implementation of the principle of equal opportunities and equal treatment of men and women in matters of employment [2006] OJ L 204/24.
[36] This is different now under the EU conflict law regimes of Article 1(2)(i) of Regulation 593/2008 (Rome I) [2008] OJ L 176/6, and Article 12 of Regulation 864/2007 (Rome II) [2007] OJ L 199/1, even though the applicable law will be that of the contract entered into.

This rather trivial amount of compensation did not suffice in the eyes of the Court, which instead insisted on the principle of effectiveness in a *positive, remedial sense* for the provision of a remedy:[37]

> "[Compensation must] be such as to guarantee real and effective judicial protection, [...] have a real deterrent effect on the employer [and] must in any event be adequate in relation to the damages sustained [...] purely nominal [compensation] e.g. the reimbursement of expenses incurred by them [the candidates] in submitting their application, would not satisfy the requirement of an effective transposition of the directive."

In this judgment, which is still very important and continues to be frequently cited, the Court rejected a merely symbolic compensation as incompatible with the principle of effectiveness in a positive sense, also including the scope of the remedy under contact law (or pre-contractual obligations as under German *culpa* principles). It is not quite clear on what legal principle the Court based its principle of full compensation since the Directive was silent on this point, especially as the Court held at the same time that Mrs von Colson did not have the right to a contract. In light of this it would be difficult to explain the claimant's right to full compensation on the basis of a traditional contract law theory. In my opinion, the damage which the Court strived to remedy in its ruling was primarily "moral". This raises the question of whether EU law should require non-material damages to be awarded more generally for breaches of EU prohibitions on gender-based discrimination; I think this would be justified, provided a certain threshold of injury is met.[38] The overall context of this case law on compensation, as inaugurated by *Von Colson*, certainly has – even if it is not phrased in these terms – a constitutional dimension, which is now well settled under Article 47 of the Charter as mentioned, in combination with the prohibition on gender-based discrimination in Article 23 of the Charter.

4.13 The case law that followed *Von Colson* tried to develop the effectiveness principle further; there is no need to go into details.[39] It will suffice to mention the issues that arose in some leading cases:

---

[37]   Case 14/83 *Von Colson and Kamann v Land Nordrhein-Westfalen* [1984] ECR 1891, paras 23–24.

[38]   The Court recognises this with regard to compensation for "lost holiday" on package tours: see case C-168/00 *Simone Leitner v TUI Deutschland* [2002] ECR I-2631; there is no reason to treat discrimination cases less stringently.

[39]   For details under German law before 1996 see E. Steindorff, *EG-Vertrag und Privatrecht*, 1996, 375; N. Reich, 'Effective Private Law Remedies in Discrimination Cases', in: R. Schulze (ed.), *Non-Discrimination in European Private Law*, 2011, 57; D. Poelzig, *supra* note 1, at 272, insisting on a "functional creation of subjective rights (*funktionale Subjektivierung*)" as a structural principle of Union law to enforce EU market legislation.

- liability does not depend on the fault of the offender;[40]
- the head of damage to be compensated includes interest as "adequate compensation";[41]
- upper limits to compensation in cases of multiple victims are subject to a strict proportionality test;[42]
- discrimination may occur not only before getting or in the duration of the job, but also after it is over.[43]

5.2. AN OPEN CONSTITUTIONAL DIMENSION: *KÜCÜKDEVICI*

4.14   The question of an effective remedy in cases of discrimination matters clearly arose in the case of *Kücükdevici*.[44] In this case, however, the remedial issue was not so much to do with compensation or restitution, but to do with precluding the application of a provision in national contract law which shortened the notice period for young employees, thereby violating the Framework Directive 2000/78[45] that forbids age discrimination. The problem with this remedy was that it stood in contrast to well-established principles that do not allow a "horizontal direct effect" of directives even in a "negative" exclusionary sense. In the prior *Mangold* case[46] the ECJ had seemingly allowed such an effect based on an alleged "general principle against age discrimination", but the reasoning remained shaky and controversial (details on age discrimination at 3.6), even though it was upheld by the German Constitutional Court (3.7).

The question in *Kücükdevici* concerned the dismissal periods in a contract for employment which would increase with age, but beginning only after the age of 25 years. The ECJ in its judgment of 19 January 2010, referring to Article 21 (but not Article 47) of the Charter,[47] required the national court in accordance

---

40   Case 177/88 *Dekker v Stichting Vormingscentrum voor Jong Volwassenen (VJV-Centrum) Plus* [1990] ECR I-3941, para 23.

41   Case C-271/91 *Marshall v Southhampton Health Authority* [1993] ECR I-4367, paras 26 and 31.

42   Case C-180/95 *Draempaehl v Urania* [1997] ECR I-2195, para 37; for discussion see U. Magnus/W. Wurmnest, *Casebook Europäisches Haftungs- und Schadensrecht*, 2002, 101.

43   Case C-185/97 *Coote v Granada Hospitality* [1998] ECR I-5199; for a discussion of the issues see H.-W. Micklitz, *The Politics of Judicial Co-operation*, 2005, 210–13, 269–70.

44   Case C-555/07 *Seda Kücükdevici v Swedex GmbH* [2010] ECR I-365, recently confirmed in case C-447/09 *R. Prigge et al v Lufthansa* [2011] ECR I-(14.09.2011), para 38; the broad approach of the Court has been criticised by M. Dougan, 'In Defence of *Mangold*?', in: A. Arnull et al. (eds.), *A Constitutional Order of States – Essays in Honour of A. Dashwood*, 2011, 219 ff., S. Weatherill, in: D. Leczykiewicz/S. Weatherill (eds.), *The Involvement of EU Law in Private Law Relationships*, 2013, 24.

45   Council Directive 2000/78/EC of 27 November 2000 establishing a general framework for equal treatment in employment and occupation [2000] OJ L 303/16.

46   Case C-144/04 *Werner Mangold v Rüdiger Helm* [2005] ECR I-9981.

47   Case C-555/07 *Seda Kücükdevici v Swedex GmbH* [2010] ECR I-365, para 22.

the principle of "full effectiveness" to disapply the discriminatory provision without the necessity to first refer the case to the Court.[48] The Bundesarbeitsgericht (the Federal Labour Court) followed suit and in its judgment of 9 September 2010 simply set aside the contested German provision (§622 (2) para 2 BGB, which discriminated against young employees because of its notice period for termination of employment) by excluding from calculation the employment period accrued before the age of 25.[49] In its stead the court used the general rule contained in §622(2) para 1 BGB on the calculation of the length of employment.

5.3. EFFECTIVE PROTECTION AGAINST UNFAIR TERMS IN CONSUMER CONTRACTS: *INVITEL/CAMINO/AZIZ*

4.15   The Unfair Terms Directive 93/13/EEC[50] has led to a number of surprising ECJ judgments that have insisted on the principle of effective protection justified by the unequal bargaining power of the parties, lately highlighted by the *Invitel* and *Aziz* judgments.[51] This results in the requirement for national courts to apply *ex officio* certain protective provisions, in particular Article 6 of the Directive. The case law began with *Océano*, concerning jurisdiction clauses,[52] was continued in *Claro*[53] and *Asturcom*,[54] in relation to arbitration clauses in consumer contracts, and was confirmed and refined in *Pannon* as follows:[55]

> "The court seised of the action is therefore required to ensure the effectiveness of the protection intended to be given by the provisions of the Directive. Consequently, the

---

[48]   Ibid., at para 54.
[49]   BAG, 2 AZR 714/08, Zeitschrift für Wirtschaftsrecht (ZIP) 2011, 444.
[50]   Council Directive 93/13/EEC of 5 April 1993 on unfair terms in consumer contracts [1993] OJ L 95/29.
[51]   Case C-472/10 *Nemzeti Fogyaszróvédelni Hatóság v Invitel* [2012] ECR I-(26.04.2012); comment H.-W. Micklitz/N. Reich, 'AGB-Recht und UWG – (endlich) ein Ende des Kästchendenkens nach Pernivoca und Invitel', EWS 2012, 257; the prior opinion AG Trstenjak of 6 December 2011 has been commented on by H.-W. Micklitz/N. Reich, EuZW 2012, 126.
[52]   Joined Cases C-240–244/98 *Océano Grupo ed. v Quintero et al* [2000] ECR I-4941.
[53]   Case C-168/05 *E.M.M. Claro v Centro Movil Milenium* [2006] ECR I-10421.
[54]   Case C-40/08 *Asturcom v Christina Rodrigues Nogueria* [2009] ECR I-9579; comment H. Schebasta, 'Does the National Court Know European Law', in: H.-W. Micklitz/N. Reich (eds,), 'The Impact of the Internal Market on the Private Law of Member Countries', EUI Working Papers 2009/22, 47 = ERPrL 2010, 847, insisting that in *Asturcom*, which concerned a consumer who "in total inertia" did not raise any defence against arbitration proceedings, including the *res iudicata* of the final award against her (para 34), the ECJ did not apply the effectiveness principle, but rather the less stringent equivalence test.
[55]   Case C-243/08 *Pannon v Erzsébet Sustikné Győrfi* [2009] ECR I-4713, para 32; see also case C-137/08 *VB Penzügyi Lizing v Ferenc Schneider* [2010] ECR I-10847, para 56, concerning investigation on its own motion whether the court has jurisdiction or not according to the disputed clause.

role thus attributed to the national court by Community law in this area is not limited to a mere power to rule on the possible unfairness of a contractual term, but also consists of the obligation to examine that issue of its own motion, where it has available to it the legal and factual elements necessary for that task, including when it is assessing whether it has territorial jurisdiction."

The problem with this approach is its apparent conflict with the principle of procedural autonomy of Member States; however, in the *Van Schinjdel* case,[56] which is cited as the clearest recognition of this principle in civil proceedings that depend on the initiative of the parties, a reservation had already been made. It is often overlooked that the Court in this judgment already expressed an exception for a court intervention on its own motion based on a *public interest* test. A joint paper by AG Trstenjak and Boysen[57] has justified this case law with the following remarks:

> "[A] less stringent application of the concept of procedural autonomy of the Member States can be observed in the case law of the ECJ with regard to the enforcement of consumer rights under the different consumer protection directives."

The case to be discussed here concerns the effects of an action for an injunction by the Hungarian consumer protection office against the fixed-line telephone network *Invitel* whose general business conditions (GBC) introduced clauses on fees for money orders (and additional postal fees) without specifying the calculation of these fees; these clauses were thus as accused of being unfair under Article 3 and the (indicative) Annex of the Unfair Terms Directive. Two questions were submitted to the Court, one concerning the fairness of these clauses (which will not be discussed in this context), and the other, more interesting for our present purposes, on the effects of a successful injunction on individual consumer contracts.

Under German law, this problem is seemingly "solved" by the so-called *Einredelösung* of §11 *Unterlassungsklagengesetz* (Law on injunctions against unfair terms): once the judgment prohibiting the use of such a clause has attained *res iudicata* force, the consumer can object to its further use, but only with future effect and only with regard to the specific defendant, not other businesses, even if they are using the same disputed clause.[58] In practice this solution has not played a role and has not proved to be an effective remedy for an individual consumer who has been the object of a disputed clause.

---

56   Case C-430–432/93 *Van Schijndel and Van Veen v Stichting Pensionenfonds* [1995] ECR I-4705, para 21; for a detailed discussion of the later case law, narrowing the *Van Schijndel* formula, see A. Hartkamp, *supra* note 30, at paras 124–130.
57   V. Trstenjak/E. Beysen, *supra* note 30, at 119.
58   Criticised by H.-W. Micklitz/N. Reich, *supra* note 51, at 261, with further references.

4.16 *Invitel* offers a much more far-reaching solution to this problem through an implicit principle of "remedial effectiveness", which means that German law will have to be changed. In *Invitel* the Court first insists on "the deterrent nature and dissuasive purpose of the measures to be adopted" under Article 7(2) of the Unfair Terms Directive (para 37). It then goes on to say:[59]

> "[W]here the unfair nature of the term included in the GBC of consumer contracts has been recognised in an action for an injunction [...] the national courts are required, of their own motion, and also as regards to the future, to draw all the consequences provided for by national law in order to ensure that consumers who have concluded a contract to which those GBC apply will not be bound by that term."

It is clear that these consequences must be attached to national law, as suggested in the hybridisation approach, but they must take two forms:

- one concerns the individual contract in which the disputed clause is "not binding on the consumer" according to Article 6, which as a consequence means that money paid under the unfair clause must be returned to the consumer under the national doctrines of unjust enrichment or restitution; and
- the second is concerned with the future effect of the unfair terms whose continued used must be prohibited under Article 7(1).

National – in this context German – law has to be updated accordingly. The so-called *Einredelösung* will have to be substituted by an *Unwirksamkeitslösung,* that is the non-binding term has to be disapplied *ex officio* by the competent German court and to be not dependent on a motion brought by a consumer.

The recent *Aziz* case (4.5) was concerned with the remedies available to the consumer against the execution of a mortgage containing unfair terms that disadvantage a defaulting consumer:[60]

> "It follows from the above that, under Spanish rules of procedure, the final vesting of mortgaged property in a third party is always irreversible, even if the unfairness of the term challenged by the consumer before the court hearing the declaratory proceedings results in the annulment of the mortgage enforcement proceedings, except where that consumer made a preliminary registration of the application for annulment of the mortgage before that marginal note. In that regard, taking into account the progress and the special features of the mortgage enforcement proceedings at issue in the main proceedings, such an eventuality must however be regarded as remote because there is a significant risk that the consumer in question will not make that preliminary registration within the period prescribed for that purpose, either because of the rapidity of the enforcement proceedings in question or because he is unaware of or does not appreciate the extent of his rights [...] It must therefore be held that such

---

[59]   Case C-472/10 *Nemzeti Fogyaszróvédelni Hatóság v Invitel* [2012] ECR I-(26.04.2012), para 43.
[60]   Case C-415/11, *Aziz v Catalunyacaixa* [2013] ECR I-(14.04.2013), paras 57–59.

procedural rules impair the protection sought by the directive, in so far as they render it impossible for the court hearing the declaratory proceedings – before which the consumer has brought proceedings claiming that the contractual term on which the right to seek enforcement is based is unfair – to grant interim relief capable of staying or terminating the mortgage enforcement proceedings, where such relief is necessary to ensure the full effectiveness of its final decision."

The inflexibility of the Spanish enforcement proceedings violated the effectiveness principle from the consumer's (not the bank's) point of view because the consumer did not have a remedy like interim relief to escape the consequences of an unfair clause. Under existing Spanish law, the court could not of its own accord – as required by the case law of the ECJ (4.16) – stay the execution proceedings even if the contract contained unfair clauses concerning acceleration, unilateral determination of the amount of unpaid debt, and default interests to be determined by the court (paras 73–75). The Court also referred to the risk in execution proceedings that the consumer may lose his home without the possibility of recovering it, even if the term was unfair; the mere possibility of obtaining reparation would violate the principle of effectiveness:[61]

"That applies all the more strongly where, as in the main proceedings, the mortgaged property is the family home of the consumer whose rights have been infringed, since that means of consumer protection is limited to payment of damages and interest and does not make it possible to prevent the definitive and irreversible loss of that dwelling."

4.17 On the other hand, the remedy provided must be commensurate to the purpose the directive, as the Court insisted in *Camino*, and may therefore exclude the remedy of adaptation of the incriminated clause:[62]

"[I]f it were open to the national court to revise the content of unfair terms included in such contracts, such a power would be liable to compromise attainment of the long-term objective of Article 7 of Directive 93/14. That power would contribute to eliminating the dissuasive effect on sellers or suppliers of the straightforward non-application with regard to the consumer of those unfair terms [...] in so far as those sellers or suppliers would remain tempted to use those terms in the knowledge that, even if they were declared invalid, the contract could nevertheless be modified, to the extent necessary, by the national court in such a way as to safeguard the interest of those sellers or suppliers."

In the same judgment, the ECJ insisted that the principle of effectiveness is not excluded by a simplified procedure for the recovery of debts:[63]

"In that context, it must be stated that such a procedural arrangement, which completely prevents the court before which an application for order for payment has

---

[61]   Ibid., para 61.
[62]   Case C-618/10 *Banco Español de Credito v Camino* [2012] ECR I-(14.06.2012), para 69; comment P. Rott, ERCL 2012, 470 at 475.
[63]   Ibid., paras 53–54.

been brought to assess of its own motion, *in limine litis* or at any other stage during the proceedings, even though it already has all the legal and factual elements necessary for that task available to it, whether terms contained in a contract concluded between a seller or supplier and a consumer are unfair where that consumer has not lodged an objection, is liable to undermine the effectiveness of the protection intended by Directive 93/13. In the light of the order for payment procedure [...], its progress and its special features, viewed as a whole, there is a significant risk that the consumers concerned will not lodge the objection required either because of the particularly short period provided for that purpose, or because they might be dissuaded from defending themselves in view of the costs which legal proceedings would entail in relation to the amount of the disputed debt, or because they are unaware of or do not appreciate the extent of their rights, or indeed because of the limited content of the application for the order for payment submitted by the sellers or suppliers, and thus the incomplete nature of the information available to them."

The judgment does not seem to require the court to always examine *ex officio* the unfairness of a term in an expedited proceeding. The ECJ is not criticising the existence of such proceedings for the rapid recovery of debts, but the strict prohibition on the judge not to examine the merits of the claim even if there is evidence before him of the use of unfair terms.

5.4. THE EXTENT OF STRICT LIABILITY IN SALES LAW: *WEBER-PUTZ*

4.18 The facts of the litigation in the *Weber* and *Putz* cases[64] decided by the ECJ on 16 June 2011 against the critical opinion of AG Mazak of 18 May 2010 are probably well known and need not be discussed in detail here; they are a good, and at the same time controversial, example of the impact of EU law on traditional ideas on remedies in sales law beyond the wording of Directive 99/44 (2.8). They concern reimbursement of additional costs by the consumer for replacing a defective product and installing an improved one, for example by tearing off and replacing defective tiles used for floor panelling, or by disconnecting and reconnecting a dishwasher that did not function. AG Mazak rejects this claim under EU law, but the ECJ upheld it as a causal consequence of the seller's obligation to deliver a product that conforms to its specifications. The reasoning of the Court is surprisingly short and based on the rather vague provisions in the Directive that repair and replacement should be done within "a reasonable time", "free of charge" and "without significant inconvenience to the consumer", even if the contract did not include installation services. This creates a *strict liability regime* for the seller, not only for the act of replacing the defective product itself, but also for the resulting follow-up costs even after the transfer of

---

[64]   Joined Cases C-65/09 + C-87/09, *Gebr. Weber et al v J. Wittmer et al* [2011] ECR I-5257.

the risk. In order to avoid the seller being over-charged, the Court referred to the possibility of bringing a recourse action against the previous seller or producer according to Article 4 of Directive 99/44 (para 48). The Court was also asked whether Article 3(3) of Directive 99/44 was to be read as an "absolute" or as a "relative" defence for the seller in relation to the impossibility of repairing or replacing the defective product. The "dominant opinion" (*herrschende Meinung*) of German law of the time under the implementing provision of §439 BGB understood it as an "absolute proportionality test": if one of the remedies was impossible and the other disproportionate in terms of cost, this had the consequence of a total loss of first-stage remedies under sales law; the consumer could only terminate the contract or receive a price reduction; damages could only be recovered under existing (German) law requiring that the seller be at fault, a possibility that would usually be excluded because the seller did not produce the good himself and did not know (nor should he have known) of the defect. The Court however opted for a "relative proportionality defence" as corroborated by recital 11: even if one remedy (repair) would be impossible and the other (replacement) result in disproportionate costs for the seller, the consumer would not completely lose his first-stage remedies; the disproportionate cost of replacement (including costs for disconnecting and reconnecting) would only allow the seller to reduce them "to an amount proportionate to the value the goods would have if there were no lack of conformity and the significance of the lack of conformity" (para 74). The reference point is not therefore the (possibly much higher) cost of removal of the defective product or/and the installation of a conforming product, but its lower net value. This seems to be a fair balancing of the different interests of the parties (for details on balancing, see Chapter 5).

4.19   The German Federal Court (BGH), in its judgment of 21 December 2011[65] followed suit, under the principle of consistent interpretation, by extending the scope of replacement from merely meaning disconnection to also including reconnection, a possibility thus far rejected in its earlier case law. The BGH also followed suit concerning the "relative proportionality test" under Article 3(3) of Directive 99/44, and interpreted §439 BGB restrictively using the method of "teleological reduction" of German law which it had already applied in its follow-up judgment to *Quelle*.[66] It discussed in detail the different proposals in legal writing on how to implement the proportionality criteria; it found a reimbursement of €600 to be adequate for the value of non-defective tiles (€1200).

---

[65]   BGH, VIII ZR 70/08 NJW 2012, 1073; the BGH however did not extend this principle to B2B transactions, VIII ZR 226/11 of 17.10.2012, EuZW 2013, 157.

[66]   BGH NJW 2009, 427.

I will not discuss the *efficiency* problems of the judgment, particularly concerning its possible negative effects on distance selling. In the present context, I am instead concerned with the *effectiveness* argument with reference to the consumer protection objective of the Directive. This is given a broad reach by the Court, but is at the same time reduced by a balancing element that takes into account the economic situation of the seller, or rather of the specific transaction. Under the "relative proportionality test", the Court avoids a complete loss of the consumer's first-stage remedies (which would have been the consequence of the "absolute test"), thereby seriously undermining the principle of effective consumer protection under Article 47 of the Charter read together with Directive 99/44. Under these criteria, the judgment certainly has the effect of deterring the sale of defective goods, especially when they need to be installed, like a dishwasher, or put into place, like the tiles, something of which the seller is well aware. At the same time, the Court used a proportionality argument based on a "fair balancing" (para 75) principle that the consumer has to bear some of the risks of this transaction. Such a balancing is also possible under a strict liability regime for compensation of costs incurred as result of the delivery of defective goods. Thus, the effectiveness argument leads to a *specific risk-sharing and risk-distribution* between the seller and the consumer, protecting at the same time the consumer's rights under Directive 99/44 without excessively increasing the risks of the seller. Effectiveness of consumer protection does not mean that the consumer's transaction is completely risk free – but he should at least not carry all its risks, so as to avoid a result that violates the emerging EU good faith principle (7.8).

5.5. A MISSED OPPORTUNITY: THE *HEININGER* SAGA

4.20   This chapter may tend to exaggerate the importance in EU civil law of the effectiveness principle of the ECJ case law. There are however also judgments where the Court did not seem to be ready to take a more forward-looking approach to providing remedies in order to protect EU law rights. The best and most often discussed example concerns the so-called *Heininger* saga,[67] where the effects of a withdrawal from a mortgage credit agreement with a bank entered into by the consumer at the doorstep on the developer's financed real estate transaction were considered by the Court. The BGH was very quick at giving its answer based on the policy that real estate and credit transactions are legally separate from each other.[68] The withdrawal of one (the mortgage credit agreement) does not affect the other (purchase of real estate). The only consequence of withdrawal from the credit contract is that it becomes void.

---

[67]   C-481/99 *Heininger v Bayr. Hypo und Vereinsbank* [2001] ECR I-9945.
[68]   BGH NJW 2002, 1884.

What are the consequences of the contract becoming void? Does the consumer have to pay back the credit in full and without the privilege of instalments, as the case law of the BGH seemed to suggest? Does he have to pay the interest stipulated in the contract, including interest which will accrue over time? Does it make any difference if he has not been informed about an eventual right of withdrawal? Could he raise a claim of compensation against the bank for not adequately informing him under the German theory of *culpa in contrahendo*?[69] Or could it even be argued that the credit and the purchase contract form an economic unit which must be judged together, even though they are formally separated?

4.21 These were the questions which came to the ECJ on reference from the lower courts, which were opposed to the restrictive case law of the BGH in the follow-up cases of *Schulte*[70] and *Crailsheimer Volksbank*.[71] In its reasoning, the Court put forward the following legal doctrines:

- Starting from a formal approach in following the opinion of AG Léger,[72] it held that the consumer's withdrawal voided the credit transaction and that therefore the parties had to return to the original state of affairs, namely that the consumer had received the credit without justification and therefore had to pay back the money immediately and in full (*Schulte*, para 87).
- The purpose for which the credit was used was of no relevance; the ECJ indirectly rejected the idea of "linked contracts" as a principle of EU law, which would however not be precluded under national law (*Schulte*, para 80).
- The consumer had to pay market interest for the credit money used without justification, thus restoring the *status quo ante* (*Schulte*, para 92).
- However, States have to "ensure that their legislation protects consumers who have been unable to avoid exposure to such risks (loss of rental income and property value incurred because of not knowing of their right of cancellation under the Directive), by adopting suitable measures to allow them to avoid bearing the consequences of the materialisation of those risks" (*Schulte*, para 101).

---

69 For a discussion see N. Reich, 'Balancing in Private Law and the Imperatives of the Public Interest: National Experiences and (Missed?) European Opportunities', in: R. Brownsword et al. (eds), *Modern Tendencies in Private Law*, 2011, 221 at 230; H. Unberath/A. Johnston, 'The Double Headed Approach of the ECJ Concerning Consumer Protection', CMLRev 2007, 1237 at 1261; T. Möllers/P. Grassi, 'Die Europarechtswidrigkeit der Schrottimmobilienrechtsprechung zur Haustürwiderrufs-RiLi 85/577/EWG durch deutsche Gerichte', VuR 2010, 4.

70 Case C-350/03 *Schulte* [2005] ECR I-9215.

71 Case C-229/04 *Crailsheimer Volksbank* [2005] ECR I-9294.

72 Opinion of AG Léger in *Crailsheimer Volksbank*, ibid. (2 June 2005), paras 54, 72.

In the end this meant that the consumer's economic situation is not improved after withdrawal; a claim for compensation will be difficult to prove in practice. The Court did not attach any importance to the effectiveness principle it had used in other cases.[73] Instead, it relied on the theory of a formal separation of transactions, as confirmed in the opinion of AG Léger of 29 October 2004 in *Schulte*:[74]

> "I think a purposive interpretation of the Directive, just like its practical effect, do not permit a requirement that the cancellation of the secured credit agreement should produce an effect, in one way or another, on the validity of the property purchase contract."

Whether the effectiveness paradigm used here would allow different answers remains an open question; even so, it will not give easy answers. This paradigm is to some extent caught in between the "full autonomy" of Member States to protect citizens in whatever way they wish under their national rules of remedies and procedures, unless there has been express EU legislation (the *Heininger* saga being an example of this because the Doorstep Lending Directive 85/577/EEC[75] left the provision of remedies to national law), and the seemingly contradictory "full effectiveness" approach that is relevant whenever there is a deficiency in the available remedies under national or EU law as in the cases studied here. But even under the "full effectiveness" approach compromise solutions must and will be sought by the ECJ; this will often result in the *balancing of different interests*.[76] This balancing should not be done so much using formal competence considerations, but rather using substantive proportionality criteria, as has been recently demonstrated in *Weber/Putz*.

In future litigation, the *Heininger* saga will not be repeated, because Article 3(3)(d) of the Consumer Rights Directive 2011/83/EU (2.5) has expressly excluded financial services from its scope of application.

---

[73] See H.-W. Micklitz, 'The ECJ between the Individual Citizen and the Member States – A Plea for a Judge Made European Law on Remedies', in: H.-W. Micklitz/B. de Witte (eds.), *The ECJ and the Autonomy of Member States*, 2012, 349 at 386; for a more positive view, A. Hartkamp, *supra* note 30, at para 174: "unexpected outcome".

[74] Case C-350/03 *Schulte* [2005] ECR I-9215, para 95.

[75] [1985] OJ L 372/31.

[76] See my paper, *supra* note 69; also criticised by H. Rösler, *Europäische Gerichtsbarkeit auf dem Gebiet des Zivilrechts*, 2012, 156: "der EuGH (hat) die wirkliche Dimension und dogmatische Komplexität des Problems wohl nicht recht erfasst" ("the ECJ probably did not understand the real dimension and dogmatic complexity of the problem").

5.6. SUMMARY OF THE CASE STUDIES

4.22   This table shows the different approaches in the ECJ case law:

ECJ case	EU rights	National remedies	National procedures	EU "upgrade"
Von Colson	No sex-based discrimination: Directive 76/2007	*Culpa in contrahendo*: token compensation		Adequate compensation, deterrent effect
Kücükdevici	No age-based discrimination: Directive 2000/78	No special dismissal protection for young employees		Preclusive effect of Directive 2000/78 read together with Article 21 of the Charter
Invitel/Camino/Aziz	No unfair terms: Directive 93/13; *ex officio* control by national court	No adaptation of unfair clause, only compensation	"Abstract" injunction of consumer office; no defence against execution	Spill-over effect to individual consumer contract; effective defence of consumer
Weber/Putz	Conformity of product and installation: Directive 99/44	Replacement only; earlier BGH case law: only disconnection – §439 BGB: absolute proportionality: if one remedy is disproportionate the other also fails		Strict liability for disconnection and reconnection – "relative proportionality test" – limited to either repair/replacement; proportionate reduction of recoverable costs
Heininger saga as an antidote	Withdrawal from doorstep mortgage credit; no time limit in case of non-information; consequences of withdrawal left to national law: Article 7 of Directive 85/577; now repealed by Directive 2011/83	Rejection of remedies: no *Einwendungs-durchgriff*	Necessity to pay back the amount credited in full with market interest	No EU remedies, Article 4(4) "appropriate measures of consumer protection"; ECJ: limited to compensation because of non-information of right of withdrawal

6. PRIMARY UNION LAW: RULES ON COMPETITION

6.1. DIRECT EFFECT OF THE COMPETITION RULES

4.23 The most important EU rules on accountability of undertakings are concerned with competition. This is a direct result of the insistence of EU law on open markets, which protects not just competition as an institution but also competitors and other market participants as individuals. Although autonomy of undertakings is a basic value of Community and now Union law and is indirectly guaranteed by the competition rules (1.14), it should nevertheless not be distorted by undertakings co-operating through anti-competitive agreements or by abusing their dominant position in the market. The sanctioning system of this fundamental principle of EU law is twofold:

- primary EU law provides that anti-competitive agreements are void *ex lege* and cannot be enforced in actions before courts of law or in recognition proceedings of international arbitration awards (1.15);[77]
- Regulation 1/2003[78] provides for administrative sanctions to be imposed either by the Commission or by national anti-trust administrations; however, it says nothing about civil sanctions such as damages and injunctions.

There is agreement that the Union rules on assuring accountability with the competition provisions are insufficient and defective with regard to civil law remedies. This is particularly true in the case of abuses of dominant positions. These are forbidden but, under primary EU law, do not as such entail civil law consequences, in particular actions for damages. The Commission is empowered to impose considerable fines or take administrative measures, but these instruments do not provide for adequate compensation to injured competitors nor to businesses up- or down-stream who have suffered loss due to anti-competitive behaviour. This is not to mention consumers or purchasers (in the case of public procurement) who have paid excessive prices due to restrictive practices.

4.24 It became clear to the Court in its formative years that this situation is unsatisfactory. Indeed, the Court tried to remedy it by developing three additional instruments to overcome the existing state of *lex imperfecta* of Union law:

---

[77]   Cf. Case C-126/97 *Eco Swiss China Time v Benetton International NV* [1999] ECR I-3055; details are discussed by W. van Gerven, in: J. Stuyck/H. Gilliams, *Modernisation of European Competition Law*, 2002, 93, with a proposal for a Council regulation.

[78]   Council Regulation (EC) No. 1/2003 of 16 December 2002 on the implementation of the rules on competition laid down in Articles 81 and 82 of the Treaty [2003] OJ L 1.

- the competition rules enjoy *direct effect* among private parties, that is, they can be invoked not only in administrative proceedings but also in civil law disputes before national courts of law;[79]
- Member State law should provide similar sanctions against anti-competitive behaviour in violation of EU law provisions as are available under national law; and
- these sanctions are, like state liability, subject to the (mostly "negative") principles of "equivalence" and "effectiveness" (4.3).

In its early case law, later repeated by the Court of First Instance (now General Court) in its *Automec II* decision,[80] it was made clear that these sanctions are based on *national, not Union, law*. It followed that all restrictions on them can be invoked equally in the event of EU law violations if the aforementioned principles of equivalence and effectiveness were respected. The legal situation of sanctions against anti-competitive behaviour resembled very much the situation of state liability for breaches of Union law before *Francovich*.[81]

It was clear that the traditional approach had a number of drawbacks:

- similar violations of identical rules were treated differently depending on the law that governed the violation;
- different treatment of violations resulted in additional distortions of competition that Union law wanted to avoid;
- the principles of "equivalence" and "effectiveness" provided for some, but only very vague and mostly "negative", guidance;
- Member State courts were very hesitant in private enforcement actions of the competition rules, unlike their American partners;[82] and
- with the shift in Community, now Union, policy to rely more on private enforcement of competition rules, the remedies available to injured parties needed to be more effective and the parties given an incentive for action.

This dilemma has to some extent been overcome by a paradigm shift *from lex imperfecta to lex perfecta* as the *leitmotif* of the new case law of the ECJ.

---

[79] Case 127/73 *BRT v SV SABAM* [1974] ECR 314.
[80] Case T-24/90 *Automec Srl v Commission* [1992] ECR II-2224.
[81] Cases C-6 and 9/90 *Francovich et al v Italy* [1991] ECR I-5357; as a follow-up see cases C-46 and C-48/93 *Brasserie du Pêcheur v Germany and the R v Secretary of State for Transport ex parte Factortame Ltd* [1996] ECR I-1029.
[82] Cf. the study by C. Jones, *Private Enforcement*, 1999.

6.2. NEW TRENDS IN COMPETITION LAW: THE *COURAGE* DOCTRINE AND ITS FOLLOW-UP BY *MANFREDI*

4.25   In the area of competition law, a change of paradigms has been witnessed similar that of 1991 with respect to state liability. This was prepared by a sweeping opinion of AG van Gerven in the *Banks* case where he said:[83]

> "[T]hose prohibitions [regarding anti-competitive behaviour] are aimed at safeguarding undistorted competition and the freedom of competition for undertakings operating in the common market, with the result that such a breach of that system must be made good in full."

AG van Gerven based his opinion on the existing principles of state liability for breach of directly effective Union law provisions and applied them to breaches of the competition rules. In his opinion, it is not the national law that determines compensation but EC law itself. This stood in stark contrast to what the CFI had previously ruled in *Automec II*. The doctrine of direct effect had to be followed up by a Community system of effective compensation, possibly also of prevention. This should not depend on the different state of development of Member State law. His arguments are based on legal policy, like those advanced in *Francovich*, since the Treaty itself does not give an answer and former case law was satisfied with a simple reference to national law.

The Court at the time of *Banks* did not take up this argument, because it denied direct effect of the competition rules under consideration, that is, rules of the ECSC, not the EC Treaty itself. It took a later case, *Courage*,[84] to set in motion the still undeveloped EU doctrine of liability for breaches of competition law. That case concerned an English rule of *nemo auditur propriam turpitudinem allegans* forbidding a partner to an anti-competitive agreement from claiming damages. The Court set aside this rule because it prevented the full effectiveness of Community law. It went beyond this merely negative answer and made the following sweeping statement with regard to compensation for breaches of the Community competition rules:[85]

> "It follows from the foregoing considerations that *any individual* can rely on a breach of Article 85(1) [now Article 101 TFEU, ex-Article 81 EC] before a national court even where he is a party to a contract that is liable to restrict or distort competition within the meaning of that provision. Indeed, the existence of such a right strengthens the working of the Community competition rules and discourages agreements or practices, that are frequently covert, that are liable to restrict or distort competition. From that point of view, actions for damages before the national courts can make a significant contribution to the maintenance of effective competition within the Community."

---

[83]   Case C-128/92 *H.J. Banks & Co. Ltd v British Coal Corporation* [1994] ECR I-1209, 1260.
[84]   Case C-453/99 *Courage Ltd v Bernhard Crehan* [2001] ECR I-6297.
[85]   Ibid., paras 25–27 (emphasis added).

The Court makes it very clear that actions for damages are an important contribution to the accountability of undertakings in the field of competition. This action is based directly on Union law, not on national law,[86] even though the procedural features, as well as the determination of the competent court, are subject to national law.

4.26   As a sequel, the later *Manfredi* case (4.5)[87] tried to clarify some aspects which were left open in *Courage*. The Court reiterated the importance of civil law remedies in enforcing the competition rules, including absolute nullity under Article 81(2) EC (now Article 101(2) TFEU) of claims for compensation by "any individual" (para 61), in the case at hand individual consumers having to pay premium increases in their car insurance because of a price cartel. There must be a *causal relationship* between that harm and an agreement prohibited under Article 81 which is for the national courts to establish. The compensation must include *damnum emergens* and *lucrum cessans* (lost profit) as well as interest under the effectiveness principle (para 95). Punitive damages are only owed if similar national law provides for them under the equivalence principle (para 93). Community law does not entail the unjust enrichment of those who enjoy a right of compensation (para 94). Limitation periods must not make practically impossible the exercise of the right to seek compensation, particularly when the limitation period begins to run from the day on which the agreement or concerted practice was adopted (para 78).

6.3. THE CONSEQUENCES OF *COURAGE/MANFREDI*: EXTENT AND LIMITS OF COMPENSATION

4.27   The highly general and sweeping statement of the ECJ in *Courage* and it development in *Manfredi* must be seen as the beginning of a series of cases similar to those litigated after *Francovich*. This of course would imply that economic actors are making use of the new case law of the ECJ, which does not yet seem to be the case. The following points still need to be clarified, without going too deeply into a still very open debate:[88]

---

[86]   A. Komninos, CMLRev 2002, 473; cf. the differing opinions of N. Reich/H.-W. Micklitz, *Europäisches Verbraucherrecht,* 4th ed. 2003, paras 4.74 and 29.12.

[87]   Joined Cases C-295–298/04 *Vicenzo Manfredi et al v Lloyd Adriatico Asssicurazioni SpA et al* [2006] ECR I-6619.

[88]   For details, see N. Reich, CMLRev 2005, 35; J. Basedow (ed.), *Private Enforcement of EC Competition Law,* 2007; J. Basedow et al. (eds.), *Private Enforcement of EU Competition Law* 2011; J. Keßler, *Schadenersatz und Verbandsklagerechte im Deutschen und Europäischen Kartellrecht,* 2009; S.E. Keske, *Group Litigation in European Competition Law,* 2010; reviewed N. Reich, CMLRev 2011, 1758; contributions to O. Remien (ed.) *Schadenersatz im Europäischen Privat- und Wirtschaftsrecht,* 2012.

- Due to the similarities of the liability of states and of undertakings for breaches of Union law obligations, the standards for determining a wrongful act should be the same. There needs to be a *sufficiently serious breach* to provoke a claim for compensation. Minor offences will not be sufficient, especially when the basic data on which the breach is based are contested, for instance market determination. Clear and obvious breaches will be subject to an action for damages. Examples would include breaches of provisions contained in so called "blacklisted clauses" of exemption regulations such as horizontal or vertical price-fixing agreements, market segregation, territorial restrictions or unjustified refusal to supply. Violations of this kind may give rise to damages actions by those protected by these directly applicable regulations.

- It is not yet clear who can be a plaintiff in a damages action. The Court very broadly spoke of "any individual", but this formula seems to be rather imprecise. In his opinion of 22 March 2001, AG Mischo mentioned third parties as victims, most notably consumers and competitors (para 38). The criterion of *direct causation* used for determining state liability may be of help in allocating compensation in a vertical chain of distribution. In the *Otis* judgment of 6 November 2012,[89] the Court gave standing to the European Commission for economic damage it suffered from an anti-competitive act in a procurement case, even if as a regulator it had imposed a considerable fine on the undertaking that was in breach; such a potential conflict of interest was not judged to be contrary to Article 47 of the Charter.

- A judgment of the German Bundesgerichtshof (BGH) of 28 November 2011[90] also allowed indirect buyers in the chain of distribution to claim for damages, in contrast to US anti-trust law which restricted compensation to direct purchasers.[91]

- The burden of proof of a violation of Article 101(1) TFEU and of the existence of "hardcore restrictions" lies upon the injured plaintiff, but there may be a *prima facie* case against the defendant for a violation if he participated in some way in the anti-competitive behaviour of the other party to the distribution contract.[92]

- The amount of damages must be proportionate to the loss caused by the breach, thus excluding punitive damages, but allowing the skimming off of profit. Comparative law studies could be helpful, as with Union or state liability, to set EU-wide thresholds for compensation.

---

[89] Case C-199/11 *Europese Gemeenschap v Otis et al* [2012] ECR I-(06.11.2012).

[90] BGH, NJW 2012, 928; comment R. van den Bergh, ZEuP 2013, 147; V. Soyez, EuZW 2012, 100; A. Fuchs, in: O. Remien (ed.), *Schadenersatz im Europäischen Privat- und Wirtschaftsrecht*, 2012.

[91] *Hannover Shoe v United Shoe Machinery*, 392 US 481 (1968); *Illinois Brick v Illinois* 431 US 720 (1977).

[92] Case C-49/92P *Commission v Anic* [1999] ECR I-4125 at para 96.

–   Whether the defendant can argue that the plaintiff was able to "pass on" the damage downstream depends on the market in question. The above mentioned judgment of the BGH – the first one in a European jurisdiction to discuss the issue – ruled that "benefits that have accrued to the plaintiff as a consequence of the passing-on of higher cartel prices may be taken into account in the analysis of comparative benefits in order to avoid unjust enrichment. The burden of proof regarding the passing-on lies upon the cartel infringer". In procurement cases like the above mentioned *Otis* case,[93] the victim of cartel prices will be able to recover what he has been over-charged, since no passing-on is possible. The same would be true with end-consumers, even though causation will be almost impossible to prove due to the wide distribution of damages. As for other indirect victims of a cartel, a "secondary burden of proof upon the counterparty requires a careful and complete analysis of all relevant circumstances to check its necessity and reasonableness", according to the BGH, thus coming close to a rejection of the passing-on defence.[94]

–   It is not clear how far injunctions or enforcement actions are possible under Community and now Union law. Examples here would include a refusal to conclude a contract because a refusal would amount to an anti-competitive practice against the potential partner. In its *Automec II* decision the Court of First Instance left this to Member State law. However, following the trend in decentralised enforcement, Union law will have to develop its own rules here. It is submitted that injunctions should be possible against anti-competitive behaviour under the principle *ubi ius, ibi remedium*.[95]

7. COMPENSATION FOR VIOLATIONS OF DIRECTLY APPLICABLE PROVISIONS OF PRIMARY UNION LAW

4.28   The *Courage* case was concerned only with violations of competition law. However, its logic can be extended to all rules of primary Union law that apply directly between private parties. In the recent case law of the Court, this is particularly true with regard to free movement of workers and the freedom to provide services. In its *ASBL v Bosman* judgment,[96] the Court made this clear in

---

93   Case C-199/11 *Europese Gemeenschap v Otis et al* [2012] ECR I-(06.11.2012).
94   Comment R. van den Bergh, *supra* note 90, at 161. See now Article 12-15 of the Commission proposal of a Directive on damages actions for infringements of the EU competition rules, COM (2013) 404 final of 11.06.2013.
95   See AG Jacobs, opinion of 22 May 2003 in Joined Cases C-264/01 etc. *AOK-Bundesverband v Ichthyol-Gesellschaft Cordes et al* [2004] ECR I-2493, para 104.
96   Case C-415/93 *ASBL v Bosman* [1995] ECR I-4921.

regard to rules of professional football associations, and in *Angonese*[97] with regard to language tests by private undertakings. Moreover, in *Wouters* the Court extended this rule to all Community law provisions protecting free movement of persons against collective restrictions.[98] This case law has been extended to certain types of industrial action infringing the freedom to provide services by posting workers, like in the *Viking* and *Laval* cases.[99] In the words of the Court in *Viking*:[100]

> "Articles 39 EC, 43 EC and 49 EC [now Articles 45, 49 and 56 TFEU] do apply not only to the actions of public authorities but extend also to rules of any other nature aimed at regulating in a collective manner gainful employment, self-employment and the provision of services."

This is justified by an *effet utile*-oriented interpretation and is indirectly confirmed by referring to Article 47 of the Charter. In *Viking* this is justified by the fact that in some Member States working conditions are governed by law, and in others by collective agreements; an exemption of the latter from the applicability of the fundamental freedoms would "risk inequality in its application". In *Laval* a more functional argument was used, namely that the abolition of "obstacles to the freedom to provide services would be compromised if the abolition of State barriers could be neutralised by obstacles resulting from the exercise of their legal autonomy by associations and organisations not governed by public law".[101] Articles 43 and 49 EC (now Articles 49 and 56 TFEU) therefore take direct effect and confer rights on individuals whose freedoms are violated by social action of labour unions.[102]

The latest case concerns an action brought by an Italian researcher, *Raccanelli* (*supra* 3.4) who, having received a doctoral stipend from the Max Planck-Gesellschaft, complained that unlike his German colleagues in a similar situation he could not get a more profitable and permanent work contract and thus was being discriminated against contrary to Article 39 EC (now Article 45 TFEU):[103]

> "The Court has thus held, with regard to Article 39 EC, which lays down a fundamental freedom and which constitutes a specific application of the general prohibition of discrimination contained in Article 12 EC, that the prohibition of

---

[97]   Case C-281/98 *Roman Angonese v Cassa di Risparmio di Bolzano SpA* [2000] ECR I-4139.
[98]   Case C-309/99 *Wouters, Savelbergh, Price Waterhouse Belastingadviseurs v Algemene Raad* [2002] ECR I-1577, para 120.
[99]   Case C-438/05 *ITF & FSU v Viking et al* [2007] ECR I-10779; C-351/05 *Laval et al v Svenska Bygnaddsförbundet* [2007] ECR I-11767; for a detailed analysis see N. Reich, Europarättslig Tijdskrift 2008, 851; D. Wyatt, Croatian Yearbook of EU law and Policy 2008, 1.
[100] Case C-438/05 *ITF & FSU v Viking et al* [2007] ECR I-10779, para 33.
[101] C-351/05 *Laval et al v Svenska Bygnaddsförbundet* [2007] ECR I-11767, para 99.
[102] *Viking*, para 58; *Laval*, para 97.
[103] Case C-94/07 *Raccanelli v MPG* [2008] ECR I-5939, paras 45–46.

discrimination applies equally to all agreements intended to regulate paid labour collectively, as well as to contracts between individuals [...] It must be held, therefore, that the prohibition of discrimination based on nationality laid down by Article 39 EC applies equally to private-law associations such as MPG."

These rulings also apply to the freedoms guaranteed in the EA (Association) Agreements, particularly on establishment and on non-discrimination of legally employed workers because, according to the case law of the Court, they enjoy direct effect (3.13).[104] This reasoning was upheld by AG Stix-Hackl in her opinion of 11 July 2002 and the Court in its judgment of 8 May 2003 in the *Kolpak* case that concerned discrimination against a professional handball player from Slovakia under the statutes of the German handball association. These limited the number of third-country foreigners in professional handball matches.[105]

4.29   The reasoning of AG van Gerven in *Banks* concerning the interrelationship between directly applicable Community law rules and an action for compensation in the event of "sufficiently serious breaches" is transferable here, too.[106] Mr Bosman therefore should have been able to claim damages for being driven out of his career as a professional football player by the rules of ASBL. Mr Angonese should get compensation for not being allowed to show language proficiency by other means than those prescribed by the Cassa di Risparmio di Bolzano. Mr Kolpak should be compensated by the German Handballbund for discrimination in his career as a professional sportsman from Slovakia under the protection of the EA agreement with his country. In *Laval*, the Swedish Labour Court granted compensation to the company that had suffered economic loss due to the illegal boycott by the Swedish construction workers' union which was a "sufficiently clear" violation of EU law – obviously a highly contested judgment.[107]

---

[104]   Cases C-63/99 *R v Secretary of State for the Home Department, ex parte Wieslaw and Elzbieta Gloszczuk* [2001] ECR I-6369; C-235/99 *R v Secretary of State for the Home Department, ex parte Eleanora Ivanova Kondova* [2001] ECR I-6427; C-257/99 *R v Secretary of State for the Home Department, ex parte Julius Barkoci and Marcel Malik* [2001] ECR I-6557, C-268/99 *Aldona Malgorzata Jany et al v Staatssecretaris van Justitie* [2001] ECR I-8615; C-162/00 *Land Nordrhein-Westfalen v Beata-Pokrzeptowicz-Meyer* [2002] ECR I-1049; for an overall discussion, N. Reich/S. Harbacevica, Europarättslig Tidskrift 2002, 411.

[105]   Case C-438/00 *Deutscher Handballbund eV v Maros Kolpak* [2003] ECR I-4135.

[106]   N. Reich, YEL 2010, 112; R. O'Donoghue/B. Carr, in: *Cambridge Yearbook of European Legal Studies*, 2009, 157, referring to English law. A different approach has been voiced by D. Leczykiewicz, in: D. Leczykiewicz/S. Weatherill (eds.), *The Involvement of EU Law in Private Law Relationships*, 2013, 220, referring to circumstances like the clarity of the obligation breached, the ease of finding a corresponding right of the claimant, whether a right or merely a freedom was at stake and the like – all somewhat arbitrary conditions.

[107]   See the judgment 89/09 of the Swedish Labour Court (Arbetsdomstolen) of 2 December 2009, which held the Swedish Trade Unions liable to damages in favour of Laval, totaling 2.5 million SEK = €250,000 for breach of the directly effective free movement rules, similar to the argument advocated here; the Arbetsdomstolen (p. 35) also refers to the *Raccanelli* judgment. For details see U. Bernitz/N. Reich, CMLRev 2011, 604.

In *Raccanelli*, the ECJ was asked expressly about the question of compensation, but did not give a straightforward answer and instead referred to national law which however must be interpreted in the sense of its *effet utile* which requires just compensation of the victim:[108]

> "In that regard, it must be held that neither Article 39 EC nor Regulation No 1612/68 prescribes a specific measure to be taken by the Member States or associations such as MPG in the event of a breach of the prohibition of discrimination, but leaves them free to choose between the different solutions suitable for achieving the objective of those respective provisions, depending on the different situations which may arise [...] Consequently, as the Commission indicates in its written observations, it is for the referring court to assess, in the light of the national legislation applicable in relation to non-contractual liability, the nature of the compensation which the applicant in the main proceedings would be entitled to claim. In those circumstances, the answer to the third question must be that, in the event that the applicant in the main proceedings is justified in relying on damage caused by the discrimination to which he has been subject, it is for the referring court to assess, in the light of the national legislation applicable in relation to non-contractual liability, the nature of the compensation which he would be entitled to claim."

It is not clear from the judgment whether there exists a duty for the national court to grant adequate compensation (as seems to be suggested by the wording), or whether this remedy is left completely to the discretion of national law. The latter consequence would, in my opinion, be contradictory to the *effet utile* of Article 39 EC (now Article 45 TFEU).

8. THE IMPORTANCE OF ARTICLE 47 OF THE CHARTER AND ARTICLE 19(1) TEU FOR EU CIVIL LAW REVISITED

8.1. A SUBSTANTIVE UNDERSTANDING OF THE ARTICLE 47 CHARTER/19 TEU TANDEM

4.30 The case studies should have given an impression of the complex interpretation and balancing problems behind the effectiveness requirement in EU civil law. However Article 47 of the Charter seems to be a "sleeping beauty" which has not yet been really "kissed awake" in *Alassini*.[109] The other cases where the ECJ refers to Article 47 of the Charter[110] seem to be too far away from

---

[108]   Case C-94/07 *Raccanelli v MPG* [2008] ECR I-5939, paras 50–52.
[109]   Case C-317/08 *Rosalba Alassini et al v Telecom Italia* [2010] ECR I-2214.
[110]   Cases C-432/05 *Unibet v Justiekanslern* [2007] ECR I-2271 on standing in administrative proceedings; C-279/09 *DEB Deutsche Energiehandels- und Beratungsgesellschaft mbH v*

civil law to allow remedies like compensation or restitution to have an impact. Should one therefore follow the sceptical view of Leczykiewicz?[111]

"However, the right of access to a court and the right to an effective remedy (under Article 47) are on their own incapable of overriding all limitations to the enforceability of Union rights and of empowering to the EU to introduce a harmonised general regime of remedies."

Or is the more optimistic approach of Micklitz justified?[112]

"I'm arguing for an active court, a court which takes the imbalance between the three legal orders (economic, social, citizen) seriously and which is ready to develop RRP's (rights, remedies, procedures) in the social legal order [...] Article 47 will have to play a key role in that respect."

In my opinion it must be remembered that, even though the Court refers to Article 47 of the Charter in a civil law setting in the *Alassini* and *Otis*[113] cases, the principles on which it is based have formed the "hidden agenda" of the Court ever since *Von Colson*. An express reference to Article 47 of the Charter and Article 19(1) TEU does not attach substantial new elements to the principle of effectiveness, but rather makes it conform to the more recent constitutionalisation of EU civil law.[114] Effectiveness has, as could be seen, a "negative", that is an "eliminatory", and a "positive", that is a "hermeneutical" and "remedial", side, both now enshrined in Article 47 of the Charter – at least, *negative* insofar as it allows a first test of national law on whether it makes "impossible or excessively difficult" the implementation of civil law rights under EU primary and secondary law. It still is a forceful and to some extent straightforward argument which the Court has used lately in *Alassini*. It is supplemented by the equivalence test preventing Member State law from prescribing lower standards for EU-based claims than for those under national

---

Bundesrepublik Deutschland [2010] ECR I-13849 on legal aid for legal persons; C-402 + 415/05P *Kadi et al v Council of the EU* [2008] ECR I-6351 on protection of persons charged with terror activities; C-12/08, *Mono Car Styling* [2009] ECR I-6653, para 47, with regard to workers' right of action to enforce information owed to them in case of collective redundancy; C-249/09 *Fuß v Stadt Halle* [2010] ECR I-9849, para 66, concerning protection against reprisal measures of the employer against an employee insisting on his EU rights.

111   D. Leczykiewicz, '"Where Angels Fear to Tread": The EU Law of Remedies and Codification of European Private Law', ERCL 2012, 58.

112   H.-W. Micklitz, in: H.-W. Micklitz/B. de Witte (eds.), *supra* note 73, at 392.

113   Case C-199/11 *Europese Gemeenschap v Otis et al* [2012] ECR I-(06.11.2012), where the Court refers to Article 47 of the Charter as follows: "The principle of effective judicial protection laid down in Article 47 of the Charter comprises various elements; in particular, the rights of the defence, the principle of equality of arms, the right of access to a tribunal and the right to be advised, defended and represented" (para 21). It does not expressly mention substantive remedies, but on the other hand does not exclude them.

114   In the same sense C. Mak, *supra* note 18.

law; *Asturcom* (4.15) is a good case in this respect as it concerned the *ex officio* protection of the consumer against an unfair term.

4.31   But effectiveness also has a *positive* side in interpreting existing remedies and even imposing newly shaped remedies, and the case studies should have demonstrated exactly this. It results in what I have called an "upgrading" of remedies, both in a substantive and in a procedural context. The so-called "remedial" and "procedural" autonomy of Member States is put on trial, but not completely abandoned.

Such a result conforms to the wording and the purpose of Article 47 of the Charter and Article 19(1) TEU. A somewhat closer look at the structure and contents of Article 47 (in conjunction with sentence two of Article 19(1) TEU) may be useful. It requires first that a "right" exists under Union law. Article 47 of the Charter shares the concept of protecting *individual rights as subjective rights in a liberal spirit*. In civil law this is limited to those EU law provisions which intend to create *mandatory standards* in favour of specific individuals; if EU law leaves contractual autonomy more or less untouched, Article 47(1) cannot be invoked.[115]

This mandatory nature is usually the case in contract law matters concerning worker and consumer protection, as well non-discrimination, as discussed in Chapters 2 and 3. It is however not limited to EU contract law, as has been shown by referring to *Manfredi*[116] on compensation for breaches of the competition rules. It will depend on the applicable EU law or secondary legislation as interpreted by the ECJ. In addition to their mandatory nature, these provisions should take direct effect under general principles of EU law, that is they must be sufficiently precise and unconditional.

4.32   This individual subjective right must be provided by Member States with "remedies sufficient to ensure effective legal protection". In my understanding, the English term is somewhat broader that the German translation *wirksamer Rechtsbehelf* and the French term *recours effectif*; while the German and French terminology seem to be restricted to access to and management of court proceedings, the English term includes also remedies based on substantive provisions of contract, tort and restitution law. This is corroborated by the case studies discussed at the start of this chapter. In a purpose-oriented interpretation of EU law as required by Article 52 of the Charter, I therefore prefer the broad English concept of remedy instead of the narrower German and French

---

[115]   An example would be Directive 2011/7/EU of 16 February 2011 combating late payments [2011] OJ L 47/1, referring to the freedom of contract in setting payment dates in Article 3(5) within the limits of the "gross unfairness principle" of Article 7; see *infra* 7.9.

[116]   Joined Cases C-295–298/04 *Vicenzo Manfredi et al v Lloyd Adriatico Asssicurazioni SpA et al* [2006] ECR I-6619.

understanding. Indeed, there could and would be no effective "judicial protection" without the prior grant of remedies in the area of civil law rights as well.

These remedies may relate to substance and/or to procedures. *Substantive remedies* include compensation, restitution, nullity of a contract clause and preclusion of the application of a non-conforming national rule.[117] *Procedural remedies* relate to issues of standing, injunctions, time-limits and evidence rules.[118] However it should be kept in mind that it will not always be easy to differentiate exactly between substantive and procedural remedies, and this is depends very much on applicable national law which uses different criteria to distinguish between substantive and procedural remedies, for example in the area of limitation periods. Obviously they must have their legal basis in EU law. These remedies must in the end be enforceable before a tribunal; but this does not rule out the existence of alternative dispute resolution mechanisms (ADR) if they do not preclude access to courts, as the ECJ stated in *Alassini*.

4.33   The approach advocated in this chapter results, as has been mentioned before, in a "*hybridisation" of remedies* which have to be introduced into national law using the classical method of "directive-conforming interpretation", supplemented lately by a "negative horizontal effect" of directives if they can be linked to the Charter, in particular the worker protection provision of Article 31(2) and the non-discrimination rules of Articles 21 and 24. It seems arguable that the principle of consumer protection in Article 38 of the Charter read together with Articles 12 and 169 TFEU allows a similar "preclusionary direct effect" of horizontal EU directives.[119]

To avoid possible fears of an "overextension" of the effectiveness principle, it should be remembered that this principle is only relevant in areas where EU law creates or intends to create rights, for example in favour of individuals who come under the umbrella of the competition or free movement rules, or those protecting discriminated persons, workers or consumers. This is always a matter of interpretation and requires that the provisions on which these are based are mandatory in nature.

---

[117]   A. Hartkamp, *supra* note 30, paras 113–114.

[118]   See the seminal paper by W. van Gerven, *supra* note 5, with examples on p. 522; see also A. Hartkamp, *supra* note 30, paras 115–116.

[119]   This is the interesting argument by O. Mörsdorf, 'Die Auswirkungen des neuen ,Grundrechts auf Verbraucherschutz' gem. Art. 38 GrCh auf den nationalen Verbraucherschutz', Juristenzeitung 2010, 759.

8.2. "FULL" EFFECTIVENESS: TOO "FULL", TOO "EMPTY", OR "JUST RIGHT"? THE NEED FOR A BALANCING APPROACH

4.34 Another point is concerned with a legal-political question: isn't the Court over-stepping its mandate to interpret EU law when it goes about reshaping remedies based on national law? This criticism does not so much rely on the effectiveness and equivalence principles in the negative sense – they have been recognised as general constitutional principles of EU law ever since, and are of course not limited to administrative and procedural issues but have also been extended to civil law matters, including (mandatory) contract law. Rather, the criticism is directed against the *positive full effectiveness* principle with its hermeneutical and remedial aspects, which the Court had developed in the cases analysed here and which are at odds with traditional Member State remedial and procedural "autonomy" and competence. The use (some say abuse) of compensation for deterrence purposes, the abrogation of the fault principle for compensation in contract law substituted by strict liability rules, the limitation of party autonomy in proceedings concerning unfair terms, the extension of seller's liability in consumer sales beyond the transfer of risk, the recognition of ADR instruments as a prerequisite for later proceedings before courts of law under certain qualifying conditions – not much "autonomy" of Member States seems to be left. Isn't the ECJ acting *ultra vires*, as was argued by the plaintiffs in the *Honeywell* litigation before the German Constitutional Court, criticising *Mangold*, but finally rejected by the same BVerfG (3.7) which confirmed the wide scope and competence the ECJ enjoys in interpreting, and in the end developing, EU law, even to the detriment of traditional principles of Member States' law?

It must also be remembered that even in cases where the ECJ required an "upgrading" of national remedies and procedures to protect rights granted under EU law, it left a wide margin of discretion to national courts to accomplish the right balancing between conflicting interests. The best example is the *Putz/Weber* case. Even if the extension of the strict seller's liability beyond the mere "bodily" quality of the goods sold at the time of transfer of risk itself may seem "revolutionary", the ensuing remedies for the consumer are nonetheless still limited by a proportionality argument taking into account the legitimate interests of the seller and the character of the transaction itself. It is of no surprise that the BGH[120] in its follow-up judgment quite straightforwardly divided the risk between seller and consumer to one half for each!

A similar approach can also be seen in discrimination cases (4.13). As a prerequisite in all cases granting compensation to victims of discrimination, there must be at the outset a national rule in this regard; the original EU Directive 76/207 did not provide for such a remedy and left it as an option to Member

---

[120]   *Supra* note 65.

States. Once the States had made use of this option, it was "upgraded" in the case law of the ECJ to meet the standards of effectiveness. Only later legislation, in particular Directive 2002/73/EC,[121] expressly provided for the remedy of compensation as also mandatory under EU law. Article 6(2), now replaced by Article 13 of the Recast Directive 2006/54,[122] to some extent codified as mandatory what the ECJ had developed alongside it as an effective remedy, thus completing what had originally been the only optional compensation regime.

8.3. RELEVANCE OF THE EFFECTIVENESS PRINCIPLE FOR COLLECTIVE REMEDIES?

4.35   The effectiveness of collective remedies like injunctions by consumer organisations or labour unions has been recognised in the opinions of several AGs. In her opinion of 6 December 2011 in the *Invitel* case AG Trstenjak wrote:[123]

> "The collective action as a means of enforcing collective rights not only provides access to this legal remedy but also has characteristics that make it an effective deterrent. As can be seen from the abovementioned judgment, this assessment is shared by the Court. Collective actions offer many advantages over individual actions. By bundling consumers' common interests together, they make it possible to enforce them judicially. By means of collective actions, consumer protection associations give consumers a voice and a weight that they would often not have in this form in isolated proceedings because of their generally weaker position. Lastly, a collective action helps to enhance the status of the consumer at the procedural level and relieves him of the risk of costs in civil proceedings if he is unsuccessful, which may deter a consumer from individually asserting his rights just as much as a low value in an individual case, for which it would not be worthwhile for an individual to incur the expense. The successful enforcement of rights by way of a collective action creates a just balancing of the interests of consumers and undertakings, ensures fair competition and shows that collective actions are just as necessary as individual actions in order to protect the consumer."

However, the effectiveness principle in this context is not linked to protecting individual rights as under Article 47 of the Charter, but rather as an "abstract

---

[121]   Directive 2002/73/EC of the EP and of the Council of 23 September 2002 amending Council Directive 76/207/EEC on the implementation of the principle of equal treatment for men and women as regards access to employment, vocational training and promotion, and working conditions [2002] OJ L 269/15.

[122]   *Supra* note 35.

[123]   Case C-472/10 *Nemzeti Fogyasztróvédelni Hatóság v Invitel* [2012] ECR I-(26.04.2012), para 41; in a similar vein, AG Jacobs, opinion of 27 January 2000, in case C-195/98 *Öst. Gewerkschaftsbund, Gewerkschaft öffentlicher Dienst v Republik Österreich* [2000] ECR I-10497, para 47.

remedy" intended to "clear the market" from unfair contract terms or unfair commercial practices, but also to sanction discriminatory practices. But what are the effects on the individual consumer who has been subject to them? Is there an obligation on Member States' law to rectify the consequences of unfair terms or practices (*Folgenbeseitigungsanspruch*)?[124] Wouldn't this be the consequence of a correct understanding of Article 47 of the Charter in its remedial function? Shouldn't there be a right of the injured to reclaim sums unduly paid as a general principle?[125] *Invitel* could be understood as a first step in this direction.[126] There the Court wrote:[127]

> "It follows that, where the unfair nature of a term included in the GBC of consumer contracts has been recognised in an action for an injunction, such as that here at issue in the main proceedings, the national courts are required, of their own motion, and also as regards the future, to draw all the consequences provided for by national law in order to ensure that consumers who have concluded a contract to which those GBC apply will not be bound by that term."

A similar consequence for the injunction under Directive 2005/29 seems to be excluded by Article 3(2), but in its recent *Pereničová* judgment the Court insisted that:[128]

> "a finding that a commercial practice is unfair is one element among others on which the competent court may base its assessment of the unfairness of contractual terms under Article 4(1) of Directive 93/13."

The Court seems to suggest a link between collective and individual remedies which must be developed in the future.

4.36 Another example of emerging collective remedies can be observed in non-discrimination law, particularly where an individual victim of a discriminatory act cannot be identified. Member States are under an obligation to sanction unjustified discriminations in civil law relations leading to the denial of contracting with a group of incriminated persons, whether or not they provide for civil law remedies.[129] Civil law, as Steindorff already insisted 20 years ago,[130] has a *Sanktionsaufgabe* – the task of providing sanctions. They must also be effective in cases of discrimination against a group of persons with certain characteristics like race under Directive 2000/43 (3.7), a requirement highlighted by AG Poiares

---

124   This is discussed by H.-W. Micklitz/N. Reich, 'Von der Missbrauchs- zur Marktkontrolle', EuZW 2013, 457.
125   A. Hartkamp, *supra* note 30, at para 134.
126   H.-W. Micklitz/N. Reich, *supra* note 51, at 264.
127   Case C-472/10 *Nemzeti Fogyaszróvédelni Hatóság v Invitel* [2012] ECR I-(26.04.2012), para 43.
128   Case C-453/10 *Pereničová and Perenič v SOS financ* [2012] ECR I-(15.04.2012), para 42.
129   N. Reich, YEL 2010, 112 at 141.
130   E. Steindorff, *EWG-Vertrag und Privatrecht*, 1996, 303 ff.

Maduro in his opinion of 12 March 2008 in the Belgian *Feryn* case.[131] The case concerned ethnic discrimination by a producer and installer of "up-and-over" doors, who publicly declared that he did not employ immigrants (in the circumstances mostly persons of Arabic origin) in order to attract clients who, because of their fear of theft, would be unwilling to employ the defendant otherwise. AG Poiares Maduro pointed out that:[132]

"On the issue of sanctions, Article 15 of the Directive [2000/43] provides that 'Member States shall lay down the rules on sanctions applicable to infringements of the national provisions adopted pursuant to this Directive and shall take all measures necessary to ensure that they are applied. The sanctions, which may comprise the payment of compensation to the victim, must be effective, proportionate and dissuasive [...]' Moreover [...] national courts have a duty to take all appropriate measures to ensure fulfilment of the Member States' obligation to achieve the result envisaged by the Directive. It is for the referring court to determine, in accordance with the relevant rules of domestic law, which remedy would be appropriate in the circumstances of the present case. However, [...] purely token sanctions are not sufficiently dissuasive to enforce the prohibition of discrimination. Therefore, it would seem that a court order prohibiting such behaviour would constitute a more appropriate remedy. In sum, if the national court finds that there has been a breach of the principle of equal treatment, it must grant remedies that are effective, proportionate and dissuasive."

In the judgment of 10 July 2008 the Court largely followed AG Poiares Maduro's opinion, while allowing the employer to prove that in his actual recruitment policy he did not discriminate (a somewhat problematic defence, since it does not eliminate the effect of his public statements which were clearly discriminatory). With regard to remedies, the Court allowed the national jurisdiction a wide range of alternatives, provided that the principles of effectiveness, proportionality and dissuasiveness were respected:[133]

"If it appears appropriate to the situation at issue in the main proceedings, those sanctions may, where necessary, include a finding of discrimination by the court or the competent administrative authority in conjunction with an adequate level of publicity, the cost of which is to be borne by the defendant. They may also take the form of a prohibitory injunction, in accordance with the rules of national law, ordering the employer to cease the discriminatory practice, and, where appropriate, a fine. They may, moreover, take the form of the award of damages to the body bringing the proceedings."

In its recent *ACCEPT* judgment of 25 April 2013 (3.38) concerning discrimination on grounds of sexual orientation, the Court insisted that a

---

[131] Case C-54/07 *Centrum voor gelijkheid van kansen en voor racismebestrijding (CGKR) v Firma Feryn NV* [2008] ECR I-5187; N. Reich, EuZW 2008, 229.

[132] Case C-54/07 *Centrum voor gelijkheid van kansen en voor racismebestrijding (CGKR) v Firma Feryn NV* [2008] ECR I-5187, paras 27–29.

[133] Ibid., para 39.

"purely symbolic sanction cannot be regarded as being compatible with the correct and effective implementation of Directive 2000/78" (para 64).

4.37   On the other hand, Article 47 of the Charter cannot be "upgraded" to a mechanism of providing collective remedies of its own without any basis in secondary law. Such an interpretation would clearly be contrary to the limited scope of the EU Charter under Article 51(1) and to the understanding of "general principles" as excluding any direct effect. Article 47 must be viewed together with existing EU law and implementing Member State law on collective remedies. It allows, as was said before, an "upgrading" of existing remedies, but not a creation of new ones.[134] The difference between the two concepts may be difficult to draw as the *Feryn* case shows, but this is again part of the ECJ's competence of interpretation under Article 267 TFEU. Therefore, an extension of the existing collective remedy of injunction to individual compensation in consumer protection and anti-discrimination cases is certainly within the jurisdiction of the ECJ, but not the creation of a free-standing group action for compensation in competition or discrimination cases. Of course, Article 47 of the Charter may serve as a legal-political argument in adopting EU legislation on collective redress.

As an example, "collective remedies" in discrimination cases sought by NGOs (associations, organisations or other legal entities which have, in accordance with national law, a legitimate interest in ensuring that the provisions on non-discrimination are complied with) are foreseen in Article 7(2) of Directive 2000/43, Article 9 (2) of Directive 2000/78 and Article 8(3) of Directive 2004/114. However, these NGOs may only bring actions in limited circumstances, exclusively in order to support individuals who have suffered from discrimination, and such actions require their approval. Injunctions, unlike in consumer cases, are not expressly foreseen, a regrettable lacuna of non-discrimination law, but this gap cannot be filled by an interpretation based on the effectiveness principle of Article 47 of the Charter. Such an interpretation would clearly contradict the will of the legislator. On the other hand, however, since the Directive imposes only a minimum requirement in the area of remedial protection as well, Member States may go beyond what is envisaged in the directive and allow "independent" actions and injunctions by NGOs. Under the equivalence principle (4.3), collective remedies for infringements of rights based on national law must also be available for violations of EU-based rights. But this extension does not create a new general principle of EU law; it only aims to treat EU law rights in an identical way to national rights.

---

[134]   N. Reich, *Individueller und kollektiver Rechtsschutz*, 2012, 50 ff.

9. CONCLUSION: HOW EFFECTIVE IS THE EFFECTIVENESS PRINCIPLE?

4.38 The effectiveness principle, as could be shown throughout in this chapter by relying on the case law of the ECJ, has certainly had a deep influence on Member State civil law insofar as it comes within the scope of EU law. The remedies reshaped under the impact of EU law have become a "hybrid" because they start from the substantive or procedural settings of Member State law and therefore respect their "remedial and procedural autonomy". EU law will make them conform to the principles enshrined in Article 47 of the Charter and Article 19(1) TEU. Member State courts are required to apply the remedies as reshaped by the ECJ and to set aside conflicting national law. This approach will also allow directives to have something of a horizontal direct effect by generalising the approach of the ECJ in *Kücückdevici*. However, this broad extension of the effectiveness principle falls short of collective remedies, which merely follow the less strict equivalence approach: rights under EU law must enjoy the same means of protection as rights under national law. Collective remedies under EU law depend on whether they are available for similar claims under national law.[135]

---

[135] See now the Recommendation of the Commission, 'Towards a Horizontal Framework for Collective Redress', COM (2013) 401/2 of 11.06.2013.

CHAPTER 5

THE PRINCIPLE
OF BALANCING

Contents

Bibliography 131
1. Introduction: a dialogue on balancing in EU civil law 132
2. Balancing in unfair term jurisprudence: transparency, "core terms"
   and the unfairness test 134
   2.1. A commercial law approach to balancing by the UK Supreme
        Court 135
   2.2. Balancing as applied by the German Federal Court 137
   2.3. The EU preference for "decentralised balancing" 138
3. Balancing to avoid "over-protection" 141
   3.1. "Principles of civil law" against alleged "over-protection" and
        its limits? 141
   3.2. Balancing in worker protection: the fuzzy concept of *abus de
        droit* in *Paletta I* and *II*. 144
4. Role of balancing in social conflicts: fundamental rights vs.
   fundamental freedoms? 146
   4.1. The ECJ as final arbiter in social conflicts? 146
   4.2. Opinion of AG Poiares Maduro 147
   4.3. The ECJ's approach in *Viking*. 148
        4.3.1. The situation of FSU 149
        4.3.2. The special case of ITF 149
        4.3.3. How to balance the balancing in "horizontal conflicts"
               involving different autonomous entities? 150
5. Conclusion 153

Bibliography

L. Azoulai, 'The Court of Justice and the Social Market Economy: The Emergence of an Ideal and the Conditions for its Realization', CMLRev 2008, 1335; C. von Bar/E. Clive/H. Schulte-Nölke (eds.), *Principles, Definitions and Model Rules of European Private Law, Draft Common Frame of Reference (DCFR)*, outline ed. 2009, full ed. 2009, Vol I-VI; R. Brownsword et al. (eds.), *The Foundations of European Private Law*, 2011; F. Cafaggi (ed.), *The Institutional Framework of*

European Private Law, 2006; R. de la Feria/S. Vogenauer (eds.), *The Prohibition of Abuse in EU Law*, 2011; M. Hesselink, 'The General Principles of Civil Law: Their Nature, Role and Legitimacy', in: D. Leczykiewicz/S. Weatherill (eds.), *The Involvement of EU Law in Private Law Relationships*, 2013, 131; D. Kennedy, 'A Transnational Genealogy of Proportionality in Private Law', in R. Brownsword et al. (eds.), *The Foundations of European Private Law*, 2011; K. Lenaerts/J. Gutiérrez-Fons, 'The Constitutional Allocation of Powers and General Principles of EU Law', CMLRev 2010, 1629; L. Niglia, *The Transformation of Contract in Europe*, 2003; H.-W. Micklitz, *The Politics of Judicial Cooperation*, 2005; H.-W. Micklitz (ed.), *The Many Concepts of Social Justice in European Private Law*, 2011; H.-W. Micklitz/N. Reich/P. Rott, *Understanding EU Consumer Law*, 2009; H.-W. Micklitz/F. Cafaggi (eds.), *European Private Law after the Common Frame of Reference*, 2010; H.-W. Micklitz/B. De Witte (eds.), *The ECJ and the Autonomy of Member States*, 2012; M.-A. Moreau, 'Labour relations and the concept of social justice in the EU', in: H.-W. Micklitz (ed.), *The Many Concepts of Social Justice in European Private Law*, 2011, 303; N. Reich, 'Fundamental Freedoms versus Fundamental Rights – Did *Viking* get it Wrong?', Europarättslig Tijdskrift 2008, 851; K. Riesenhuber (ed.), *Europäische Methodenlehre*, 2nd ed. 2010; R. Schulze (ed.), *Common Frame of Reference and Existing EC Contract Law*, 2008; R. Schulze/H. Schulte-Nölke, *European Private Law – Current Status and Perspectives*, 2011; C. Willet, 'Social Justice in the OFT v. Commutative Justice in the Supreme Court', in: H.-W. Micklitz (ed.), *The Many Concepts of Social Justice in European Private Law*, 2011, 359; V. Trstenjak/E. Beysen, 'European Consumer Protection Law: *Curia Semper Dabit Remedium?*', CMLRev 2011, 95.

1. INTRODUCTION: A DIALOGUE ON BALANCING IN EU CIVIL LAW

5.1 This chapter takes up some ideas that are well known in EU constitutional law, namely the need to balance seemingly contradictory positions that each claim protection of their interests in one of the many "rights" or "principles" of the Charter. Take as starting point the ECJ's *Promusicae* case (1.8)[1] which concerned the balancing of the right to protection of intellectual property under Articles 17 and 47 of the Charter on the one hand with the right to privacy and personality protection under Articles 7 and 8 on the other. The Court wrote:[2]

> "The present reference for a preliminary ruling thus raises the question of the need to reconcile the requirements of the protection of different fundamental rights, namely the right to respect for private life on the one hand and the rights to protection of property and to an effective remedy on the other [...] That being so, the Member States must, when transposing the directives mentioned above, take care to rely on an interpretation of the directives which allows a fair balance to be struck between the various fundamental rights protected by the Community legal order. Further, when implementing the measures transposing those directives, the authorities and courts of the Member States must not only interpret their national law in a manner consistent with those directives but also make sure that they do not rely on an interpretation of

---

[1] Case C-275/06 *Productores de Música de España (Promusicae) v Telefónica de España SAU* [2008] ECR I-271.
[2] Ibid., paras 65 and 68.

them which would be in conflict with those fundamental rights or with the other general principles of Community law, such as the principle of proportionality."

A similar approach was taken in the more recent *Sky* case (1.13):[3]

"In the light, first, of the importance of safeguarding the fundamental freedom to receive information and the freedom and pluralism of the media guaranteed by Article 11 of the Charter and, second, of the protection of the freedom to conduct a business as guaranteed by Article 16 of the Charter, the European Union legislature was entitled to adopt rules such as those laid down in Article 15 of Directive 2010/13, which limit the freedom to conduct a business, and to give priority, in the necessary balancing of the rights and interests at issue, to public access to information over contractual freedom."

It will be argued in this chapter that the principle of balancing as a constitutional principle of EU law also has importance and relevance for EU civil law. In this context, it may useful to refer to the thoughts of the American legal theorist Duncan Kennedy reflecting on interesting conflicting parallel developments in civil law methodology from a transnational perspective. In his words, "[i]n balancing we understand ourselves to be choosing a norm (not choosing a winning party) among a number of permissible alternatives on the ground that it best balances or combines conflicting normative considerations".[4] Such methodology, well known in constitutional law, has allowed in civil law a rather conflicting and incoherent "opening" of legal thought to extra-legal considerations, which, for many adherents to a more abstract legal reasoning (which Duncan Kennedy calls "Classical Legal Thought" (CLT)), comes close to policy-making. There is a fear that as part of this "opening", civil law, particularly in countries with a tradition of codified law, loses its "innocence", namely the guaranteeing of the enforcement of the "free will" of parties to a contract in the interest of an efficient market economy. Instead of the prevalence of default rules, which to some extent put into legal norms what reasonable parties aiming to minimise transaction costs would have included in their contract themselves had they known about the potential conflict,[5] civil law becomes "corrupted" by mandatory rules that protect weaker parties (Chapter 2) and impose constitutional values like non-discrimination on free transactions (Chapter 3) that must be effectively implemented (Chapter 4).

5.2   Even the Draft Common Frame of Reference (DCFR: see 0.10 and 6.6)[6] to which Kennedy refers seems "contaminated" by this trend towards a more

---

3   Case C-283/11 *Sky Österreich v Österreichischer Rundfunk* [2013] ECR I-(22.01.2013), para 66.
4   D. Kennedy, 'A Transnational Genealogy of Proportionality in Private Law', in: R. Brownsword et al. (eds), *The Foundations of European Private Law*, 2011, 185.
5   For an economic approach to harmonisation, see F. Gomez/J. Januza, 'The Economics of Private Law Harmonised Law-making: Mechanisms, Modes and Standards', in: R. Brownsword et al. (eds), *The Foundations of European Private Law*, 2011, 115.
6   C. von Bar/E. Clive/H. Schulte-Nölke (eds), *Principles, Definitions and Model Rules of European Private Law, Draft Common Frame of Reference (DCFR)*, outline ed. 2009.

substantive justice in civil law, based on balancing.[7] "Balancing" in this context becomes a highly complex and at the same time controversial issue going beyond the traditional two-party scheme of civil law based on nearly unfettered private autonomy (*in dubio pro libertate*), which I have rejected because of the concept of "framed autonomy" as a characteristic of EU civil law distinguishing it from Member State private law (1.3). As I will show later, balancing can be found in a multi-level system of European jurisdictions – always in confrontation with CLT – based on abstract, formal, "principled" legal reasoning that defends private autonomy against the intrusion of extra-legal principles and values. My approach will be based on a discussion of three areas where balancing has found differing and to some extent conflicting expressions:

- the so-called "price argument" in controlling unfair terms in consumer contracts under Directive 93/13 (5.3–5.8);
- the seemingly paradoxical and incoherent emergence of countervailing "(general) principles of civil law" against a potential "over-protection" of weaker parties" (5.9–5.11); and
- the conflict of the "collective autonomy concept" as a fundamental right or principle in EU labour relations with the free movement provisions of the Treaty (5.12–5.17).

2. BALANCING IN UNFAIR TERM JURISPRUDENCE: TRANSPARENCY, "CORE TERMS" AND THE UNFAIRNESS TEST

5.3 One of the most difficult and most discussed problems in EU civil law has been to define the limits of private autonomy, as discussed in Chapter 1 under the heading of "framed autonomy". Recent litigation concerning the application and interpretation of the EU unfair terms Directive 93/13/EEC[8] can be useful in this context. The problem concerns the understanding of Article 4(2) of the Directive, which posits that:

> "Assessment of the unfair nature of the terms shall relate neither to the definition of the main subject matter of the contract nor to the adequacy of the price and remuneration, on the one hand, as against the services or goods supplied in exchange, on the other, in so far as these terms are in plain intelligible language."

---

[7] See the joint paper by H. Eidenmüller et al., 'Der Gemeinsame Referenzrahmen für das Europäische Privatrecht – Wertungsfragen and Kodifikationsprobleme', Juristenzeitung 2008, 529; English version OJLS 2008, 659; see also contributions to R. Schulze (ed), *Common Frame of Reference and Existing EC Contract Law*, 2008.

[8] Council Directive 93/13/EEC of 5 April 1993 on unfair terms in consumer contracts [1993] OJ L 95/29.

The legislative history of this last-minute amendment is somewhat confusing and difficult to use for interpretation purposes.[9] The EU legislator seems to be combining two important principles which are said to govern any market economy based on effective competition:

- the principle of transparency in pre-formulated terms in consumer contracts; and
- the exclusion of so-called "core-terms" from the unfairness test of Article 3(2) once the requirement of transparency is fulfilled.

Recent litigation in three jurisdictions – the UK, Germany and the EU – permits an analysis of the different *Vorverständnisse* ("pre-conceptions": 0.2) with which judges tackle the problem put before them by the EU legislator. Again, it is necessary to cut a long story short.

2.1. A COMMERCIAL LAW APPROACH TO BALANCING BY THE UK SUPREME COURT

5.4 The interpretation of Article 4(2) was an issue addressed by the UK Supreme Court (formerly the House of Lords) in the judgment of 25 November 2009 in the case of the *Office of Fair Trading v Abbey National et al.*[10] This concerned the highly controversial practice of UK banks debiting the following charges for consumers "not in credit":

- "overdraft excess charges", to some extent similar to "overrunning" in the sense of Article 12 of Directive 2008/48;[11]
- "guaranteed paid item charges";

---

[9]   L. Niglia, *The Transformation of Contract in Europe*, 2003, 139; H.-W. Micklitz/N. Reich/ P. Rott, *Understanding EU Consumer Law*, 2009, para 3.11; the "origin" of the amendment is frequently seen in the paper by H. Brander/P. Ulmer, 'The Community Directive on Unfair Terms in Consumer Contracts – some critical remarks on the proposal submitted by the EC Commission', CMLRev 1991, 647 at 656, insisting that any control by the courts of the reasonableness or equivalence of the relationship between price and the goods or services provided was "anathema to the fundamental tenets of a free market economy".

[10] *Office of Fair Trading v Abbey National et al* [2009] UKSC 6 (on appeal from [2009] EWCA Civ 116), critical comments by S. Whittaker, 'Unfair Contract Terms, Unfair Prices and Bank Charges', ModLR 2011, 106; M. Kenny, 'Orchestrating Consumer Protection in Retail Banking: *Abbey National* in the Context of Europeanized Private Law', ERPrL 2011, 43. The Supreme Court was referring to its earlier decision in *Director General of Fair Trading v First National Bank* [2001] UKHL 52; [2002] 1 AC 481; for a critical analysis see H.-W. Micklitz, 'Case note: House of Lords – *Fair Trading v National Bank*', ERCL 2006, 471; H.-W. Micklitz, 'Zum englischen Verständnis von Treu und Glauben in der Richtlinie 93/13/EWG', ZEuP 2003, 865; H.-W. Micklitz, *The Politics of Judicial Co-operation*, 2005, 418.

[11] For an overview see H.-W. Micklitz/N. Reich/P. Rott, *supra* note 9, at para 5.8.

- "unpaid item charges"; and
- "paid item charges".

These charges made up about 30 per cent of the banks' revenue from payment services; to some extent, those clients "not in credit" – and therefore those who were more needy – heavily subsidised those "in credit" – that is those who were better off and did not have to pay these charges – as Lord Mance recognised in his speech (para 105). Starting from the premise that the clauses setting out the different charges fulfilled as such the requirement of transparency, the question arose as to whether they could be challenged as unfair, or whether they should come under the exclusion of Article 4(2) as "core terms".

5.5   Both the High Court and the Court of Appeal, in very detailed judgments, rejected the application of Article 4(2) (or the UK equivalent in its implementation of Directive 93/13)[12] to these charges, thus using a well-known principle of EU law to interpret exceptions narrowly and to take account of the consumer protection objective of Directive 93/13, which had been reiterated by the ECJ several times.[13] They argued, along more or less the same lines, that some of these clauses concerned additional charges either for services not rendered, or that they did not relate to the "core terms" of the transaction, that is for services based on the contractual *quid pro quo*.

5.6   The approach of the Supreme Court turned the matter upside down. The speeches of the Law Lords show a purely market-oriented, commercial *Vorverständnis* of consumer protection. Viewed in this way, Directive 93/13 is more or less concerned with consumer choice, not with protecting him or her from unfair terms. As Lord Walker said in his speech, '[t]he services that banks offer to their current account customers are a comparable package of services' (para 40). This view was shared by Lord Phillips (para 89). Lord Mance, in a detailed analysis of the legislative history of the clause, rejected the distinction between "essential" and "non-essential" terms (para 112). The consumer "buys" this package inclusive of all the mentioned charges if not in "credit", and therefore "any monetary price or remuneration payable under the contract" is exempted from the unfairness test. Only ancillary provisions come under this test.

The judgment has been criticised on a number of points: one is certainly the failed reference to the ECJ under Article 234(3) EC (now Article 267(3) TFEU); another is the dramatic narrowing of the unfairness test, which is excluded for

---

12   Unfair Terms in Consumer Contract Regulations 1994, S.I. No. 3159, as adjusted by S.I. 1999 No. 2083; for details see G. Howells/S. Weatherill, *Consumer Protection Law*, 2nd ed. 2005, para 5.3 at pp. 267.
13   For an example, see Case C-243/08 *Pannon* [2009] ECR I-4713, para 22.

any term even if only indirectly relating to the "price of the package". What is more important is the *Vorverständnis* of the Law Lords concerning the function of consumer law, which they took to be not about balancing an unequal distribution of power between banks and consumers in favour of the weak party (2.1), but about understanding consumers as rational market agents making a choice on a take-it-or-leave-it basis a package of services into whose overall "value for money" the judge does not want to interfere.

2.2. BALANCING AS APPLIED BY THE GERMAN FEDERAL COURT

5.7   The Bundesgerichtshof (BGH) had to decide similar cases, but arrived at different results. The starting point was a neat distinction between "price clauses", which contain the "core terms" to which the unfairness test cannot be applied under German law (which is drafted somewhat differently from the EC Directive, but has a similar legislative purpose), and ancillary clauses (*Preisnebenabreden*).[14]

In a bank charges case similar to the one before UK Supreme Court, the BGH did not refer to Article 4(2) of Directive 93/13, but rather to a provision in German – and to some extent EU law – that controls lump-sum payments for damages clauses. This conceptual trick allowed the BGH to control the bank charges by redefining them as clauses on penalties and damages, not as price clauses.

But this reconceptualising of "conflicting interests" did not go very far. It is interesting to note that the BGH, in its later judgment of 14 October 1997[15] concerning the control of pre-formulated clauses by banks and credit card providers for a special charge on the use of credit cards abroad (*Entgelt für Auslandseinsatz*), used a somewhat modified version of its earlier conceptual argument to deny such control. Without any reference to EU law and in particular to Article 4(2) of Directive 93/13,[16] it stated that not only were general clauses concerning the consideration for a service excluded from unfairness control, but so were clauses for a special service (*Sonderleistung*) for which there is no legal regulation. The BGH insisted on the principle of private autonomy

---

[14]   BGHZ 124, 254, judgment (30 November 1993), confirmed more recently by judgment of 13 November 2012, VuR 2013, 105, prohibiting extra charges for a so-called "P-account" (*Pfändungsschutzkonto* – a special account introduced by the legislator to protect customers against seizure); the negative effects of this case law from an efficiency argument based on risk-distribution have been criticised by M. Kenny, *supra* note 10, at 58.

[15]   BGHZ 137, 27 at 30.

[16]   For criticism, J. Basedow, 'Die Klauselrichtlinie und der EuGH – eine Geschichte der verpassten Gelegenheiten', in: H. Schulte-Nölke/R. Schulze (eds), *Europäische Rechts-angleichung und nationales Vertragsrecht*, 1999, 277, 285.

which allows banks to shape their price clauses as they wish. Since all providers ask for a special charge in an almost cartel-like fashion, the consumer will usually take it for granted that he has to pay such charges for the use of his card abroad.

A later widely publicised judgment of the BGH of 24 March 2010[17] concerned clauses in gas supply contracts with final consumers, linking the price of gas to the market price of light oil. The BGH did not discuss the problem of price clauses in general, that is in relation to Article 4(2) of Directive 93/13, but simply held that the clause was void because it unduly disadvantaged the consumer (*"unangemessene Benachteiligung der Kunden des Versorgungsunternehmens"*), which is prohibited by §307(I)(1) BGB.

These different judgments of the BGH show that the *Vorverständnis* of judges on the adequacy and fairness of the relevant clauses is seemingly more important in deciding a case than the conceptual framework referred to in the judgment. Such a method may not help legal clarity, but it at least allows an open deliberation as to which approach to take, aimed at finding a just result in a specific case before the judge.

2.3. THE EU PREFERENCE FOR "DECENTRALISED BALANCING"

5.8   On this understanding, it is not the "fairness test" of Article 3(2) of Directive 93/13 but the transparency test of Article 4(2) that becomes the decisive control instrument of unfair terms relating to price clauses. In his earlier analysis, Niglia pointed out the changes that Directive 93/13 made to European contract law:[18]

> "[T]he vocabulary of a market-oriented contract law has been replacing the traditional rule-based one whenever judges decode the Directive's set of market factors to be taken into account, is increasingly evident in various respects."

The *Ausbanc* case[19] before the ECJ allows an analysis of the *Vorverständnis* of consumer protection in the EU. The opinion of AG Trstenjak of 29 October 2009 helps in understanding the scope and importance of the litigation. The AG had already made significant contributions to an EU-specific theory of balancing with regard to both the extent and limits of private autonomy in several areas of

---

[17]   Case VIII ZR 178/08, NJW (Neue Juristische Wochenschrift) 2010, 2789; for more details see H.-W. Micklitz, *Brauchen Konsumenten und Unternehmen eine neue Architektur des Verbraucherrechts? Gutachten A zum 69. Deutschen Juristentag*, 2012, A 73–75.

[18]   L. Niglia, *supra* note 9 at 190.

[19]   Case C-484/08 *Caja de Ahorros y Monte de Piedad de Madrid v Asocación de Usuarios de servicios bancarios (Ausbanc)* [2010] ECR I-4785; see the case note by J Stuyck, ERCL 2010, 449.

private law, for example in recent ECJ case law concerning doorstep selling,[20] consumer sales[21] and unfair commercial practices,[22] which were all adhered to in the final judgments of the ECJ.

The *Ausbanc* case concerns the question implicitly decided by the Law Lords, namely the place of Article 4(2) of Directive 93/13 in the functioning of the unfairness control of pre-formulated terms. Spanish law had not implemented Article 4(2) under the principle of minimum harmonisation hitherto part of EC law. The Spanish Tribunal Supremo wanted to know whether this exclusion prevented a control of the unfairness of "core terms" on the price. AG Trstenjak clearly put Article 4(2) at the centre of the conflict between private autonomy on the one hand, and the protection of the weaker party – the consumer – on the other (para 39). Are Member States prevented from also extending control of unfair terms to the core elements of the transaction, or is the consumer sufficiently protected by competition and transparency, as the UK Supreme Court seemed to suggest?

The argument of the AG is to a large extent a legal discussion of the principle of minimum harmonisation. The concept of minimum harmonisation allows Member States a broad margin of appreciation in how they protect consumers and, at the same time, forbids a reduction in the level of protection (para 86). Even more important are the AG's remarks on the balancing of "interests" undertaken by Directive 93/13 and the specific role of EU law in this context. As a result, the general principles of EU law, such as open market economy, competition and the fundamental freedoms, do not make Article 4(2) mandatory. The AG argues for a restrictive and not – as decided by the UK Supreme Court – an extensive interpretation of Article 4(2), which does not cover all aspects of price clauses (para 41).

The ECJ followed suit, insisting on the consumer protection objective of Directive 93/13 (2.5):[23]

> "[A]ccording to settled case-law, the system of protection introduced by the Directive is based on the idea that the consumer is in a weak position vis-à-vis the seller or supplier, as regards both his bargaining power and his level of knowledge. This leads to the consumer agreeing to terms drawn up in advance by the seller or supplier without being able to influence the content of those terms."

---

[20] Case C-227/08 *Martin*, opinion of AG Trstenjak, paras 79–83, concerning a balancing approach to the consequences of the *ex officio* protection of the withdrawal right of the consumer under Directive 85/577.

[21] Case C-404/06 *Quelle v Bundesverband der Verbraucherzentralen* [2008] ECR I-2685, opinion of AG Trstenjak, para 51.

[22] Case 207/07 *Gysbrechts* [2008] ECR I-9949, opinion of AG Trstenjak of 17 July 2008; critique H.-W. Micklitz/N. Reich, VuR 2008, 349.

[23] Case C-484/08 *Caja de Ahorros y Monte de Piedad de Madrid v Asocación de Usuarios de servicios bancarios (Ausbanc)* [2010] ECR I-4785, para 27.

Its existing case law follows the line of AG Trstenjak and clearly had made the point of importance for consumer protection rules. Some authors have even argued for an interpretation of EU law as *in dubio pro consumatore*.[24] However, it is uncertain whether this line of argument can be continued in future; there are signs that the ECJ supports full harmonisation to the detriment of Member State consumer protection.[25] If one follows the UK Supreme Court's interpretation, this would dramatically narrow the unfairness control and reduce consumer protection to consumer choice.

The recent *RWE* case[26] concerned unilateral price increase clauses for household gas supplies. A regional consumer advice centre (*Verbraucherzentrale Nordrhein-Westfalen*) brought a representative action for 25 consumers against one of the biggest German gas supply companies which in their general conditions for special contracts referred to legislation to vary gas prices unilaterally without stating the grounds; this legislation referred to in Article 1(2) of Directive 93/13 only applied to standard tariff contracts and in the opinion of the Court could not be applied to special contracts. The Court then, upon reference of the BGH, examined the price variation clause both under the transparency requirement of Articles 4(2) and 5 of Directive 93/13 and of similar provisions of the second Gas Directive 2003/55 (3.19). The Court stated:[27]

> "A standard term which allows such a unilateral adjustment must, however, meet the requirements of good faith, balance and transparency laid down by those directives."

The supplier had to give the consumer notice and information about the right to terminate the contract in good time before the price increase. The Court insisted on the effectiveness of this information and the right to termination, thus following earlier case law (4.16):[28]

> "Those strict requirements as to the information to be given to the consumer, both at the stage of the conclusion of a supply contract and during the performance of the contract, as regards the right of the supplier unilaterally to alter the terms of the contract, correspond to a *balancing of the interests of the two parties*. To the supplier's legitimate interest in guarding against a change of circumstances there corresponds

---

24   H. Rösler, 'Auslegungsgrundsätze des Europäischen Verbrauchervertragsrechts in Theorie und Praxis', RabelsZ 2007, 495; K. Tonner/M. Tamm, 'Zur Auslegung des europäischen Verbrauchervertragsrechts – insbesondere zur Auslegungsregel "in dubio pro consumatore"', in: L. Thévenoz/N. Reich (eds), *Liber amicorum B. Stauder*, 2006, 527; for criticism, see K. Riesenhuber, 'Kein Zweifel für den Verbraucher', Juristenzeitung 2005, 831; K. Riesenhuber, *Europäische Methodenlehre*, 2006, 264, pleads for a different approach to the consumer *leitbild* as a basis for interpretation. See also the recent paper by V. Trstenjak/E. Beysen, 'European Consumer Protection Law: *Curia Semper Dabit Remedium*?', CMLRev 2011, 95.

25   For an overview, see N. Reich, 'Von der Minimal- zur Voll- zur "Halbharmonisierung"', ZEuP 2010, 7 at 10.

26   Case C-92/11 *RWE Vertrieb v Verbraucherzentrale NRW* [2013] ECR I-(21.03.2013).

27   Ibid., para 47.

28   Ibid., paras 53–54 (emphasis added).

the consumer's equally legitimate interest, first, in knowing and thus being able to foresee the consequences which such a change might in future have for him and, secondly, in having the data available in such a case to allow him to react most appropriately to his new situation. With respect, in the second place, to the consumer's right to terminate the supply contract he has concluded in the event of a unilateral alteration of the tariffs applied by the supplier, it is of fundamental importance [...] that the right of termination given to the consumer is not purely formal but can actually be exercised. That would not be the case if, for reasons connected with the method of exercise of the right of termination or the conditions of the market concerned, the consumer has no real possibility of changing supplier, or if he has not been informed suitably in good time of the forthcoming change, thus depriving him of the possibility of checking how it is calculated and, if appropriate, of changing supplier. Account must be taken in particular of whether the market concerned is competitive, the possible cost to the consumer of terminating the contract, the time between the notification and the coming into force of the new tariffs, the information provided at the time of that communication, and the cost to be borne and the time taken to change supplier."

The Court seems to put great confidence in the individual capacity of the consumer to check the legitimacy of the price increase. Such optimism reaffirms the above mentioned criticism of the ECJ's purely individualistic concept of protection of weaker parties (1.15). On the other hand, such information is also necessary to protect the collective interests of consumers, for example through the actions of consumer or user associations as taken in the *RWE* case by the *Verbraucherzentrale NRW*. Seen in this broader context, the balancing element seems to become central in the control of pre-formulated clauses and allows a more far-reaching interference of EU law into standard B2C contracts, thus implementing the principles of "good faith" and transparency (7.5).

3.   BALANCING TO AVOID "OVER-PROTECTION"

3.1. "PRINCIPLES OF CIVIL LAW" AGAINST ALLEGED "OVER-PROTECTION" AND ITS LIMITS?

5.9   Another area where the method of balancing has been used by the ECJ is concerned with situations where the protection of the weaker party under an EU Regulation or Directive – mostly concerned with consumer protection as part of a concept of "framed autonomy" (1.20) – has led, at least in the eyes of the referring court, to an "over-protection" to be corrected by some method of "balancing" allowed in national law, such as rules on good faith, abuse of rights or avoidance of unjust enrichment. Take as a starting point the *Messner* case,[29]

---

[29]   Case C-489/07 *Messner v Firma Stefan Krüger* [2009] ECR I-7315.

which concerned the question of whether the consumer, having made inappropriate use of a product ordered under a distance contract from which he later withdrew, could be asked for compensation under national law. The relevant EU Directive 97/7/EC seemed to exclude such a right which was still granted by national law (in the case before the ECJ, German law). The ECJ responded with the following rather cryptic words:[30]

> "However, although Directive 97/7 is designed to protect the consumer in the particular situation of a distance contract, it is not intended to grant him rights going beyond what is necessary to allow him effectively to exercise his right of withdrawal. Consequently, the purpose of Directive 97/7 and, in particular, the prohibition laid down in the second sentence of Article 6(1) and Article 6(2) thereof do not preclude, in principle, a legal provision of a Member State which requires a consumer to pay fair compensation in the case where he has made use of the goods acquired under a distance contract in a manner incompatible with the principles of civil law, such as those of good faith or unjust enrichment."

The formulation "principles of civil law like good faith or unjust enrichment" has given rise to an extensive discussion on how far such principles can be said to exist in EU civil law and, if this is said to be the case, where they originate from, because they do not exist in all legal orders of EU Member States (0.3). In particular, English law does not contain a principle of "good faith", even though it has been spelled out in some recent EU "soft law" documents like the Common Frame of Reference.[31] The issue will be discussed in more detail in Chapter 7.

Later cases used similar formulations, although in somewhat different contexts. In *Hamilton*[32] the Court considered the lapse of the right of withdrawal according to the Doorstep Selling Directive 85/577:

> "[T]he provision which governs the exercise of the right of cancellation – namely, Article 5(1) of the doorstep selling directive – provides, inter alia, that '[t]he consumer shall have the right to renounce the effects of his undertaking'. The use in that provision of the term 'undertaking' indicates [...] that the right of cancellation may be exercised as long as the consumer is not bound, at the time that the right is exercised, by any undertaking under the cancelled contract. That logic flows from one of the general principles of civil law, namely that full performance of a contract results, as a general rule, from discharge of the mutual obligations under the contract or from termination of that contract."

---

[30] Ibid., paras 25–26.
[31] See the references of AG Trstenjak in her opinion of 18 February 2009, at para 85 of the *Messner* case.
[32] Case C-412/06 *Hamilton v Volksbank Filder* [2008] ECR I-2383, para 42.

A similar reference can be found in *Friz*[33] concerning the consequences of withdrawal from a closed-end property fund which will not free the consumer entirely from his obligations under the wording of Directive 85/577:

> "[T]here is nothing in the Directive to preclude the consumer, in certain specific cases, from having obligations to the trader and, depending on the circumstances, from having to bear certain consequences resulting from the exercise of his right of cancellation. It is necessary to ascertain in the light of those considerations whether the Directive does not preclude a national rule that the consumer who cancels his membership of a closed-end real property fund established in the form of a partnership is the owner of a right in respect of that partnership calculated according to the value of his interest at the date of his retirement from membership of it. That seems to be the case as regards the national rule at issue in the main proceedings. As the [referring court] observed in its decision for reference, that rule is intended to ensure, in accordance with the general principles of civil law, a satisfactory balance and a fair division of the risks among the various interested parties."

It seems clear from the context of these cases that the ECJ does not intend to establish new (general) principles of civil law, despite the many critical voices against this case law,[34] but rather to allow the national court to balance interests according to the Member State's own law, against the seemingly strict wording of the relevant EU law instruments aimed at avoiding an unintentional "over-protection" of the consumer. As a consequence, the Consumer Rights Directive 2011/83 (which revised Directives 85/577 and 97/7) (2.1) takes over the results of the case law of the ECJ in Article 10 (limitation of the right of withdrawal in case of non-information to 12 months, against *Heininger* (3.20) and following *Hamilton*) and Article 14(2) (limited liability of the consumer for diminished value of the goods, following *Messner*).

5.10 The case law of the ECJ is however far from consistent. The recent *McDonagh* case[35] concerned the question of the extent of airlines' obligation of to provide assistance to passengers in the event of cancellation of a flight due to "extraordinary circumstances" (in this case, the eruption of the Icelandic volcano Eyjafjallajökull leading to the closure of airspace). Article 9 of the Air Passenger Regulation (EU) No 261/2004[36] requires such assistance and does not contain a limitation based on "exceptionally extraordinary circumstances", as

---

[33]   Case C-215/08 *Friz GmbH v Carsten von der Heyden* [2010] ECR I-2947, paras 45–48.
[34]   This is my main criticism of the otherwise brilliant analysis of the case law by M. Hesselink, 'The General Principles of Civil Law: Their Nature, Role and Legitimacy', in: D. Leczykiewicz/S. Weatherill (eds.), *The Involvement of EU Law in Private Law Relationships*, 2013, 131 at 139.
[35]   Case C-12/11 *D. McDonagh v Ryanair* [2013] ECR I-(31.01.2013).
[36]   [2004] OJ L 46/1.

the airline argued. The Court refused to apply the balancing principle to introduce such a general limitation by way of "teleological restriction" of the regulation and gave the consumer/passenger a right to claim compensation for costs incurred if such assistance had been denied. However the Court allowed a limitation on a case-by-case basis:[37]

> "None the less, an air passenger may only obtain, by way of compensation for the failure of the air carrier to comply with its obligation referred to in Articles 5(1)(b) and 9 of Regulation No 261/2004 to provide care, reimbursement of the amounts which, in the light of the specific circumstances of each case, proved necessary, appropriate and reasonable to make up for the shortcomings of the air carrier in the provision of care to that passenger, a matter which is for the national court to assess."

3.2. BALANCING IN WORKER PROTECTION: THE FUZZY CONCEPT OF *ABUS DE DROIT* IN *PALETTA I* AND *II*

5.11   The extensive grant of rights to European citizens, especially in the area of free movement as the strongest pillar of EU law, should according a theory of "socialisation of law" at least be protected against unilateral abuse. This is particularly true in the area of worker protection where EU law has been quite worker-friendly (2.4). However, the ECJ must at the same time either prevent abuses by the worker himself which would conflict with the very objective of the rights granted to him, or allow Member States to take measures against such unilateral abuse. The legal concept for such "countervailing balancing" has been – at least in the continental tradition – the concept of *abus de droit*.[38] There is a clear pronouncement in this direction in the "old" *Van Binsbergen* case of 1974[39] concerning limits to the freedom to provide services:

> "Likewise, a Member State cannot be denied the right to take measures to prevent the exercise by a person providing services whose activity is entirely or principally directed towards its territory of the freedom guaranteed by Art. 59 EEC (now Art. 56 TFEU, ex-Art. 49 EC) for the purpose of avoiding the professional rules of conduct which would be applicable to him if he were established within that state."

---

[37]   Case C-12/11 *D. McDonagh v Ryanair* [2013] ECR I-(31.01.2013), para 51.

[38]   For an overview see the contributions to R. de la Feria/S. Vogenauer, *Prohibition of Abuse of Law*, 2011, in particular the paper by A. Metzger at 235 and the commentary by S. Whittacker at 253.

[39]   Case 33/74 *Van Binsbergen v Besteuur von de Bedrijfsverening voor de Metaalnijverheid* [1974] ECR 1299, para 12; confirmed in case C-23/93 *TV10 v Commissariaat v.d. Media* [1994] ECR I-4795, para 20.

This inherent limitation is part of the guarantee of the freedom to provide services itself. It authorises Member States to take measures against potential abuse, for instance by invoking the rules on establishment that allow a stricter control of activities in its territory.

This rhetoric has been continued but at the same time considerably narrowed down by the Court in later cases. Take as an example the controversial *Paletta II* decision concerning an Italian family residing in Germany and taking their vacation in Italy, where they regularly fell ill at the end of their vacation and asked for paid sick leave under German law by presenting a note from an Italian doctor. Could this, as German law seemed to suggest, be regarded as an "abuse" of the right of Mr Paletta to sickness compensation, especially after repeated "sickness" in Italy? The Court verbally accepted the argument of "abuse" but substantially narrowed it by referring to having

> "consistently held that Community law cannot be relied on for purposes of abuse or fraud [...] Although the national courts may, therefore, take account – on the basis of objective evidence – of abuse or fraudulent conduct on the part of the worker concerned in order, where appropriate, to deny him the benefit of the provisions of Community law on which he seeks to rely, they must nevertheless access such conduct in the light of the objectives pursued by those provisions."[40]

At the same time, the Court insisted that the defence of *abus de droit* should not rule out the exercise of Community rights. Therefore, it is up to the person alleging "abuse or fraudulent conduct" – in the *Paletta* case, the employer – to give adequate proof that this is the case; mere allegations are not sufficient in that respect. The Court however did not try to develop objective criteria for defining *abus de droit*, such as preventing a circumvention of protective provisions justified by fair labour conditions. It seemed to take a rather narrow view of *abus de droit*, insisting on a strong subjective element based on behavioural factors like "abuse or fraudulent conduct" – conditions difficult to prove without allowing a "prima facie evidence" rule in the case of repeated absence after vacation due to alleged sickness, a possibility which the Court rejected.[41]

---

[40] Case C-206/94 *Brennet v Paletta* [1996] ECR I-2357, paras 24–25; comment K. Ziegler, '"Abuse of Law" in the Context of Free Movement of Workers', in: R. de la Feria/S. Vogenauer, *supra* note 38, at 309; cf. also AG Cosmas in his *Paletta* opinion relying on the Roman law principle of *fraus omnia corrumpit* at 2373 para 51; in Case C-36/96 *Günaydin v Freistaat Bayern* [1997] ECR I-5143 the Court did not find an *abus de droit* by Turkish migrant workers who had signed a paper only for temporary work permits and who later wanted to remain in the receiving country. Cf. also Case C-367/96 *Kefalas et al v Greece* [1998] ECR I-2843; criticised by D. Triantafyllou, CMLRev 1999, 157; F. Ranieri, ZEuP 2000, 165.

[41] See K. Ziegler, *supra* note 40, at 310.

4. ROLE OF BALANCING IN SOCIAL CONFLICTS: FUNDAMENTAL RIGHTS VS. FUNDAMENTAL FREEDOMS?

4.1. THE ECJ AS FINAL ARBITER IN SOCIAL CONFLICTS?

5.12   In his above-cited contribution,[42] the American legal theorist Duncan Kennedy wonders how the "European proportionality analysis" relates to the American version of balancing in constitutional law. Some of the different cases mentioned above tried to show that there is really no such thing as a "European" concept of proportionality, but that its use depends very much of the *Vorverständnis* of judges in the litigation before them. This can be demonstrated by a short analysis of the *Laval*[43] and *Viking*[44] litigation which *in nuce* concerns the applicability of EU free movement rules to social action undertaken or supported by trade unions and their head associations against the posting of workers from one EU country (Latvia) to another (Sweden), or against the re-flagging of a ferry from a country with higher wages (Finland) to one with lower wages (Estonia). The outcome of this litigation has provoked violent reactions in the scholarship.[45] I will not go into the many aspects of this

---

[42]   D. Kennedy, *supra* note 4.

[43]   Case C-341/05 *Laval un Partneri Ltd v Svenska Byggnadsarbetareförbundet* [2007] ECR I-11767; the order for reference is based on a prior judgment: 49/05 case A 268/04 of 29 April 2005. For earlier discussions of the litigation, see N. Reich, 'Diskriminierungsverbote im Gemeinschaftsprivatrecht', in: *Jahrbuch Junger Zivilrechtswissenschaftler*, 2005, 9; C. Barnard, *EC Employment Law*, 4th ed. 2012, 283; N. Wahl/P. Cramér (eds), *Swedish Studies in European Law*, 2006, 129; C. Woolfson/J.W. Summer, 'Labour Mobility in Construction: European Implications of the Laval Dispute with Swedish Labour', European Journal of Industrial Relations 2006, 49; V. Hatzopoulos/T. Uyen Do, 'The Case Law of the ECJ concerning the Free Provision of Services', CMLRev 2006, 978.

[44]   Case C-438/05 *The International Transport Workers' Federation (ITF) & The Finnish Seamen's Union (FSU) v Viking Line ABP & Oü Viking Line Eesti* [2007] ECR I-10779. The High Court established jurisdiction because the headquarters of ITF were in London and therefore jurisdiction was conferred to the English Court under Article 2 of Regulation 44/2001, without the parties being able to raise *forum non conveniens* objections as held by the ECJ in case C-281/02 *Andrew Owusu v NB Jackson et al* [2005] ECR I-1383. The High Court granted an injunction against ITF and FSU which was quashed by the Court of Appeal in its decision to refer the case to the ECJ: [2005] EWCA Civ 1299 (Waller LJ). The litigation is explained by B. Bercusson, 'The Trade Union Movement and the EU: Judgment Day', ELJ 2007, 279.

[45]   C. Joerges/F. Rödl, 'Informal Politics, Formalised Law, and the "Social Deficit" of European Integration: Reflections after the Judgments of the ECJ in Viking and Laval', ELJ 2009, 1; P. Rodière, 'Les arrêts Viking et Laval, le droit de grève et le droit de négociation collective', RTD Eur 2008, 47; J. Malmberg/T. Sigman, 'Industrial Actions and EU Economic Freedoms: The Autonomous Collective Bargaining Model Curtailed by the ECJ', CMLRev 2008, 1115; L. Azoulai, 'The Court of Justice and the Social Market Economy: The Emergence of an Ideal and the Conditions for its Realization', CMLRev 2008, 1335; S. Deakin, 'Regulatory Competition after Laval', in: *Cambridge Yearbook of European Legal Studies*, 2008, 581.

litigation, which I have done elsewhere.[46] I will also limit myself to the *Viking* litigation which confronted the owner of the ferry *Rosella* in Finland (Viking Line) against the Finnish Seafarers Union (FSU), which took social action against the re-flagging, with support and solidarity action by the International Transport Workers Federation (ITF).

The following discussion will take as settled case law that the EU fundamental freedoms, in particular the freedom of establishment in Article 43 EC (now Article 49 TFEU) in *Viking* (and the freedom to provide services in Article 49 EC (now Article 56 TFEU) in *Laval*), were also applicable "horizontally" (4.28) against social action by trade unions, which was regarded as a "restriction of these freedoms", and that the decisive question therefore was whether these actions (restrictions) could be justified under the general "public interest" test as developed in the consistent case law of the ECJ.

4.2. OPINION OF AG POIARES MADURO

5.13   AG Poiares Maduro gave his opinion in the *Viking* litigation on 23 May 2007 and insisted that, in the absence of secondary law, the case must be resolved according to a balancing test, which he set out with great clarity.[47] The question was how far trade unions can take social action against acts of relocation by undertakings protected by the free movement rules. On the one hand, workers (and their unions) must accept the recurring negative consequences that are inherent to the internal market's creation of increasing prosperity, in exchange for which society must commit itself to the general improvement of their living and working conditions and to the provision of economic support to those workers who, as a consequence of market forces, get into difficulties (para 59).

This balancing is performed not by applying a proportionality test, but via the classical argument of market segregation. A coordinated policy of collective action among unions normally constitutes a legitimate means to protect the wages and working conditions of seamen However, collective action that has the effect of dividing the labour market and that impedes the hiring of seamen from certain Member States in order to protect the jobs of seafarers in other Member States would strike at the heart of the principle of non-discrimination on which the common market is founded.[48]

In my opinion, this simple test as proposed by AG Maduro has a number of drawbacks, as the *Viking* case clearly shows. The collective actions of the ITF and FSU seemingly divide the labour market by attacking the re-flagging and thereby

---

[46]   N. Reich, 'Fundamental Freedoms versus Fundamental Rights – Did Viking get it Wrong?', Europarättslig Tijdskrift 2008, 851.

[47]   Case C-438/05 *The International Transport Workers' Federation (ITF) & The Finnish Seamen's Union (FSU) v Viking Line ABP & Oü Viking Line Eesti* [2007] ECR I-10779, paras 57–72.

[48]   Ibid., at para 62.

preventing the hiring of (cheaper) Estonian seafarers. However, on the other hand, this is in the eyes of labour unions acting in solidarity, justified by a general policy against flags of convenience, not against Estonian workers in particular. Who is to judge the legitimacy of this social policy, even if it may have a detrimental effect on free movement? These effects may also be purely accidental and an unavoidable consequence of social action if there is desire for it to be effective. The AG also seems to exaggerate the parallels between social actions in *Commission v France*[49] and *Viking*: while the first made free movement impossible through wildcat actions blocking roads in France against Spanish fruit exporters, Viking Line could continue run the ferry *Rosella* (as indeed it has done for more than four years during protracted negotiations with the FSU, though perhaps without making the expected profit – not that making a profit is as such protected under the free movement rules). These economic disadvantages of social action may also materialise in any other conflict concerning relocation of business within the EU. In my opinion, Viking Line cannot expect special protection against social actions established to impede re-flagging, unless this action is in itself disproportionate (as in *Commission v France*), which, in my opinion, it was not.

4.3. THE ECJ'S APPROACH IN *VIKING*

5.14   The ECJ based its argument on the premise that, under EC law, the most important limitation of the right to social actions – as now guaranteed in Article 28 of the Charter referred to in *Viking* (para 44) – is provided by the rules on free movement, as spelled out in the *Schmidberger*[50] and *Omega*[51] judgments.[52] The exercise of the right to collective actions must be "reconciled with the requirements relating to rights protected under the Treaty and in accordance with the principle of proportionality".[53]

The Court expressly recognises the right of labour unions to take collective action "for the protection of workers as a legitimate interest", which is also justified by the fact the Community has "thus not only an economic but also a social purpose", expressly provided for in Article 136 EC[54] (now Article 3(3) TEU, insisting on a "social market economy aiming at full employment and social progress"). These general principles must be applied to the different

---

49 Case C-381/93 *Commission v France* [1994] ECR I-5145.
50 Case C-112/00 *Eugen Schmidberger v Austria* [2003] ECR I-5659.
51 Case C-36/02 *Omega Spielhallen- und Automatenaufstellungs-GmbH v Oberbürgermeisterin der Bundesstadt Bonn* [2004] ECR I-9609.
52 Case C-438/05 *The International Transport Workers' Federation (ITF) & The Finnish Seamen's Union (FSU) v Viking Line ABP & Oü Viking Line Eesti* [2007] ECR I-10779, at para 45.
53 *Viking*, para 46; see also *Laval*, para 95.
54 *Viking*, paras 77 and 79; *Laval*, paras 103 and 105.

circumstances. In *Viking* the Court found it necessary to distinguish between the social action of FSU on the one hand, and the call for solidarity action by ITF on the other.

4.3.1. *The situation of FSU*

5.15   The collective action of FSU would be justified if it "could reasonably be considered to fall, at first sight, within the objective of protection the workers" (para 81). This is a matter of the national court to determine. But the ECJ makes a number of qualifications which are to some extent new and put additional restrictions on the right to strike.

The social actions must truly serve the aim of protection of workers; this would not be the case "if it were established that the jobs or conditions of employment at issue were not jeopardised or under serious threat" (para 81), for example if the undertaking which takes over the re-flagged vessel would be bound by the prior collective agreement or statutory provisions protecting workers. The mere reference to the policy of avoiding flags of convenience would not be enough. A similar argument could be invoked against strikes to avoid the outsourcing of an undertaking.

The action taken by FSU, which is as such a legal means for defending workers' rights, must meet the requirements of proportionality. This, again, must be established by the national court; the ECJ can only give guidance. In particular, the ECJ stressed the *ultima ratio* principle to justify social actions against re-flagging as an infringement of the freedom of establishment (para 87).

4.3.2. *The special case of ITF*

5.16   The case of ITF is somewhat different because it is a head organisation of labour unions of seamen with a special objective, namely that of combating flags of convenience. The ECJ was indirectly asked whether this policy was justified under free movement rights. The judgment is ambiguous on this point since the Court, on the one hand, insisted on the restrictive character of this policy, but on the other referred to the opinion of the national court that "the objective of that policy is also to protect and improve seafarers' terms and conditions of employment" (para 88). The Court resolves this conflict in the following words:[55]

> "However, as is apparent from the file submitted to the Court, in the context of its policy of combating the use of flags of convenience, ITF is required, when asked by one of its members, to initiate solidarity action against the beneficial owner of a vessel which is registered in a State other than that of which that owner is a national, irrespective of whether or not that owner's exercise of its right of freedom of

---

[55]   *Viking*, para 89.

establishment is liable to have a harmful effect on the work or conditions of employment of its employees. Therefore, as Viking argued during the hearing without being contradicted by ITF in that regard, the policy of reserving the right of collective negotiations to trade unions of the State of which the beneficial owner of a vessel is a national is also applicable where the vessel is registered in a State which guarantees workers a higher level of social protection than they would enjoy in the first State."

What exactly does the Court mean where it suggests it does not entrust the task of judging the legitimacy of solidarity action to the national court? The ECJ seems to take an overall critical stance against social action to defend and support the policy against flags of convenience since there is no proof that that policy is automatically pursuing the objective of protecting the interests of workers. The national court will have to establish that the solidarity action indeed pursued this objective, which is a matter for ITF to prove. In the end, this seems to curtail severely the right to engage in solidarity action in a certain area before a concrete social conflict arises. This interpretation seems highly problematic because it implies that labour unions and their head associations can take social action only for the concrete purpose of protecting workers, not to support policies which in the long run may improve the social wellbeing of their members, or avoid "social dumping" by indirect actions by undertakings, in particular via outsourcing. This limitation of the right of strike even goes beyond what AG Poiares Maduro had argued for, namely to prevent a segregation of markets via social action, but not to put a general limit on social action to avoid outsourcing. What is even more regrettable is that the Court does not really explain the reasons for its opinion despite its insistence on the social purpose of the EU and the broad guarantee of the right to social action as a fundamental right.

4.3.3. How to balance the balancing in "horizontal conflicts" involving different autonomous entities?

5.17 The *Viking* and *Laval* judgments have aroused a lively debate among lawyers – with divergent views from both a national labour and an EU free movement perspective – on the "spill-over effect" of the EU free movement rules on traditional social policy objectives and collective action by labour unions of Member States.[56] Both judgments certainly tend towards a more "liberal" and less "social" approach, by invoking a degree of precedence of free movement rights over the fundamental right to strike, despite the "social rhetoric" of the ECJ. This is however really nothing new to observers of the recent development of the case law of the ECJ. The *Viking* judgment seems to be particularly

---

[56]   See the articles cited *supra* note 45; a more nuanced position has been taken by the German judge at the ECJ; T. von Danwitz, 'Grundfreiheiten und Kollektivautonomie', EuZA 2010, 6, 11.

characteristic of that tendency. This stems first from its unclear reasoning with regard to both the strike by FSU (which seems to be limited to specific protection of workers if threatened, even though it can be argued that there was no real danger of the loss of workplaces and/or income), and the solidarity action of ITF. Secondly, there is concern that action in support of a policy which may only in the long run improve the situation of workers, but which does not directly relate to collective bargaining and simply has an indirect negative effect on company mobility by making re-flagging more difficult and costly, will fall foul of the overarching EU principle of free movement. Such a reading of the right to strike and to engage in solidarity action has not really been explained by the Court in interpreting the fundamental freedoms or the fundamental right to collective action, even if the Court seemingly wants to protect both using a balancing test. This balancing is clearly on the side of free movement and against social rights – a problematic consequence.

It is obvious that the *Viking* judgment may be used against other types of social action that directly or merely indirectly infringe free movement, if it cannot be established that the action serves to improve the (concrete) protection of workers. Furthermore, the use of the concept of "proportionality" – originally developed in response to actions by the State or the Union that limit fundamental freedoms or fundamental rights – gives rise to uncertainty, which in the end will prevent, or at least make more difficult, collective action and make the judge (whether national or European) the final arbiter in social disputes.[57]

5.18   The basic problem of the reasoning of the ECJ is not so much the question of a hierarchical relation between fundamental freedoms and fundamental rights – which must, in my opinion, be put on the same level – but the problematic reference of the ECJ to the proportionality argument, which is now seemingly transferred to action by private associations. The ECJ seems to have forgotten that the latter derive their legitimacy from the freedom of association as protected under Article 11 ECHR read in conjunction with Article 6 TEU and Article 28 of the Charter, and that therefore their margin of discretion in determining the course of action in following their legitimate social objectives must necessarily be greater than that of Member States. They are not bound by a similar obligation of loyalty as Member States under Article 10 EC (now Article 3(4) TEU). The strict proportionality test with which the ECJ monitors any state action that has negative effects on free movement – with some nuances to allow Member States a considerable margin of appreciation in delicate areas like the protection of children[58] – cannot simply be taken over to private

57   See the article by R. Rebhahn, 'Europäisches Gericht bringt Bewegung in das Arbeits-kampfrecht', Frankfurter Allgemeine Zeitung (19 December 2007), 23, which seemed to take a positive view of this approach of the ECJ.
58   See case C-244/06 *Dynamik Medien Vertriebs GmbH v Avides Media AG* [2008] ECR I-505 where the ECJ refers to Article 24(1) providing that children have a right to protection of their

associations without in effect curtailing their autonomy of action. European Union law can only set the outer limits of action; it must leave social partners a wide margin of discretion as to how they realise them. Negative side effects of free movement therefore have to be accepted in the interests of a democratic society, as spelled out in Article 11(2) ECHR.

5.19 European Union law, as implemented by the ECJ, can therefore set only the outer limits of action in horizontal ("apparently private") relations. If collective action by labour unions (or by business associations) tends to negate this very freedom, for example by a policy of "closed shops" or by grossly violating the "negative freedom of association",[59] that action cannot be justified, because it goes beyond the principle of proportionality. The same would be true in the case of social action that aims to defend discriminatory conditions of work, for example with regard to nationality, gender, race or similar reasons expressly condemned by human rights and EU law (for details see Chapter 3). On the other hand, it must remain a matter for social partners themselves to decide whether and how their actions "truly serve the protection of workers", whether the policy of the ITF against flags of convenience is legitimate or not (provided there are no elements of discrimination, as AG Poiares Maduro correctly pointed out), how far solidarity action is legitimate, and what concrete steps they want to take regarding strikes, boycotts, picketing or lock-outs, without giving notice of their industrial action. The reference to *Schmidberger* and *Commission v France* is misleading with regard to the proportionality criteria: both cases concern state (non-)action, not social action by private associations as such. And it is obvious that the differences in Member State laws and social relations must be taken particularly seriously in this respect, as the ECJ recognised in *Omega* with regard to fundamental rights.[60] The EU fundamental freedoms, however fundamental they may be, cannot have unlimited supremacy over fundamental rights.[61] Balancing has two sides: it must reject an unrestricted priority of fundamental freedoms as well as of fundamental rights. Both are "too fundamental" to be forced into a hierarchical relation with each other in whatever direction.[62] This can be done neither directly, as argued above, via a "reserved area" for social action beyond the reach of the fundamental freedoms, nor indirectly through a presumption against

---

wellbeing; it is a matter for the Member States to define the level of protection.

[59] F. Sudre et al., *Les grands arrêts de la Cour Européenne des droits de l'homme*, 2003, 482, referring to the case law of the European Court of Human Rights in Strasbourg.

[60] Case C-36/02 *Omega Spielhallen- und Automatenaufstellungs-GmbH v Oberbürgermeisterin der Bundesstadt Bonn* [2004] ECR I-9609, para 37.

[61] Likewise: see C. Joerges/F. Rödl, *supra* note 45, at 17, fearing a "loss of power" (*Entmachtung*) of Finnish labour unions.

[62] Likewise: P. Rodière, *supra* note 45, at 57; L. Azoulai, *supra* note 45.

social action going beyond a narrowly defined area of "protection of workers" as set *ex post* in court litigation. Indeed, judicial restraint[63] is necessary in this area.

5. CONCLUSION

5.20 What is the result of this discussion on balancing as a general principle of EU civil law, including collective action in horizontal relations? From a methodological point of view, courts seem to use different methods of reaching decisions which they regard as just and fair. They will refer to "Classical Legal Thought" (CLT) in the sense of *Begriffsjurisprudenz* (conceptual jurisprudence) to find seemingly coherent solutions to legal problems within the conceptual limits of their thinking, or use the more open reasoning of a standard of "proportionality" that allows a balancing of different norms and societal interests to fill "gaps in law". Neither method can avoid the "indeterminacy" paradox which has been so dear to legal realists and critical legal studies.[64] The hermeneutic realism of Esser insists on a broadening of legal reasoning by *Durchgriff* (piercing the veil) to "principles". This approach was later taken up by Dworkin who pointed, as will be remembered, to the difference between "rules" and "principles" (or standards) (0.2).[65]

But even such methodological fine-tuning may not always be satisfactory, as the analysis of the case law of different European courts based on different *Vorverständnisse* has shown. The case law of the ECJ, in particular concerning social action, can be explained only from a liberal *Vorverständnis*, even if it uses some "social rhetoric", as shown in the analysis of the *Viking* litigation. In consumer protection matters, a similar observation was possible with regard to the UK Supreme Court (5.6). The ECJ has been somewhat hesitant and unclear, not using the full scope of argument which balancing would have allowed it. In Germany, a notable difference could be found in the approach of the same BGH in cases concerning unfair terms of price clauses (5.7) on the one hand, and its restrictive approach, on the other hand, towards consumer protection in the *Heininger* saga, which was basically supported by the ECJ (4.20). From a methodological point of view, most relevant has been the recent case law on balancing contractual arrangements between consumers and businesses by reference to "principles of civil law" (5.9). This will be relevant in the more in-depth analysis of "good faith" later on (Chapter 7). Finally, the most complex and controversial use of the balancing test has been the attempt by the ECJ in its *Viking* and *Laval* judgments to define the limits of collective autonomy (of trade

---

63   See C. Joerges/F. Rödl, *supra* note 45, at 21.
64   See D. Kennedy, *A Critique of Adjudication (fin de siècle)*, 1997, 169 ff.
65   R. Dworkin, *Taking Rights Seriously*, 1977, 2.

unions) in the context of EU free movement provisions. As Lenaerts (now the Vice-President of the ECJ) and Gutiérrez Fons have written:[66]

> "[T]he ECJ must be respectful of the constitutional traditions of the Member States, but not to the extent of giving up the basic constitutional tenets of the Union [...] Beyond the bounds of a core nucleus of key shared values vital to the Union's integrity, however, the ECJ should have recourse to a 'margin of appreciation' analysis which would strike the right balance between 'European commonality' and 'national particularism'."

---

[66]   K. Lenaerts/J. Gutiérrez-Fons, CMLRev 2010, 1629 at 1668.

CHAPTER 6

THE PRINCIPLE
OF PROPORTIONALITY

Contents

Bibliography 156
1. Importance of the principle of proportionality for EU civil law:
   some general remarks 157
   1.1. "Hard look" in reviewing of national measures 157
   1.2. "Proportionality" of Union measures 158
   1.3. A "positive" approach to proportionality? 161
2. The Draft Common Frame of Reference 162
   2.1. A general assessment of the DCFR 162
   2.2. (Limited) legal effects of the principles and model rules
        of the DCFR 164
   2.3. Selective reference to the DCFR in ECJ case law? 168
3. The "feasibility study" and draft Common European Sales Law 169
   3.1. The steps taken towards the CESL 169
   3.2. Structure of the CESL 170
   3.3. The CESL as a hybrid contract law 173
        3.3.1. No necessity for B2SMU cross-border transactions 175
        3.3.2. Is there a real "need" for the CESL in B2C transactions? 176
4. Open method of coordination, convergence and improved law-making
   in reflexive contract governance in the EU 180
5. The "positive proportionality" principle in EU civil legislation: two
   examples 182
   5.1. Unfair terms in B2B contracts 182
   5.2. Improving the coherence of B2C legislation with the "help of
        the CESL": digital contracting 184
6. Conclusions on the principle of proportionality as an instrument
   of legal control and support of EU measures 187

Bibliography

J. Basedow, *The Law of Open Societies*, 2013; C. Busch, 'From European Sales Law to Online Contract Law: The CESL in the European Parliament', EUVR 2013, 33; D. Caruso, 'The Baby and the Bath Water: The American Critique of European Contract Law', American JCompL 2013, 479; H. Eidenmüller et al., 'The Common Frame of Reference for European Private Law – Policy Choices and Codification Problems', OJLS 2008, 659; E. Ellis (ed.), *The Principle of Proportionality in the Laws of Europe*, 1999; B. Fauvenarque-Cosson et al., *Principes contractuals commun – Projet de cadre commun de référence*, 2008: T. Harbo, 'The Function of the Proportionality Principle in EU Law', ELJ 2010, 158; A. Hartkamp, *European Law and National Private Law*, 2012; M. Heidemann, 'European Private Law at the Crossroads', ERPrL 2012, 1128; N. Helberger et al., 'Digital Content Contracts for Consumers', JCP 2013, 37; N. Helberger et al., *Digital Consumers and the Law*, 2013; C. Joerges/T. Ralli (eds.), *European Constitutionalism without Private Law – Private Law without Democracy*, 2011: K. Lenaerts, 'The European Court of Justice and Process Oriented Review', YEL 2012, 3; E. Letowska, 'Is the Optional Instrument (CESL) consistent with the principle of subsidiarity?', EUVR 2013, 28; M. Loos/H. Schelhaas, 'Commercial Sales: CESL Compared to the Vienna Sales Convention', ERPrL 2013, 105; U. Magnus (ed.), *CISG vs. Regional Sales Law Unification*, 2012; H.-W. Micklitz/F. Cafaggi (eds.), *European Private Law after the Common Frame of Reference*, 2010; H.-W. Micklitz/B. De Witte (eds.), *The European Court of Justice and the Autonomy of Member States*, 2012; H.-W. Micklitz/ N. Reich, 'The Commission Proposal for a Regulation on CESL – Too Broad or not Broad Enough?', EUI/Law Working Papers 2012/04, available at <www.ssrn-id2013183[1].pdf>; L. Moccia (ed.), *The Making of European Private Law: Why, How, What, Who*, 2013; F. Möslein/K. Riesenhuber, 'Contract Governance – A Research Agenda', ERCL 2009, 248; MPI (Max Planck Institut für ausländisches und internationals Privatrecht), 'Policy Options for Progress Towards a European Contract Law', RabelsZ 2011, 373; L. Niglia (ed.), *Pluralism and European Private Law*, 2013; N. Reich, 'How Proportionate is the Proportionality Principle? – Some critical remarks on the use and methodology of the proportionality principle in the internal market case law of the ECJ', in: H.-W. Micklitz/B. De Witte (eds.), *The European Court of Justice and the Autonomy of Member States*, 2012, 83; N. Reich, 'EU Strategies in Finding the Optimal Consumer Law Instrument', ERCL 2012, 1; N. Reich, 'Critique of the Draft Regulation for a Common European Sales Law (CESL) under the Concept of Reflexive Governance in the EU', Revija za Evropsko Pravo 2012, 5; H. Rösler, *Europäische Gerichtsbarkeit auf dem Gebiet des Zivilrechts*, 2012; G. Rühl, 'Regulatory Competition in Contract Law: Empirical Evidence and Normative Implications', ERCL 2013, 61: C. Schmid, *Die Instrumentalisierung des Privatrechts durch die EU: Privatrecht und Privatrechtskonzeptionen in der Entwicklung der Europaischen Integrationsverfassung*, 2009: M. Schmidt-Kessel (ed.), *Der Gemeinsame Referenzrahmen*, 2009; M. Schmidt-Kessel (ed.), *Der Entwurf für eine Gemeinsames Europäisches Kaufrecht – Kommentar*, 2013; R. Schulze (ed.), *Common European Sales Law (CESL) – Commentary*, 2012; A. Somma (ed.), *The Politics of the Draft Common Frame of Reference*, 2009; V. Trstenjak/E. Beysen, 'Das Prinzip der Verhältnismäßigkeit in der Unionsrechtsordnung', EuR 2012, 265; C. Twigg-Flesner, *A Cross-Border Regulation for Consumer Transactions in the EU – A Fresh Approach to EU Consumer Law*, 2012; S. Whittaker, 'The Optional Instrument of European Contract Law', ERCL 2011, 371.

1. IMPORTANCE OF THE PRINCIPLE OF PROPORTIONALITY FOR EU CIVIL LAW: SOME GENERAL REMARKS

1.1. "HARD LOOK" IN REVIEWING OF NATIONAL MEASURES

6.1 The principle of proportionality as a constitutional principle of EU law – including EU civil law – was first developed to justify restrictions by Member States on free movement under the public policy or general interest proviso. The Court summarised the basic principles in *Gebhard* mentioned earlier within the context of "framed autonomy" (1.9):[1] Member State restrictions on autonomy of contracting which have a negative impact on fundamental freedoms must be justified not only by a legitimate public interest, but they must also be *suitable* for attaining the given objective (relationship between means and end), and be *necessary* for achieving the proposed goal, without putting an *excessive burden* on the individual. In general terms, this amounts to the "less restrictive alternative" test.[2] A state measure which puts an unreasonable burden on the individual and which can easily be substituted by a less intrusive measure capable of attaining the same objective will not be regarded as being "necessary".

The *Gebhard* test has been used many times in later cases, sometimes with slight variations in the wording, which I will not follow up here. Its impact on (mandatory) contract law of Member States restricting free movement of goods, services or capital has been mentioned above with some examples from ECJ practice (1.10–1.11). With regard to the "imperative requirements in the general interest", the catalogue of these interests – consumer or worker protection, environmental concerns, fairness of commercial transactions – is an open-ended one, with the exception of "purely economic interests", which do not justify restrictions. Member States will usually be able to find a justified public interest which legitimates restrictions on the exercise of fundamental freedoms by EU market citizens. The debate in the many cases which have been decided under the *Gebhard* test, or closely related tests, will therefore usually concentrate on:

– first, the *adequacy* of a certain restrictive regulation (is it suitable for attaining the proclaimed general interest objective?);

---

[1] Case C-55/94 *Gebhard v Consiglio dell'Ordine degli Advocati e procuratori di Milano* [1995] ECR I-4165, para 37.

[2] T. Tridimas, *The General Principles of Community Law*, 2nd ed. 2006, 209–220 (Proportionality – review of national measures); N. Reich, in: H.-W. Micklitz/B. de Witte, *The ECJ and the Autonomy of Member States*, 2012, 83 at 97; V. Trstenjak/E. Beysen, EuR 2012, 269, regarding *Angemessenheit* as third stage of the proportionality exam.

- second, its *necessity* with regard to its intrusive elements (does it go beyond what is required to attain this objective, for example as in the case of "information" vs. "regulation" to protect consumers or guarantee fair commercial practices?);
- third – somewhat beyond the *Gebhard* test – whether state restrictive measures contribute to the regulation of cross-border health or gambling services in a "consistent and systematic manner".[3]

6.2 The proportionality principle applies on a case-by-case basis. In some cases, the Court takes the necessary value-judgment itself, while in others it leaves the matter to Member State courts, usually providing them with some guidance on the application of the proportionality principle in the case at hand. As a general rule, the more severe the restriction to free movement appears to be, and the less it is justified,[4] the more readily the Court will intervene. The principle of proportionality has become the most important instrument in reviewing national measures against the fundamental freedoms, including those based on mandatory civil law. The case law is abundant and has only been mentioned to give an overview of the "hard look" the ECJ takes at restrictions justified by a legitimate public interest. It is not part of this study to go deeper into this control mechanism and its impact on the civil law of Member States.

1.2. "PROPORTIONALITY" OF UNION MEASURES

6.3 More important in the context of this book will be the impact of the proportionality principle on developing a separate body of Union civil law. This is first of all a question of competence under the internal market (Article 114 TFEU), the anti-discrimination (Articles 18, 19 and 153 TFEU) or social policy (Article 153 TFEU) provisions (0.10). The competence provisions have been used for measures relating to civil law, in particular contract law, have withstood any challenges as to their proportionality,[5] and have been mentioned in this study in order to find general principles emerging from them. The guarantees of

---

[3] Case C-169/07 *Hartlauer Handelsgesellschaft v Wiener Landesregierung et al* [2009] ECR I-1721, para 55; Case C-238/08 *Ladbrokes Betting & Gaming Ltd et al v Stichting de Nationale Sportstotalisator* [2010] ECR I-4757, para 28; Case C-46/08 *Carmen Media* [2010] ECR I-8149, para 64.

[4] N. Reich/S. Harbacevica, CMLRev 2003, 615 at 629.

[5] See case C-58/08 *Vodafone* [2010] ECR I-4999, para 69, concerning the mandatory setting of wholesale and retail roaming charges: "in the light of the importance of the objective of consumer protection within the context of Article 95(3) EC [now Article 114(3) TFEU], intervention that is limited in time in a market that is subject to competition, which makes it possible, in the immediate future, to protect consumers against excessive prices, such as that at issue, even if it might have negative economic consequences for certain operators, is proportionate to the aim pursued."

fundamental rights and principles contained in the Charter expressly exclude additional Union powers in this area (Article 6(1) TEU and Article 51(2) of the Charter), even though they can be used for interpreting such legislative and implementing measures, as well as for filling eventual gaps left by the legislator.

How far can these powers under the specific enabling provisions be extended to more general areas of civil law, including, for instance, rules on contracting, unfair terms, compensation and restitution not limited to specific groups of persons or directed against discriminatory practices (3.2)? Provisions on general civil law are usually left to Member States and only coordinated by Union rules on conflict of laws in contracting[6] and in non-contractual obligations.[7] Does the principle of proportionality exclude Union powers in this area? The question is a more fundamental one concerning the role of the Union in legislating civil law matters:

- is it confined to legislating on specific problem areas, resulting on the one hand on some "general principles" (perhaps with the addition of some "soft law" mechanisms), and on the other hand in a piecemeal approach; or
- should it be extended to cover general contract law matters, similar to Member State contract law, but allowing a "second" regime *parallel to* applicable national law according to conflict rules, or a "28/29th" regime *in addition to* existing national law of the originally 27 – now with Croatia 28 – Member States for contracting in the EU?[8]

There has been a debate going on for more than ten years on the feasibility and extent of Union powers in civil law, in particular contract law, matters which has resulted in the proposal of a Regulation on a Common European Sales Law of 11 October 2011 based on the Internal Market competence of the Union under Article 114 TFEU (CESL, 6.12).[9] An enormous amount of legal literature has emerged from this proposal which will not be analysed in this context.[10]

6.4 It will be suggested that this question should be answered not so much under the competence dilemma described above (0.11), but in a more targeted way under the proportionality principle as it applies to Union law. It has become part of positive EU law in Article 5(4) TEU (slightly modifying Article 5(3) EC), which reads:

---

[6] Regulation (EC) No. 593/2008 of the EP and the Council of 17 June 2008 on the law applicable to contractual obligations (Rome I) [2008] OJ L 176/6.

[7] Regulation (EC) No. 864/2007 of the EP and the Council of 11 July 2007 on the law applicable to non-contractual obligations (Rome II) [2007] OJ L 199/1.

[8] For a discussion of the issues involved, see now J. Basedow, *The Law of Open Societies*, 2013, 229.

[9] COM (635) final.

[10] Overview by E. Hondius, ERPrL 2013, 3.

Under the principle of proportionality, the content and form of Union action shall not exceed what is necessary to achieve the objectives of the Treaties.

In linking Union action to the achievement of Treaty objectives, proportionality provides a relatively precise test to evaluate and eventually challenge the legality of, for example, Community/Union directives. It was used extensively in the tobacco advertising judgment as an argument for annulment (0.11).[11] In its later tobacco manufacture judgment and related cases concerning mandatory EU standards mostly related to product marketing,[12] but exceptionally also to contract terms,[13] the Court took a more cautious approach, insisting on the broad discretion of the legislature:[14]

> "Consequently, the legality of a measure adopted in that respect can be affected only if the measure is manifestly inappropriate having regard to the objective which the competent institution is seeking to pursue."

It has recognised that "the Community legislature must be allowed a broad discretion in areas which involve political, economic and social choices on its part, and in which it is called upon to undertake complex assessments", even though in principle limited by the proportionality principle according to the then Article 5(3) EC (now Article 5(4) TEU).

According to Harbo,[15] the Court has so far used a very "moderate" approach in controlling Community (now Union) law measures under the proportionality test, while it uses much more restrictive language with regard to Member State measures allegedly restricting fundamental freedoms. The Vice-President of the ECJ, Koen Lenaerts, has limited the proportionality principle to a mere "process-oriented" review; for him it is sufficient that the legislature can produce some kind of "impact statement" or impact assessment" justifying EU action.[16] I have criticised this rather reductionist approach as compared to the strict proportionality control of Member State measures restricting the fundamental freedoms.[17]

---

11 Case C-376/98 *Germany v EP and Council* [2000] ECR I-8419, para 84.

12 Case C-491/01 *R v Secretary of State for Health ex parte British American Tobacco (Investments) Ltd et al* [2002] ECR I-11453; C-380/03 *Germany v EP and Council* [2005] ECR I-11573, para 145; referring to earlier cases like C-84/94 *United Kingdom v Council* [1996] ECR I-5755, para 58; C-233/94 *Germany v Parliament and Council* [1997] ECR I-2405, paras 55–56; C-157/96 *National Farmers' Union et al* [1998] ECR I-2211, para 61.

13 C-344/04 *IATA and ELFAA v Department for Transport* [2006] ECR I-403, para 80, recently confirmed in C-58/08 *Vodafone, supra* note 5.

14 Case C-491/01, *supra* note 12, para 123.

15 T.-I. Harbo, 'The Function of the Proportionality Principle in EU Law', ELJ 2010, 166, 172, 177.

16 K. Lenaerts, 'The European Court of Justice and Process-Oriented Review', YEL 2012, 3 at 7.

17 See N. Reich, in: H.-W. Micklitz/B. de Witte (eds.), *The European Court of Justice and the Autonomy of Member States*, 2012, 110.

1.3. A "POSITIVE" APPROACH TO PROPORTIONALITY?

6.5 How far does this discretion of EU institutions under the proportionality principle extend? What are the limits on EU legislation in civil law under the proportionality test? What are possible alternative methods? Does it matter that EU law not only intrudes into matters left to private autonomy and free movement like the cases mentioned above but also to Member State legislation as in general civil law?

In what follows it will be suggested that we should give the proportionality principle *more positive content*. The question should not be what the Union *cannot do* under a more or less strictly applied proportionality test, but what is *"necessary to achieve the objectives of the Treaty"*. Obviously the EU legislature will have a broad discretion to set its priorities and to take the appropriate measures, always subject to review under the general constitutional principles developed in this book. One of the criteria for review and criticism is the effectiveness principle mentioned in Chapter 4: measures which are not effective in achieving the objectives of the Treaty are not necessary; on the other hand, if it can be shown that certain measures are more effective than others, then there is a necessity to take them.

This positive approach towards the EU-specific proportionality principle will be applied to two initiatives currently under discussion to create a more coherent civil law regime in the EU. So far, there has been no legislation. Two initiatives stand out:

- the Draft Common Frame of Reference (DCFR) (6.6–6.11); and
- the Proposal for a Common European Sales Law (CESL) (6.12–6.19).

Both initiatives are mainly concerned with general contract law, namely both so-called B2C (business to consumer) and B2B (business to business) relations. Once put on the EU statute books in whatever form, this would substantially widen the scope of Union civil law. The DCFR is much broader than CESL in four important aspects:

- it aims to cover C2C relations;
- it takes over the EU *acquis* also in the area of non-discrimination legislation;
- it goes beyond contracting by also including provisions on non-contractual liability; and
- it covers security interests in movables on the crossroads between contract and property law.

Employment law has so far not been affected by the different initiatives and will be mentioned in this context only insofar as spill-over effects on general civil law principles can be presumed to exist.

The focus will however not only be on formal legislation but also on other methods of making private law,[18] for example:

- the conflict-of-laws methods to coordinate, not to harmonise, legislation (6.18);
- "soft law" instruments like "codes of practice", voluntary standards and contract terms;
- "open methods of coordination" and convergence (6.20);
- *de lege ferenda* in the form in the form of a directive or even a regulation based on the existing competence regime of the EU (0.10), implementing a "positive proportionality principle" through legislative action (6.22–6.23); and
- development of an emerging general principle in civil law, namely "good faith" (Chapter 7).

It will be shown that EU institutions have a whole set of actions available to them to make civil law more coherent with the objectives of the Treaty without unduly stretching the proportionality principle. An analysis of the DCFR as well as the CESL draft regulation will give some examples (although not an exhaustive list) of how this could be done in the future.

2. THE DRAFT COMMON FRAME OF REFERENCE

2.1. A GENERAL ASSESSMENT OF THE DCFR

6.6 The term "Common Frame of Reference" (CFR) (0.10) was on the EU agenda for some time, and a large group of European civil law scholars had been assembled under the two headings of Study Group and *Acquis* Group.[19] In 2007/8 a first interim draft CFR[20] was presented to the Commission, which was followed in 2008/9 by a final version,[21] supplemented by six copious volumes of notes and

---

18 N. Jansen, 'Dogmatising Non-Legislative Codifications', in: R. Brownsword et al. (eds.), *The Foundations of European Private Law*, 2011, 31.

19 For an overview see C. Twigg-Flesner, *A Cross-Border Regulation for Consumer Transactions in the EU – A Fresh Approach to EU Consumer Law*, 2012, 46.

20 C. von Bar/E. Clive/H. Schulte-Nölke (eds.), *Principles, Definitions and Model Rules on European Private Law – DCFR*, interim outline ed. 2008.

21 C. von Bar/E. Clive/H. Schulte-Nölke (eds.), *Principles, Definitions and Model Rules on European Private Law – DCFR*, outline ed. 2009.

explanations.[22] An intense academic debate followed.[23] It is not necessary to go further into this discussion. However, three points should be remembered because they are of relevance for the following discussion on EU civil law:

- The principles and provisions of the DCFR go far beyond mere contract law; they contain rules on the law of obligations in general (for example on non-contractual obligations like tort and unjust enrichment), on a number of specific contracts beyond sales law, particularly in the area of services, and on transfer of property and security interests in movables. Some scholars made the criticism that the authors "over-fulfilled" the mandate given by the Commission.
- The DCFR aims to integrate and in some cases to improve mandatory consumer law provisions, particularly those from the *acquis* into the general rules of EU civil law. Therefore, Article I. – 1:105(1) of the DCFR provides: "A 'consumer' means any natural person who is acting *primarily* for purposes which are not related to his or her trade, business or profession". This definition is broader than the traditional one used in the *acquis* to allow the inclusion of so-called "double purpose contracts" which would usually not come within the scope of the consumer protective provisions of EU law according to the *Gruber* case law of the ECJ (2.9).[24]
- The legal character of the DCFR remains unclear. In its early communications, the Commission regarded it as a "toolbox" for future legislation – a somewhat dismissive term for the enormous scholarly work which went into it. But the Commission certainly did not want to endorse the work formally because of a "competence gap" in the EU Treaties regarding general contract law, and even more so private law, legislation in the EU (0.11).[25] This had not been changed by the Lisbon Treaty on European Union; on the contrary, Article 5 TEU insisted on a narrow reading of EU competences based on the principle of "conferral" and limited by the provisions on subsidiarity and proportionality mentioned above (6.5).

---

[22] C. von Bar/E. Clive/H. Schulte-Nölke (eds.), *Principles, Definitions and Model Rules on European Private Law – DCFR*, full ed. 2009.

[23] See F. Cafaggi/H.-W. Micklitz (eds.), *European Private Law after the CFR*, 2010; H. Eidenmüller et al., 'The CFR for European Private Law – Policy Choices and Codification Problems', OJLS 2009, 659–708; N. Jansen/R. Zimmermann, 'A European Civil Code in all but name', ELJ 2010, 98; M. Hesselink, 'The CFR as a source of European Private Law', Tulane LRev 2009, 919–971; O. Cherednychenko, 'Fundamental Rights, Policy Issues and the DCFR', ERCL 2010, 39; S. Vogenauer, 'CFR and UNIDROIT-Principles of International Commercial Contract: Coexistence, Competition, or Overkill of Soft Law', ERCL 2010, 143; P. Larouche/F. Chirico (eds.), *Economic Analysis of the DCFR*, 2011; G. Wagner (ed.), *The CFR – A View from Law and Economics*, 2009; not to mention the many French, German, and Italian contributions.

[24] C-464/01 *Johann Gruber v Bay Wa AG* [2005] ECR I-439, decided under the mechanism of the Brussels Convention.

[25] See my earlier remarks in N. Reich, 'A European Contract Law – Ghost or Host for Integration', WisIntLJ 2006, 425 at 437–449.

2.2. (LIMITED) LEGAL EFFECTS OF THE PRINCIPLES AND MODEL RULES OF THE DCFR

6.7   Could the provisions of the DCFR not be used – at least partially – for an "optional instrument" of EU contract law based on a concept of regulatory competition?[26] Indeed, for many supporters of an EU-specific civil law the idea of an optional instrument looked like a panacea for the "competence gap" described above, and numerous academic and political contributions discussed matters of competence, scope and relation to national law of an EU optional instrument, filling an entire issue of the European Review of Contract Law (ERCL) after a conference in Leuven in 2010.[27] This debate was to some extent kicked off by a Commission Green Paper of 1 July 2010[28] which has been reviewed elsewhere.[29] Many questions had controversial answers:

- the competence basis: internal market under Article 114 or "reserve competence" of Article 352 TFEU, the first being subject to majority voting, the second needing unanimity in the Council and the consent of the European Parliament?
- the personal scope: only B2C or B2B or both?
- the territorial scope: only cross-border or both internal and cross-border?
- use of a so called "blue button" approach proposed by Schulte-Nölke specially to meet the needs of e-commerce?[30]

---

[26]   For an overview see now G. Rühl, 'Regulatory Competition in Contract Law: Empirical Evidence and Normative Implications', ERCL 2013, 61, concerning competition in Member State contract law without including EU aspects.

[27]   Contributions by Riesenhuber, Sefton-Green, Gutman, Howells, Augenhofer, Maugeri, Meli, Twigg-Flesner, Mak, Gome and Ganuza, Hesselink, Cristas, Cartwright, Rutgers, and Castermans, in the special issue of ERCL 2011, 115–366.

[28]   COM (2010) 348 final.

[29]   C. Herrestahl, 'Ein europäisches Vertragsrecht als Optionales Instrument', EuZW 2011, 7; K. Tonner, 'Das Grünbuch der Kommission zum Europäischen Vertragsrecht für Verbraucher und Unternehmer – Zur Rolle des Verbrauchervertragsrecht im europäischen Vertragsrecht', EuZW 2010, 767; H. Rösler, 'Rechtswahl und optionelles Vertragsrecht in der EU', EuZW 2011, 1; M. Tamm, 'Die 28. Rechtsordnung der EU: Gedanken zur Einführung eines grenzüberschreitenden B2C Vertragsrecht', GPR 2010, 281; J. Cartwright, '"Choice is good" Really?', paper presented at the Leuven conference on an optional contract law, ERCL 2011, 335. A comprehensive study with detailed recommendations has been prepared by a working group of the Hamburg Max Planck Institute for Comparative and International Private Law, 'Policy Options for Progress Towards a European Contract Law', 2011, MPI paper 11/2 = RabelsZ 2011, 373; N. Reich, Revija za evropsko pravo 2012, 5–13, with further references on the questions mentioned below; see also: ESC, position paper on options for a European contract law, OJ C 84/1 of 17 March 2011.

[30]   H. Schulte-Nölke, 'EC Law on the Formation of Contract – from the Common Frame of Reference to the Blue Button', ERCL 2007, 348 ff.: "The 'Blue Button' would be an Optional Instrument enabling businesses to set up a European-wide e-shop which has only to comply with one set of rules. Such an Optional Instrument would solve most of the cases likely to arise in B2C as well as B2B and C2C relations. When buying goods in an e-shop the client

6.8 The results of this debate have to some extent culminated in the draft regulation on a Common European Sales Law (CESL) to be discussed below (6.12). The question put before the EU civil lawyer is somewhat more modest but at the same time more complex: can the DCFR be used to develop "general principles" or at least "soft law standards" of an emerging EU civil law – whether as *acquis commun* or even *acquis communautaire*? Indeed, some of the language of the DCFR itself seems to suggest such an approach, particularly in the area of an EU-specific "good faith" principle (7.13).

The DCFR is to some extent a sequel to earlier projects on the consolidation or even codification of EU private law containing extensive references to the concept of "principles". As can be shown, the concept of principles used is rather vague, has an unclear scope of application, and remains of limited value on its own. It is neither based on an analysis of the case law of the ECJ nor on constitutional values – whether contained originally in the TEU/TFEU and its predecessors, or now in the Charter. It mainly serves as a reference point for some generalised private law concepts like good faith, *pacta sunt servanda*, *rebus sic stantibus*, unjust enrichment and protection of weaker parties, which are subject to differences and even controversies in the civil law of Member States. Some principles are confused with rules, in contrast to the analysis above (0.2). In this spirit, the *Principles of European Contract Law (PECL)* have been drawn up by the so-called Lando Commission.[31] Article 1:101(1) refers to "Principles [...] intended to be applied as general *rules* of contract law in the European Union" (emphasis added).

6.9 Another initiative which to some extent preceded the DCFR is the so-called *Acquis* Principles.[32] They were drawn up by a group of legal scholars on the initiative of the European Commission in preparation of a truly EU-specific contract law based on the existing directives, mostly in consumer contract law. This was obviously not an easy task, due to the rather haphazard nature of these directives and their mandatory character which is difficult to adapt them for general contract law matters containing mostly default rules. Nevertheless, they were able to define "five possible fundamental principles",[33] namely:

---

could easily choose the application of the Optional Instrument by clicking on a 'Blue Button' on the screen showing his or her acceptance of the optional European Law [...] If the client chooses the 'Blue Button', the optional European Law would derogate the law which otherwise were applicable to the conflict of law rules"; for criticism of the "*Professorenmodell*", see H.-W. Micklitz/F. Cafaggi, *After the Common Frame of Reference*, 2010, xxv. But it is interesting to note that under this approach the consumer would be free to choose the applicable law himself: it would not be imposed upon him, as it normally is in cross border situations!

[31]   *Supra* 0.10, note 44.
[32]   Acquis Group, *Acquis Principles – Contract I*, 2007 and later parts.
[33]   Ibid., at XI.

- the general function of contract as "the basic legal instrument enabling natural and legal persons the freedom to regulate their relations which each other by agreement";
- binding force of contract;
- general functions of European contract law (in relation to EU objectives);
- freedom of contract and its restrictions; and
- information.

These are obviously imprecise formulations about the objectives of (EU) contract law which were put into rather general and unspecific rules. They may be useful to explain a piece of legislation, but cannot be used for interpreting and filling gaps in existing EU legislation or Member State implementation, as was stated in the introductory remarks in relation to "general principles" (0.2). They will therefore not be considered in the following discussion.

6.10 The interim outline edition of the DCFR (6.7) published in 2008 listed an astonishing fifteen items as "principles":

- justice;
- freedom;
- protection of human rights;
- economic welfare;
- solidarity and social responsibility;
- establishing an area of freedom, security and justice;
- promotion of the internal market;
- protection of consumers and others in need of protection;
- preservation of cultural and linguistic plurality;
- rationality;
- legal certainty;
- predictability;
- efficiency;
- protection of reasonable reliance; and
- proper allocation of responsibility for the creation of risks.

The principles were not ranked in any order of priority. A controversial debate arose on the value of such a seemingly arbitrary menu-card of principles.[34] The French Association Henri Capitant, in taking up this discussion, proposed limiting the principles to three *principes directeurs*:[35]

---

[34] See the overview in: DCFR, full edition, Vol. I, *supra* note 22, at para 12.
[35] B. Fauvenarque-Cosson et al., *Principes contractuals commun*, 2008.

- *liberté contractuelle*;
- *sécurité contractuelle*; and
- *loyauté contractuelle*.

The 2008 principles were also criticised as relating only to contract law. They were not exhaustive and were said to have a more descriptive function.[36] In the final outline edition of the DCFR in 2009, the "Underlying Principles" were shortened to just four:[37]

- freedom;
- security;
- justice; and
- efficiency.

Sub-headings with more detailed "principles" were added, for example under "Freedom" a section on "freedom of contract the starting point". It clearly acknowledges party autonomy as the guiding principle:

> "As a rule, natural and legal persons are free both to decide whether or not to contract. They should also be free to agree on the terms of their contract. [...] In normal situations there is no incompatibility between contractual freedom and justice. Indeed, it has been claimed that, in some situations freedom of contract, without more, leads to justice."[38]

There are a number of other "sub-principles" which are sometimes quite detailed and look more like broadly worded rules.

In addition, the 2009 version added a description of so called "overriding principles"[39] like:

- protection of human rights;
- promotion of solidarity and social responsibility;
- preservation of cultural and linguistic diversity;
- protection and promotion of welfare; and
- promotion of the internal market.

Again, the legal importance of these "overriding principles" is by no means clear. It probably amounts to a political and legislative statement with limited value in

---

[36]   DCFR, at para 13.
[37]   DCFR, at para 15; see the – in my opinion exaggerated – criticism by M. Hesselink, 'If You Don't Like Our Principles, We Have Others', in: R. Brownsword et al. (eds.), *The Foundations of European Private Law*, 2011, 59.
[38]   Freedom, Principle 3 – Freedom of contract the starting point.
[39]   DCFR, introductory paras 16–21.

legal disputes and with little interpretative force in case of disagreements between the parties.

On the other hand, the principle of good faith was given an important place in the rules as drafted by the DCFR (7.14).[40]

As a result of this short inquiry, the discussion on EU civil law principles in the DCFR is somewhat confusing and contradictory; it does seem to not advance the topic of this study.

2.3. SELECTIVE REFERENCE TO THE DCFR IN ECJ CASE LAW?

6.11 Even though the legal status of the DCFR is not clear – some regard it as a mere toolbox, others as a source of inspiration for law-making and law application – several AGs of the ECJ have referred to it in their opinions in cases relating to EU civil law. Particularly interesting have been opinions of AG Trstenjak in *Martin*,[41] *Friz*,[42] *VB Penzügi Leasing*[43] and *Messner*,[44] where she expressly cited several provisions of the DCFR concerning the concepts of fairness, abuse and remedies in B2C transactions. In a similar spirit, AG Poiares Maduro referred to the predecessor of the DCFR, the *Acquis* principles,[45] in his opinion in *Hamilton*.[46] The ECJ has not explicitly endorsed this approach, even though, as mentioned above (5.9), it referred to "(general) principles of civil law" like good faith, unjust enrichment and abuse of rights in several of its follow-up judgments to avoid an alleged "over-protection" of weaker parties under a merely formal application of protective provisions.[47]

The methodological approach used in this study differs somewhat since the "general principles" as defined here are linked to constitutional pronouncements contained either in primary law or in the Charter or in both, which have to be balanced with other constitutional rights and principles. I will discuss whether the different approaches to interpreting and applying EU civil law in a greater methodological context can also be directed at an emerging "good faith" principle (Chapter 7).

---

[40]   M. Mekki/M. Kloepfer-Pelesse, 'Good faith and fair dealing in the DCFR', ERCL 2008, 338, taken over a principle from PECL (Article II); criticised in H. Eidenmüller et al., 'The Common Frame of Reference for European Private Law – Policy Choices and Codification Problems', OJLS 2008, 659.

[41]   Case C-227/08 [2009] ECR I-11939, opinion of 7 May 2009, para 51.

[42]   Case C-215/08 [2010] ECR I-2947, opinion of 8 September 2009, para 69 at note 62.

[43]   Case C-137/08 [2010] ECR I-10847, opinion of 6 October 2010, para 96 at note 54.

[44]   Case C-489/07 [2009] ECR I-7315, opinion of 18 February 2009 at para 85.

[45]   Acquis Group, *supra* note 32.

[46]   Case C-412/06 [2008] ECR I-2383, opinion of 21 November 2007, at para 24.

[47]   *Supra* notes 42, 44 and 46 relating to the cases *Fritz*, *Messner* and *Hamilton*, in contrast to *Penzügi Leasing* and *Martin*.

3. THE "FEASIBILITY STUDY" AND DRAFT COMMON EUROPEAN SALES LAW

3.1. THE STEPS TAKEN TOWARDS THE CESL

6.12　The Commission, eager to push for an EU contract law after long years of only symbolic interest, did not even await the outcome of the consultation procedure on its Green Paper of 1 July 2010 (6.7) and set up an expert group to study the feasibility of producing an optional instrument on European Contract Law in April 2010.[48] The expert group presented its results in record time, after just one year of work, on 3 June 2011.[49] It proposed a draft Common European Sales Law (CESL), including provisions on general contract law, special (mostly mandatory) rules on consumer transactions, but also general, mostly default, rules on the law of obligations like damages, restitution and prescription. There was a short consultation period which ended on 1 July 2011. The Commission finally published its draft CESL on 11 October 2011 – again in record time, which obviously did not allow any in-depth discussion.

How should we approach this long, complex and many layered document? The Commission has with some modifications (particularly concerning the inclusion of "digital content" which did not figure in the feasibility study of 3 May 2011; a definition and some information-specific provisions were only included in Articles 2(11), 5(1)(g) and (h) and 6(1)(r) and (s) of the Consumer Rights Directive 2011/83/EU (2.1)) more or less taken over the content and the concrete proposals of the expert group. The proposal for an EU-specific optional instrument has a double-pronged structure:

- the *Regulation* (with an explanatory memorandum and recitals, as is common in EU legal instruments) will cover "general EU law matters" (the so-called *chapeau*), like the objectives and legal basis of the instrument, the definitions, the scope of application, the agreement to and enforcement of a fair and transparent "opt-in" procedure in B2C transactions, obligations and remaining powers of Member States, and miscellaneous technical issues; and
- *Annex I* will contain the detailed provisions (186 articles) of the CESL, and *Annex II* a "Standard Information Note" explaining an eventual consumers' opt-in; no recitals or explanations are attached to the Annex.

---

[48]　Commission Decision [2010] OJ L 105/109.
[49]　<http://ec.europa.eu/justice/contract/files/feasibility-study_en.pdf>; contributions in: R. Schulze/ J. Stuyck (eds.), *An Optional Instrument for EU Contract Law*, 2011; the feasibility study is printed on pp. 217 ff.

3.2. STRUCTURE OF THE CESL

6.13   This study will give only a short overview of the structure and the basic content both of the *chapeau* and of Annex I, trying neither to analyse their central provisions nor to go deeper into the already very controversial discussion.[50] The main focus of this chapter, besides a structural critique under the proportionality principle (6.15–6.16), will be to look at its potential contribution to improving civil law legislation in the EU in both B2B and B2C relations (6.22–6.23). C2C relations, as well employment and non-discrimination law, will have to be left out because they do not figure in the CESL.

The main points can be summarised as follows:

– The CESL is supposed to be a measure of the internal market in the sense of Article 114 TFEU and would therefore follow the ordinary legislative procedure by majority voting both in the Council and the EP – a basis certainly to be welcomed by the EP which has always resisted any competence norm where it is not an equal partner like in Article 352 TFEU.[51] According to the explanatory memorandum this is justified because the proposal removes "obstacles to the exercise of fundamental freedoms which result from differences between national law, in particular from the additional transaction costs and perceived legal complexity experienced by traders when concluding cross-border transactions and the lack of confidence in their rights experienced by consumers when purchasing from another country – all of which have a direct effect on the establishment and functioning of the internal market and limit competition".[52]

– The CESL has a limited personal scope: it is applicable to B2SMU (business-to-business contracts where one of the parties is an SMU (small or medium undertaking) as defined in Article 7(2) and which can be extended by Member States), or B2C contracts under the narrow definition of the *acquis* whereby "'consumer' means any natural person who is acting for purposes which are outside the person's trade, business, craft, or profession." This would exclude most dual-purpose contracts, contrary to recital 17 of the new Consumer Rights Directive 2011/83 (2.1) and the DCFR (6.6).[53] The Draft Report of the Legal Committee of the European Parliament of 18 February

---

[50]   M. Schmidt-Kessel (ed.), *Der Entwurf für eine Gemeinsames Europäisches Kaufrecht – Kommentar*, 2013; R. Schulze (ed.), *Common European Sales Law (CESL) – Commentary*, 2012.

[51]   See ECJ case C-436/03 *EP v Council* [2006] ECR I-3733, para 43–44, concerning the legal basis of the European Cooperative Society which was based on Article 352 TFEU and challenged by the EP, which lost its case!

[52]   Explanatory memorandum at 9; likewise, recitals 4–6.

[53]   For criticism, see H.-W. Micklitz/N. Reich, 'The Commission Proposal of a Regulation for an Optional "Common European Sales Law" – Too broad or not broad enough?', EUI Working Papers Law 2012/04: www.ssrn-id2013183[1].pdf, Part I, paras 18–22 at p. 12.

2013 wants to extend this definition "in the case of dual purpose contracts, where the contract is concluded for purposes partly within and partly outside the person's trade and the trade purpose is so limited as not to be predominant in the overall context of the contract, that person shall also be considered as a consumer".

– The CESL is supposed to be available to cross-border contracting, with the possibility of Member States to make its use also possible for purely internal transactions: Article 13(a). In B2C situations, the cross-border element is however defined very broadly in Article 4(3) depending on the address indicated by the consumer (whether or not it is identical with the habitual residence), the delivery address for goods or the billing address. It is therefore not restricted, as one could have imagined by the "blue button" concept, to distance contracts or e-commerce. This means that in a "face-to-face situation" where a consumer in Germany enters into a contract with a company established in Germany but delivery will be made in France, the CESL could be used by opting in specially, alongside normally applicable German law.[54] Is that an attractive prospect for businesses or consumers? Why allow a "journey to the unknown" when all parties are used to contracting according to their legal traditions and no real link with a cross-border element is established, except the rather superficial element of a delivery address abroad as part of the performance of a contract which under normal circumstances in conflict-of-laws matters does not have any influence on applicable law? Considering these problems the Draft Report of the Legal Affairs Committee of the European Parliament of 18 March 2013 wants to limit the CESL to online contracts.[55]

– Its substantive scope is limited to the "sale of movables", of "digital content" (6.23) and of "service contracts" related to the sale of goods. Certain combined contracts are excluded, for example those with a credit element Article 6(2).[56] This makes the use of the CESL unattractive or even impossible if the trader offers means of deferred payment or a similar financial accommodation.

– The use of the CESL in B2C transactions depends on rather complex and separate information and notification requirements as set out in Articles 8 and 9 and paralleled by a sort of warning to the consumer, the terms of which are defined in Annex II. In order to avoid cherry-picking, the parties can only choose the CESL in its entirety (Article 8(3)). Such strict rules discourage rather than encourage consumers to agree to the use of the CESL. Traders will not find these rules attractive because they are barred from using

---

[54] See the criticism by C. Twigg-Flesner, *supra* note 19, at 76.

[55] See C. Busch, EUVR 2013, 33.

[56] The Draft Report of the Legal Affairs Committee wants to make this possible; see C. Busch, *supra* note 55, at 34.

standard terms for the opt-in. The contracting will be split up into two parts: an agreement about the use of the CESL and an agreement on the contract terms within the framework of the CESL.[57] Nothing is said about how the opting-in in B2SMU transactions will be done: will Article 3 of Regulation 593/2008 be applicable here? Recital 10 of the *chapeau* seems to exclude this, but Flessner[58] rightly points out that once the CESL is chosen it will take priority as a Regulation under Article 288 TFEU and will set aside conflicting Member State law within its scope of application.

– The relation of the CESL to the EU *acquis* and to mandatory national consumer law under Article 6(2) of Regulation 593/2008 is by no means clear, unless one follows the argument of Flessner. The Commission simply writes: "Since the CESL contains a complete set of fully harmonised mandatory consumer protection rules, there will be no disparities between the law of the Member States in this area, where the parties have chosen to use the CESL." Consequently, Article 6(2) which is predicated on the existence of differing levels of consumer protection in the Member States, has no practical importance for the issues covered by the CESL". This statement appears to be incorrect, as Article 6(2) is concerned with differing Member States' rules on consumer protection, not with EU provisions. It seems inconceivable within the framework of EU law that an EU Regulation can become "nationalised" as a second contract law regime parallel to the existing Member State contract law, as recital 9 seems to suggest by arguing: "It [the CESL] harmonises the contract law of Member States not by requiring amendments to pre-existing national contract law but by creating with each Member State's national law a second contract law regime for contracts within its scope. The second regime should be identical throughout the Union and exist alongside the pre-existing rules of national contract law." How can the CESL Regulation first be transformed into a "second" (national) regime and still remain "identical" Union law – namely as a 28th (or after the accession of Croatia a 29th) regime? It seems more convincing to simply argue that the CESL where applicable takes precedence over national law, including mandatory consumer protection under Article 6(2) of Regulation 593/2008. So-called "overriding mandatory provisions" of the forum (*lex fori*) under Article 9(1) and (2) of Regulation 593/2008[59] would however not be set aside by the CESL because Member States enjoy a wide margin of discretion in this area (always subject to limitation under primary EU law).

---

[57]   H.-W. Micklitz/N. Reich, *supra* note 53, at 18.

[58]   A. Flessner, 'Der Status des Gemeinsamen Europäischen Kaufrechts', ZEuP 2012, 726.

[59]   Case C-369 + 376/96 *Arblade* [1999] ECR I-8453, para 30; for their interpretation see now the opinion of AG Wahl of 15 May 2013 in the case C-184/12 *Unamar v Navigation Maritime Belge* under Article 7 of the Brussels Convention which must be interpreted in the light of Article 9(1) of Regulation 593/2008.

– The different parts of the CESL contain quite detailed rules on B2SMU and B2C contracting within its above mentioned scope of application. A closer analysis reveals that the provisions relating to B2SMU are mostly default rules with some "micro protection" of SMUs for instance concerning good faith (Article 2(3)), remedies for fraud (Article 56(1)), "grossly" unfair contract terms (Articles 81 and 86; see 7.22), damages (Article 171), and prescription (Article 186). Consumer protection rules are meant to be mandatory, even in general contract law matters like remedies for mistake (Article 56(2)), *contra preferentem* interpretation (Article 64), terms derived from pre-contractual statements (Article 69), contracts of indeterminate duration (Article 77(2)), grey and black lists of unfair terms (Articles 84 and 85), interest for delay in payment (Article 167) and restitution (Article 177). Without saying so, *the CESL contains two completely different sets of rules*, namely mostly default rules in B2SMU transactions while in B2C contracting mandatory provisions are the standard. This tends to make the personal scope of the CESL a matter of continuing controversy, aggravated by the narrow concept of the consumer which cannot, unlike in the *acquis*, be extended by Member States. This *hybrid structure* is important for a closer analysis of CESL not so much under competence, but rather under proportionality criteria of Article 5(4) TEU to which I will turn now.

3.3. THE CESL AS A HYBRID CONTRACT LAW

6.14 The legal-political debate on the CESL concentrates on five main controversies:[60]

– the competence basis in EU law: Articles 118 or 352 TFEU;
– the methods and technicalities of the "opt-in" and the effects on national law;
– a detailed analysis of the many rules proposed to do with coherence and legal certainty, sometimes with express reference to existing national law, including proposals for improvement which have to some extent already found their place in the draft report of the Legal Affairs Committee of the EU of 18 February 2013;
– the relation between mandatory and default provisions, mostly in B2C transactions, including whether the specific level of protection is (or is not)

---

[60] The – mostly critical – literature has become impossible to follow. Just some examples: special issue of Vol. 8 ERCL 2012, Vol. 4 ZEuP 2012; Vol. 212 AcP 2012; ERPrL 2013, 1; H. Eidenmüller et al., 'Der Vorschlag für eine Verordnung über ein Gemeinsames Europäisches Kaufrecht', Juristenzeitung 2012, 269; separate publication by C. Wendehorst/B. Zöchling-Jud (eds.), *Am Vorabend eines Gemeinsamen Europäischen Kaufrechts*, 2012. The European Law Institute (ELI) has published an amended and improved version of CESL: statement of ELI on the proposal of the Regulation for a CESL, 2012; first supplement of 25 July 2013.

"high" enough under Articles 12 or 169 TFEU or Article 38 of the Charter; and

– whether the protection offered to consumers may on the contrary be "too high", so as to discourage business to opt in to the CESL in B2C transactions.[61]

Quite frankly, this debate is only of a very limited interest to me because it does not answer the preceding and more important question: do stakeholders (businesses, SMUs, consumers and other participants in cross-border trade), the Member States and the EU itself really *need* such an instrument?[62] The necessity test is not identical with the competence basis but must be met by *all measures* under Article 114 or 352 TFEU – otherwise it would not have been separately regulated in Article 5(4) TEU. The rather generous conditions of the "manifestly inappropriate" test the ECJ is applying have been mentioned above (6.5).

In the following I will argue that there is *no need for CESL as an optional instrument*, including the recent proposals of the Legal Affairs Committee of the EP, whether in B2SMU or in B2C contracting. Other adequate mechanisms for contracting in the internal market which fulfil the above mentioned dual criteria – avoiding unwarranted trade restrictions *and* guaranteeing a sufficiently high level of protection for consumers – already exist or can be envisaged within the existing EU *acquis*. This makes the CESL superfluous, even if in the legislative process it will be made "more consumer or user friendly", even if some of the technical defects debated in the extensive literature can be overcome, and even if the "market for legal regulations"[63] the Commission is hoping for will accept and make frequent use of it. When discussing the "necessity" test, some realism about contracting seems to be useful: in most cases, the active partner will propose the contract regime. In B2C transactions, this will always be the business side; the consumer is given a take-it-or-leave-it choice; the idea that he can use a "blue button" in his favour as proposed by Schulte-Nölke[64] seems somewhat far-fetched. In the area of B2SMU contracting, usually the stronger side will impose the contract terms; this is usually not the SMU, unless it is in particularly favourable position.[65]

---

[61]   This criticism has been voiced mostly by American law scholars coming from a (behavioural) law and economics background; see references in D. Caruso, American JCompL 2013, 479 at 486 with many references.

[62]   For a critique, see C. Twigg-Flesner, 'Debate on a European Code of Contracts', Contratto e Impresa Europa I-2012, 157.

[63]   S. Vogenauer, ERPrL 2013, 54; B. Lurger, 'A Radical View of Pluralism', in: L. Niglia (ed.), *Pluralism and European Private Law*, 2013, 175; G. Rühl, *supra* note 26.

[64]   H. Schulte-Nölke, *supra* note 30.

[65]   C. Twigg-Flesner, *supra* note 62 at 163.

3.3.1. *No necessity for B2SMU cross-border transactions*

6.15   However, even under the "manifestly inappropriate" criteria, it could be argued against the Commission that it has not explained why the CESL should also cover general contract law matters like the conclusion of the contract, defects in consent and interpretation of a contract, which are not specific to sales (and related services) law, and certain areas of the general law of obligations like damages, restitution and prescription, while on the other hand such important provisions as representation, capacity and legality have been left to (applicable) Member State law. CESL provisions on B2B transactions can mostly be qualified as default rules in B2B transactions which can be modified by party agreement; very few provisions of the CESL contain mandatory rules which could be invoked in particular (but not exclusively) by SMUs (6.13). These very broad and general rules, which differ among Member States, have had no proven impact on cross-border transactions so far. The "impact assessment" of the Commission staff seems to be highly speculative on this point, even if it might suffice for an ECJ review on its "manifestly inappropriate" test.[66]

In any case, eventual internal market problems can be solved by the B2SMU parties' freedom of choice under Article 3 of the Rome I Regulation within the limits of mandatory provisions of the Article's paragraphs 3 and 4 which also apply to B2SMU transactions. With regard to provisions specific to cross-border commercial sales law, most are already covered by the Convention on the International Sale of Goods of 1980 (CISG – the Vienna Convention) which will be applicable either under the "opt-out" mechanism in Article 1(1)(a)), or, for traders not established in the CISG Member States, namely in the UK, Ireland, Portugal and Malta, by an "opt-in" possibility under Article 1(1)(b). It is true that CISG is not concerned with general contract terms, which is also an important issue in B2B, in particular B2SMU, contracting. But this deficiency in EU contract regulation could easily be solved by special legislation not depending on any type of opt-in, as will be shown later (6.22)

It is also true that the EU is not party to the CISG, and that the ECJ has no explicit power to interpretation it, but may refer to and *thereby indirectly interpret* it if a link to EU law can be shown to exist.[67] Still the question remains: why put a second level on cross-border contracting in related matters when the parties to a B2SMU transaction already have an instrument at their disposal for which considerable legal expertise and experience has already been accumulated, and which may therefore increase the degree of legal certainty which the Commission invokes for B2SMU transactions in the internal market? Why

---

66   *Supra* note 13.
67   In case C-381/08 *Car Trim v Key Safety* [2010] ECR I-1255, para 36, concerning the interpretation of the concept of "place of performance" in Article 5(1)(b) of the Brussels Regulation 44/2001 where the Court referred to Article 3 CISG.

artificially separate international and EU cross-border trade, which will make transactions more complex, instead of giving the parties more clarity about their rights and obligations as promised by the Commission? Therefore, it seems highly doubtful whether under the "necessity" test the EU has jurisdiction to regulate cross-border B2SMU sales (and related service) transactions at all by adopting the CESL or a similar instrument in its present or even in an improved form.[68]

This critical analysis cannot be refuted by arguing that CESL is "only" optional in B2SMU transactions. Optional instruments have to pass the "necessity" test as any other EU legislative act. The "option" is only concerned with its specific application in a contract between B2SMU partners, not at all with the EU's competence to propose and adopt such a measure to the parties.

Against the argument of the Commission, that CESL is necessary to save (or minimise) transaction cost in internal market contracting, it should be remembered that quite probably the contrary will be true:

– the *personal scope* of the CESL is quite unclear due to the ambiguities and uncertainties of the concept of SMU in Article 7(2) itself which may not be known or available to the other contracting party, especially in an online situation;
– the *substantive scope* of the CESL is rather limited in that it excludes a number of important contract law questions from its scope of application, in particular representation, set-off, illegality etc.; parties cannot avoid a reference to applicable national law, either by choice or under other provisions of Regulation 593/2008; and
– the *options left to Member States* to extend (or not) the scope of the CESL beyond cross-border B2SMU contracting create additional disparities between the contract law of the Member States which increase rather than decrease uncertainty as to applicable law between parties.

3.3.2. Is there a real "need" for the CESL in B2C transactions?

6.16 In B2C transactions matters are more complex because of the mostly mandatory nature of provisions protecting the consumer under EU and national

---

68   I follow here the argument used in H.-W. Micklitz/N. Reich, *supra* note 53, Part I, paras 14–16, at p. 9; a similar argument has been voiced by A. Stadler, 'Anwendungsvoraussetzungen und Anwendungsbereich des CESL', AcP 2012, 473 at 489; for a discussion of the divergences of the CISG and the CESL in commercial cross-border sales transactions see the detailed analysis of U. Magnus, in: U. Magnus (ed.), *CISG vs. Regional Sales Law Unification*, 2012, 97, arguing that "there appears to be no virtual necessity to enact an instrument alongside the CISG", 121. More positive M. Loos/H. Schelhaas, 'Commercial Sales: CESL Compared to the Vienna Sales Convention', ERPrL 2013, 105, taking a more positive view, in particular with regard to the rules on standard terms, at 111.

law, reiterated in many judgments of the ECJ.[69] In cross-border transactions this problem is referred to in Article 6 of the Rome I Regulation 593/2008 (6.13) which does not seem to be a real impediment if interpreted in a way that conforms to EU policy.[70] The ongoing differences between Member State consumer protection laws despite harmonisation at the EU level may warrant the adoption of a more coherent and uniform EU regulation focusing on establishing uniform standards of cross-border B2C transactions.[71] However, the proposed provisions of the CESL must be "necessary" with regard to "content and form". In my opinion, this necessity test is also not fulfilled with regard to those provisions which try to regulate problems specific to B2C transactions and which have already been the object of EU legislation, lately in the CRD 2011/83/EU which has fully harmonised the provisions on "off-premises" and distance contracts figuring in Articles 17–19, 24–27 and 40–47 CESL. Is it really "necessary" to have *two layers of consumer protection* in EU law, one mandatory for both internal and cross-border transactions, and the other containing "optional mandatory provisions" only for cross-border contracting which however may not always have been coordinated and updated with the existing protective regime of the *acquis?*

In those areas where the CESL contains better or different rules, for instance with regard to the professional seller's liability for non-conforming digital content which was not included in the CRD but only in Articles 100–105 CESL, the protection of the consumer/user of digital content should not depend on whether or not he/she has opted in to the CESL but made part of a specific legislative initiative of the EU under the *positive proportionality principle* (6.23). Another example concerns the differences in remedies in the case of a non-conforming product under the CESL and the CRD: while the CRD limits the consumer's first-stage remedies to replacement or repair without allowing him/her a right to immediate rejection or giving the seller a "right to cure" (which however can be introduced by Member State law under the minimum harmonisation principle), such a right is foreseen in the CESL (Article 114(2)), provided that the non-conformity is not insignificant, which has to be proven by the seller. If the trader proposes to the consumer to opt in to the CESL and the consumer agrees, the trader would implicitly waive his "right to cure" and allow the consumer, like in UK law, an immediate right of rejection of a significantly non-conforming good.[72] Not surprisingly, this increase in consumer protection

---

[69] The case law has been well analysed in the opinion of AG Trstenjak of 29 November 2009 in case C-453/10 *Pereničová and Perenič v SOS financ* [2012] ECR I-(15.03.2012), paras 42–45; see the comment by H.-W. Micklitz/N. Reich, EuZW 2012, 126.

[70] N. Reich, 'EU Strategies in Finding the Optimal Consumer Law Instrument', ERCL 2012, 1 at 21.

[71] This is the main argument by C. Twigg-Flesner, *supra* note 19.

[72] H.-W. Micklitz/N. Reich, *supra* note 53, Part III, paras 16, at p. 79.

has been met with strong opposition in business circles and in academia.[73] On the other hand, isn't the possibility of immediate rejection the only realistic remedy in cross-border contracting, while repair or replacement may even be more costly to the trader?[74] Finally, why should this remedy depend on the opt-in to a complex instrument like the CESL whose impact on a protective level the "normal consumer" will usually not be able to assess? Couldn't the trader offer a right of immediate rejection on his own by a voluntary marketing action, perhaps in a soft-law instrument negotiated between business and consumer associations? Does one *need* a legislative instrument for that?[75]

6.17   On the other side of the picture, there are some provisions in the CESL which seem to reduce the extent of consumer protection granted under the CRD or the case law of the ECJ. The consumer protection objective of the remedies in Directive 99/44/EC was expressly confirmed by the ECJ in its *Quelle* judgment;[76] the question of whether the costs for disconnecting and re-installing non-conforming goods have to be borne by the seller if this has not been expressly agreed in the contract reached the ECJ in the *Weber/Putz* case (4.18).[77] In its judgment of 16 June 2011, the ECJ, against the opinion of AG Mazak, clearly placed those costs (so long as they are proportionate) on the seller, because he delivered a non-conforming product. It is not clear that this case law will be taken over by CESL; at least the consumer cannot be sure that by being encouraged or "persuaded" to opt in to the CESL (this will usually not depend on his choice but on the marketing strategy of the trader that gives the consumer the option to take it or leave it) he or she will have the same amount of protection as under the *acquis*. Even more problematic, Article 112(1) CESL seems to restrict the consequences of the *Weber/Putz* judgment in that the seller only has to take back the replaced items at his expense but does not say that the seller also must cover the costs of re-installing a non-conforming good.[78]

---

[73]   G. Wagner, 'Ökonomische Analyse des CESL', ZEuP 2012, 794 at 820 (criticism from an economic efficiency point of view), disregarding however English law, which is familiar with the consumer's right to rejection without a right to cure of the seller; there is no evidence of opportunistic behavior, see G. Howells/S. Weatherill, *Consumer Protection Law*, 2005, para 3.6.2; R. Anderson, 'UK Sales: Loss of the Right to Reject Goods, Judgment of the Scottish Outer House of 5 Feb. 2010', ZEuP 2011, 655. The Draft Report of the Legal Affairs Committee wants to limit it to a period of six months after delivery, to be raised within 30 days.

[74]   F. Zoll, 'Das Konzept des Verbraucherschutzes in der Machbarkeitsstudie für das Optionale Instrument', EUVR 2012, 9 at 21.

[75]   Proposal in the study by G. Howells/H.-W. Micklitz/N. Reich, *Optional Consumer Law Standards for Businesses and Consumers*, 2011, which was prepared for the European Consumer Association BEUC <www.BEUC.eu>.

[76]   Case C-404/06 *Quelle AG v Bundesverband der Verbraucherzentralen* [2008] ECR I-2685, confirmed by Article 112(2) CESL.

[77]   Joined Cases C-65 + 89/09 *Weber and Putz* [2011] ECR I-5257, against the opinion of AG Mazak of 18 May 2010; case note J. Luzak, EUVR 2012, 35. For the German follow-up case see the judgment of 21 December 2012 of the BGH NJW 2012, 1073.

[78]   See the comment by J. Luzak, *supra* note 77, at 40.

6.18   One could therefore argue that the EU's obligation in its internal market measures to guarantee a high level of consumer protection – referred to in recital 11 – according to Articles 114(3) and 169 TFEU and Article 38 of the Charter cannot be waived by the consumer by opting into the CESL if it contains a lower level of protection than is available under the CRD. The opt-in mechanism of the CESL would create different levels of consumer protection in the EU, which is against the principle of non-discrimination in Article 12 TFEU and Article 21 of the Charter without being justified by imperative requirements of the internal market.[79] Against recital 58 of the recently adopted CRD, the consumer could be "deprived of the protection granted by this Directive" under the opt-in mechanism of the CESL. Even if the choice of the parties to a B2C contract would also make reference to the "default" provisions of the CESL and to those mandatory provisions in general contract law which are contained in it, there is still no *need* for an optional instrument, because under conflict-of-law rules the business party has freedom of choice under Articles 3 and 6(2) of Regulation 593/2008 with its flexible principle of equivalence which can function as a long stop to protect the consumer without placing unnecessary burdens on the trader.[80] The trader can always avoid "being caught" by the consumer protection provisions of the consumer's home country by voluntarily agreeing to a high(er) level of protection. There is no "regulatory gap" and hence "no need" that must be closed by allowing the parties to opt in to the CESL under EU jurisdiction.

6.19   To sum up: it seems arguable that even if the CESL can be based on the existing EU competence provisions, in particular Article 114 TFEU, its two core elements – to regulate cross-border B2SMU and B2C transactions in the internal market – *do not comply with the necessity test* under the proportionality criteria of Article 5(4) TEU:

– in B2SMU, there is no need because of the prevalence of party autonomy and the possibility of choosing the CISG, also available to SMUs: references to national law will always be necessary in areas not covered by the CESL; as a result, the CESL will complicate cross-border B2B transactions instead of making them easier in the spirit of an internal market; and
– in B2C, there is no need for an opt-in instrument because this could create an incentive for traders to remove mandatory protective provisions under primary and secondary EU provisions; remaining differences at the level of (non-harmonised) Member State consumer protection measures do not seem to present an appreciable impediment to cross-border marketing and can be levelled out by an application of conflict-of-law provisions in the Rome I Regulation 593/2008 that conforms with the internal market.

---

[79]   B. Lurger, *supra* note 63.
[80]   N. Reich, *supra* note 70.

Even if the necessity test can be passed, the *coherence criteria* as developed by the Court to control Union measures[81] seem to be absent in the CESL. This is due to its rather arbitrary distinction between B2SMU and B2C transactions, its unclear determination of the personal and substantive scope of application of the CESL, and the options available to Member States which increase the differences in contract law in the internal market instead of contributing to eliminating them, as promised in the recitals (6. 13)

4. OPEN METHOD OF COORDINATION, CONVERGENCE AND IMPROVED LAW-MAKING IN REFLEXIVE CONTRACT GOVERNANCE IN THE EU

6.20 The criticism of the legislative approach to the CESL as an optional instrument is not meant as a complete rejection of its usefulness. This refers to a broader discussion on "contract governance" in general. In an overview paper based on comparative research in relation to the "corporate governance" paradigm, Möslein and Riesenhuber[82] distinguish four areas of research and practical relevance of contract governance

1. "governance of contract law" (institutional framework of contract law rule-making);
2. "governance of contracts" (contract law as an institutional framework for private transactions);
3. "governance by means of contracts law" (design of contract law as an instrument of steering behaviour and for achieving regulatory results – regulatory function of contract law); and
4. "governance through contract" (contracts as an institutional framework and mechanism for self-guidance by private parties).

In the context of the discussion on improved civil law-making in the EU, points 1 and 3 on contract governance are of particular relevance. The CESL is based on prior comparative law work done by academics, in particular the DCFR. This can be used without formal legislation not only as a "toolbox", but also as a "soft law" mechanism, to develop timely and legitimate solutions to ongoing contract law problems in the EU if they are not of a mandatory nature. It is not a source of law, but certainly a *source of inspiration*. In this spirit, the DCFR has already been used as a source of solutions with EU relevance (6.11) by several

---

81 See case C-239/09 *Test-Achats* [2011] ECR I-773, para 21.
82 F. Möslein/K. Riesenhuber, 'Contract Governance', ERCL 2009, 248 at 260.

AGs in cases referred to the ECJ concerning private law matters. AG Trstenjak mentioned in her *Camino* opinion of 14 February 2012[83] that the recent EU activities concerning the CESL would "have an important influence on the further development in the field of consumer protection law". Whether this is true or not will not be discussed any further here. Even though there has been no political commitment of the Commission behind this rather "incremental development" of general principles of civil law in the EU without having a formal legislative basis,[84] it comes close to what the former AG van Gerven called the "open method of convergence".[85]

6.21   The regulatory function of contract law has been broadly – some say too broadly[86] – elaborated in the CESL in its many mandatory provisions on B2C contracting, against very few on B2SMU transactions. However, this function is entirely dependent on the CESL being chosen by the stronger party, which will normally be the business side, not the consumer or the SMU. The "mandatory" regulation of the stronger party to a contract depends on its "self-subjection" to regulation – a somewhat paradoxical finding. This however does not make the CESL superfluous. It can be used as an instrument for better law-making or law application by the EU and Member States, especially their courts of law.[87] It could serve as a source of inspiration for the business and consumer community to negotiate "better contracting" practices. This approach could be the true value of the DCFR and of instruments that followed, including the CESL, as sort of guideline for "fair contracting", to be followed up by Commission reports on its practical impact, on *lacunae*, on the need for improvement of rules on digital content (Articles 100–105 CESL) and updating "black" and "grey" lists of unfair clauses (Articles 83–87 CESL).

---

[83]   Case 618/10 *Camino*, see *supra* 4.17.

[84]   For an comprehensive analysis of this development see M. Hesselink, 'The general principles of civil law: their nature, role and legitimacy', in: D. Leczykiewicz/S. Weatherill et al. (eds.), *The Involvement of EU Law in Private Law Relationships*, 2013, 131 at 175; M. Safjan/ P. Miklaszewicz, 'Horizontal effect of the general principles of EU law in the sphere of private law', ERPL 2010, 475; A. Hartkamp, *European Law and National Private Law*, 2012, 109; more critical however is S. Weatherill, 'The "principles of civil law" as a basis for interpreting the legislative *acquis*', ERCL 2010, 74; J. Basedow, 'The Court of Justice and private law: vacillations, general principles, and the architecture of the European judiciary', ERPL 2010, 443.

[85]   W. van Gerven, 'Needed: A Method of Convergence for Private Law', in: A. Furrer et al. (eds.), *Beiträge zum Europäischen Privatrecht*, 2006, 437, 456–460; W. van Gerven, 'Bringing (Private) Laws Closer to Each Other at the European Level', in: F. Cafaggi (ed.), *The Institutional Framework of European Private Law*, 2006, 37, 74–77.

[86]   See S. Grundmann, 'Kosten und Nutzen eines Europäischen Optionalen Kaufrechts', paper delivered at a special meeting of the German Zivilrechtslehrervereinigung on 20–21 April 2012 in Cologne, Archiv für die civilistische Praxis (AcP) 2012, 502.

[87]   See the discussion by M. Hesselink, 'A Toolbox for European Judges', in: A. Neergaard et al. (eds.), *European Legal Method*, 2011, 185, distinguishing European, traditional and political methods; criticised because of its immature legal character by H. Eidenmüller et al., JZ 2012, 259 at 288.

In linking parts 1 and 3 of the contract governance paradigm, the Commission could issue a *recommendation* as envisaged in option 3 of its Green Paper of 1 July 2010 and could regularly report on how that recommendation is or is not accepted in the "market for contracting". It should be remembered that even the ECJ seems to accept the indirect legal value of Commission recommendations in its *Alassini* case law.[88]

5. THE "POSITIVE PROPORTIONALITY" PRINCIPLE IN EU CIVIL LEGISLATION: TWO EXAMPLES

5.1. UNFAIR TERMS IN B2B CONTRACTS

6.22 Unfair terms in B2B contracts so far have been excluded from EU legislation, in particular Directive 93/13. An exception is Article 7 of the Late Payment Directive 2011/7/EU[89] on "unfair contractual terms and practices" – thus extending the earlier Directive 2000/35/EC[90] – which reads:

> "(1) Member States shall provide that a contractual term or practice relating to the date or period for payment, the rate of interest for late payment or the compensation for recovery costs is either unenforceable or gives raise to a claim for damages if it is grossly unfair to the creditor.
> In determining whether a contractual term or a practice is grossly unfair to the creditor [...] all circumstances of the case shall be considered, including
> – any gross deviation from good commercial practice, contrary to good faith and fair dealing;
> – the nature of the product or service;
> – whether the debtor has an objective reason tom deviate from the statutory rate of interest for late payment [...]
> (2) For the purpose of para 1, a contractual term or a practice which excludes interest for late payment shall be considered as grossly unfair.
> (3) For the purpose of para 1, a contractual terms or a practice which excludes compensation for recovery costs [...] shall be presumed to be unfair.
> (4) Member States shall ensure that, in the interest of creditors and competitors, adequate and effective means exist to prevent the continued use of contractual terms and practices which ae4 grossly unfair within the meaning of para 1."

Article 7 of Directive 2011/7, to be implemented by 16 March 2013, is the first legal extension of the concept of (grossly) unfair terms also to B2B transactions

---

[88]   Case C-317/08 *Rosalba Alassini et al v Telecom Italia* [2010] ECR I-2213, para 40.
[89]   [2011] OJ L 48/1; date of implementation by Member States: 16 March 2013 (Article 12).
[90]   [2000] OJ L 200/35.

(7.4), albeit in a much more limited scope than payment terms in favour of creditors; unfair terms that disadvantage the business debtor (for example a SMU) exclude liability and allow unilateral changes of contract terms are not included.

The concept of unfairness in B2B terms had already been developed in the DCFR in some detail in Article II. – 9:401 et seq.[91] Article II. – 9:405 defines the concept of "unfair terms" in B2B contracts as being if it "grossly deviates from good commercial practice, contrary to good faith and fair dealing", in contrast to B2C terms in Article II. – 9:403 which more or less follows Article 3(1) of Directive 93/13. Article II. – 9:402 contains a general transparency requirement whose breach only in B2C contracts means a term will be regarded as unfair.

The CESL has taken up some of the proposals of the DCFR. Under Article 81, the provisions on unfair terms are meant to be mandatory – obviously once the parties have opted into them, a rather contradictory consequence, as mentioned above. Article 86 then defines the meaning of "unfair" in contracts between traders:

> "1. In a contract between traders, a contract term is unfair for the purposes of this section only if
>   – it forms part of not individually negotiated terms […]
>   – it is of such nature that its use grossly deviates from good commercial practice, contrary to good faith and fair dealing
> 2. When assessing the unfairness of a contract for the purposes of this section, regard is to be had to
>   – the nature of what is to be provided under the contract
>   – the circumstances prevailing during the conclusion of the contract
>   – the other contract terms
>   – the terms of any other contract on which the contract depends."

It is not the objective of these lines to give an assessment of the proposals. Suffice it to say that they are limited to contracts between businesses SMUs as defined in Article 7 of the *chapeau* and relate to cross-border situations only.[92] This of course does not mean that they cannot be generalised into an EU legislation on unfair terms in B2B contracts as well, thus following the path of Directive 2011/7 with its limited scope only to creditor protection. Why should it not be extended to cases of business-debtors – in particular SMUs – who may also be in need of protection?

---

[91]   For a detailed explanation see DCFR, full edition 2009; critique had been voiced by H.-W. Micklitz/N. Reich, 'Unfair Terms in the DCFR', Juridica Int. 2008, 58 at 64.
[92]   See H.-W. Micklitz/N. Reich, *supra* note 53, paras 18–26.

5.2. IMPROVING THE COHERENCE OF B2C LEGISLATION WITH THE "HELP OF THE CESL": DIGITAL CONTRACTING

6.23   Provisions on digital content were first contained in the CRD 2011/83 (1.23): recital 19 explains the new EU policy with regard to digital content. Article 2(11) defines "'digital content' as data which are produced and supplied in digital form". Article 5(1)(g) and (h) includes information requirements for contracts other than off-premises or distance ones, while Article 6(r) and (s) includes similar ones for off-premises and distance contracts (2.7). Articles 14(4)(b) and 16(m) contain special rules concerning withdrawal from digital content contracts.

These consumer information provisions for digital content were taken over and extended, in particular with regard to conformity and remedies in case of non-conformity, by the CESL and were not contained in the feasibility study of the expert group which is the source of the CESL (6.12). This is an interesting development which however should not be limited by an opt-in mechanism. On the contrary: the "positive proportionality" principle, as explained above (6.5), requires that they are included in mandatory EU consumer legislation because there is a real need due to the expansion of digital content contracts,[93] thus continuing the path begun with the CRD.

Article 2(j) CESL is much more specific in its definition of digital content than the CRD:

> "[D]igital content means data which are produced and supplied in digital form, whether or not according to the buyer's specifications, including video, audio, picture or written digital content, digital games, software and digital content which makes it possible to personalise existing hardware of software; it excludes
> i)   financial services, including online banking services:
> ii) legal or financial advice provided in electronic form
> iii) electronic healthcare services
> iv) electronic communication services and networks, and associated facilities and service;
> v)   gambling;
> vi) the creation of new digital content and the amendment of existing digital content by consumers or any other interaction with the creation of other users."

Article 5(b) CESL seems to indicate that the EU legislator is treating the supply of digital content like software, music, video, electronic games – with or without consideration, whether supplied online or on a tangible medium like a CD or DVD – as a sort of "quasi-sales contract". This seems to be a departure from the classical approach of licencing of intellectual property rights, which was

---

[93]   N. Helberger et al., *Digital Consumers and the Law*, 2013, with rich documentation both of the legal and the technical aspects.

regarded as a contract of its own in most Member States.[94] It can be justified by the "commodification" (*Verdinglichung*) of digital content through modern technologies, in particular through downloading on the internet, which makes digital content a candidate for a standardised transaction similar to the traditional sales concept. There are some exceptions to this new approach, in particular financial services and gambling.

Article 100 CESL extends the concept of conformity expressly to "digital content". Article 102 contains rules on third-party claims, some of which are specific to digital content in B2C transactions, namely (with exceptions for digital content supplied without a price: Article 107):

> "– [...] the digital content [...] must be cleared of any right or not obviously unfounded claim of a third party [...] under the law of the contract or, in case of absence of such agreement, under the law of the buyer's residence, provided [...] the seller knew or could be expected to have known of at the time of the conclusion of the contract;
> – liability of the seller is excluded only in cases of positive knowledge of the consumer;
> – the provisions of this article may not be derogated from in B2C transactions."

It is not quite clear why the seller's obligation on conformity, which normally is a strict one, surprisingly depends on fault in contracts of digital content. It is also not clear how *use restrictions* on the consumer-buyer in general contract terms, allegedly justified by the so-called Copyright in the Information Society Directive 2001/29/EC,[95] which are quite frequent and extensive in contracts for the downloading of digital content, have to be evaluated using a "fairness" test.[96] Abuses seem to be frequent, but this needs to be studied separately, combining intellectual property with contract law concepts.[97]

Article 105(4) contains a specific mandatory clause on an obligation for updating of digital content, whereby the trader "must ensure that the digital content remains in conformity with the contract throughout the duration of the contract". This right to an update depends of course on its (express or implied) terms and therefore may simply be avoided by omitting such a clause in the contract, even though the consumer may have expectations of its inclusion.[98]

---

[94] See the study of P. Rott, 'Extension of the Proposed Consumer Rights Directive to Cover the Online Purchase of Digital Products', study for BEUC, 2009; U. Grüber, *Digitale Güter und Verbraucherschutz*, 2010; N. Helberger et al., *supra* note 93, at 21. See also the detailed "Amsterdam Study" on Future Rules for Digital Content Contracts, 2011, done for the Commission.

[95] [2011] OJ L 167/10.

[96] For a discussion of the problems under contract terms legislation in Germany, see U. Grüber, *supra* note 94, at 116. The US law situation which allows a near to complete control by copyright owners over users, in particular with regard to so called "virtual worlds" (games etc.), has been critically discussed in the excellent study by G. Lastowka, *Virtual Justice*, 2010, 93, 179 ff.

[97] For details see now N. Helberger et al., JCP 2013, 44.

[98] N. Helberger et al., *Digital Consumers and the Law*, 2013, 99 and 109.

The CESL does not seem to contain any specific remedies for non-performance of B2C contracts relating to the use of digital content even though the "digital buyer" enjoys a "right to require performance" under Article 110. Some remedies may relate to physical goods only, like repair. The right of termination in the event of non-insignificant non-performance is expressly extended also to "the supply of digital content" in Article 114(2) CESL.

If there has been a breach of information duties on digital content (Article 20(1)(g) and (h)), Article 29(1) CESL provides for liability of the trader "for any loss caused to the other party by such failure". This provision cannot be derogated from: Article 29(4). The concept of loss has been defined in Article 2(c) of the Proposal. On the other hand, once the professional seller has supplied the information as required, for example on lack of interoperability, the consumer will not have a remedy against the seller. The information requirement *de facto functions as an exclusion clause* under Article 99(3).[99]

Obviously, many other questions remain open, the most important being the relation between consumer and copyright law. The CESL does not contain any provisions concerning private copying of digital content; Member State legislation is divergent under Article 5(2)(b) of the Copyright in the Information Society Directive 2001/29/EC, where this is only optional.[100] Such limited protection of reasonable consumer expectations should be reconsidered.[101] Helberger et al. write:[102]

> "Arguably, the reasonable consumer expectations standard counterweighs the copyrightholder-centered norms on private copying that prevail in the copyright-law analysis."

In practice however, the real problem may lie with exclusion clauses which, according to Article 108 CESL, are forbidden in B2C contracts, but by an *argumentum e contrario* are allowed in B2B transactions. This makes the already difficult distinction between the types of transactions (6.13) even more crucial, but in the "virtual world" of the internet almost impossible to verify. It is therefore suggested that a presumption that digital content contracts come under the B2C provisions, unless the commercial character of the transaction is obvious, should be added.

As a result, it is submitted that a separate EU directive (or EU regulation) should be included in the consumer *acquis* regulating digital consumer content contracts, based on Directive 2011/83 and including (improved) provisions taken from the CESL as mentioned above. It is not suggested that the Consumer Sales

---

[99] N. Helberger et al., *supra* note 97, at 48.
[100] [2001] OJ L 167/10.
[101] N. Helberger et al., *supra* note 98, at 97.
[102] N. Helberger et al., *supra* note 97, at 47.

Directive 1999/44 should be amended because of the hybrid character of digital content contracts.

6. CONCLUSIONS ON THE PRINCIPLE OF PROPORTIONALITY AS AN INSTRUMENT OF LEGAL CONTROL AND SUPPORT OF EU MEASURES

6.24 The principle of proportionality has been developed into one of the most important yardsticks for controlling the compatibility of Member State measures with EU law in relation to fundamental freedoms and lately also fundamental rights, including mandatory contract law provisions that have a restrictive effect on those rights and freedoms. Similar criteria should be applied to Union measures to decide whether they are "necessary" to implementing fundamental freedoms and EU fundamental rights, despite the generous "obvious inappropriateness" test applied by the ECJ. Such a strict application of the proportionality principle on EU civil law, particularly contract law, measures will have a dual impact:

- on the *negative* side, it puts into doubt any EU measure to codify contract law beyond a strict necessity test, including recent efforts to create an optional EU CESL, as criticised by this author; however,
- on the *positive* side, it requires EU action in areas where necessary in the interest of the internal market and/or consumer protection, for example regulating unfair terms in B2B relations and with regard to harmonised provisions on digital content in B2C contracting (in a broad sense).

CHAPTER 7

AN EMERGING PRINCIPLE OF GOOD FAITH AND OF A PROHIBITION OF ABUSE OF RIGHTS?

Contents

Bibliography 189
1. Some misunderstandings about good faith in contract law:
   elements of a duty of loyal cooperation in contracting 190
2. Good faith in commercial law settings 193
3. Directive 93/13 on unfair terms 195
   3.1. The unclear unfairness test 195
   3.2. Consequences of unfairness. 200
   3.3. An EU-specific black or grey list of unfair terms 201
4. Absence of good faith obligations for the bank in B2C financial
   services 202
5. "Co-responsibility" as an indirect good faith-obligation: some
   examples 203
6. Elements of good faith in recent soft law initiatives. 206
7. Relevance of Article 54 of the Charter to an EU concept of abuse
   of rights? 208
8. Conclusion: good faith on the move? 211

Bibliography

R. Brownsword/N. Hird/G. Howells, *Good Faith in Contract: Concept and Context*, 1999; C. Calliess/M. Ruffert (eds.), *EUV-AEUV – Das Verfassungsrecht der EU mit Europäischer Grundrechtscharta, Kommentar*, 4th ed. 2011; O. Cherednychenko, 'The legal matrix for retail investment services in the EUI: where is the individual investor', in: J. Devenny/M. Kenny (eds.), *Consumer Credit, Debt, and Investment in Europe*, 2012, 253; O. Cherednychenko, 'The Regulation of Retail Investment Services in the EU: Towards the Improvement of Investor Rights?', JCP 2010, 403; H. Collins (ed.), *Standard Term Contracts in Europe, A Basis and a Challenge to European Contract Law*, 2008; R.D. Cooter/H.-B. Schäfer, *Solomon's Knot – How Law Can End the Poverty of Nations*, 2013; S. Grundmann, *European Company Law*, 2nd ed. 2012; S. Grundmann/D. Mazeaud (eds.), *General Clauses and Standards in European Contract Law: Comparative Law, EC Law, and Contract Law Codification*, 2006; M. Hesselink, 'The Concept of Good Faith', in: A. Hartkamp et al. (eds.),

Towards A European Civil Code, 4ᵗʰ ed. 2011, 619; M. Hesselink, 'The General Principles of Civil Law', in: D. Leczykiewicz/S. Weatherill (eds.), *The Involvement of EU Law in Private Law Relationships*, 2013, 131: N. Jansen, 'Legal Pluralism in Europe: National Laws, European Legislation, and Non-legislative Codifications', in: L. Niglia, *Pluralism and European Private Law*, 2013, 109–132; M. Mekki/M. Kloepfer-Pelèse, 'Good faith and fair dealing in the DCFR', ERCL 2008, 338; A. Metzger, 'Abuse of Law in EU Private Law: A (Re-)Construction from Fragments', in: R. de la Feria/S. Vogenauer (eds.), *Prohibition of Abuse of Law – A New Principle of EU Law?*, 2011, 235; H.-W. Micklitz, *The Politics of Judicial Cooperation*, 2005; H.-W. Micklitz, 'Reforming Unfair Contract Terms Legislation in Consumer Contracts', ERCR 2010, 347; H.-W. Micklitz/N. Reich/ P. Rott, *Understanding EU Consumer Law*, 2009; L. Niglia, *Pluralism and European Private Law*, 2013; F. Randolph/J. Davey, *The European Commercial Agency Law*, 3ʳᵈ ed. 2010; N. Reich, 'The Tripartite Function of Modern Contract Law in Europe: Enablement, Regulation, Information', in: F. Werro/ T. Probst (eds.), *Le droit privé Suisse face au droit communautaire européen*, 2004, 145–172; N. Reich, 'The interrelation between rights and duties in EU Law: Reflections on the state of liability law in the multilevel governance system of the Union – Is there a need for a more coherent approach in European private law?', YEL, 2010, 112; N. Reich/H.-W. Micklitz, 'Unfair Terms in the DCFR', Juridica Int. 2008, 58; G. Teubner, 'Legal Irritants: Good Faith in British Law or How Unifying Law Ends Up in New Divergencies', ModLR 1998, 1; T. Tridimas, *The General Principles of EU Law*, 2ⁿᵈ ed. 2006; S. Vogenauer/J. Kleinheisterkamp (eds.), *PICL Commentary*, 2009; S. Weatherill, 'The "principles of civil law" as a basis for interpreting the legislative *acquis*', ERCL 2010, 74; S. Whittaker, 'Assessing the Fairness of Contract Terms', ZEuP 2004, 75; R. Zimmermann/ S. Whittaker (eds.), *Good Faith in European Contract Law*, 2000.

1. SOME MISUNDERSTANDINGS ABOUT GOOD FAITH IN CONTRACT LAW: ELEMENTS OF A DUTY OF LOYAL COOPERATION IN CONTRACTING

7.1 The concept of "good faith" in contract law has been the subject of extensive legal writing in the Member States of the EU. Comparative lawyers usually distinguish between the continental approach where the general clause of good faith is part of the general law of obligations, including contracting[1], and the attitude in common law, which seems to ignore such a general concept. As a sort of "proof", Hesselink cites a prominent English judge as having said:[2]

> "In many civil law systems, and perhaps in most legal systems outside the common law world, the law of obligations recognises and enforces an overriding principle that in making and carrying out contracts parties should act in good faith [...]

---

[1] For French law, a rather cautious formulation with particular importance to consumer contracts has been given by J. Calais-Auloy, in: S. Grundmann/D. Mazeaud (eds.), *General Clauses and Standards in European Contract Law*, 2006, 189.

[2] M. Hesselink, 'The General Principles of Civil Law', in: D. Leczykiewicz/S. Weatherill (eds.), *The Involvement of EU Law in Private Law Relationships*, 2013, 173 at note 157, citing Bingham LJ in *Interfoto Picture Library Ltd v Stiletto Visual Programmes Ltd* [1989] QB 433.

English law has, characteristically, committed itself to no such overriding principle but has developed piecemeal solutions in response to demonstrated problems of unfairness."

In this context, it comes as a surprise that the ECJ, in the *Messner* case (5.9), refers to the "principles of civil law, such as those of good faith". As far as German contract law is concerned, this is of course nothing surprising, but for an English lawyer it must have been quite shocking and remained unexplained how far this refers merely to applicable, i.e. German, law or EU civil law in general, which is the object of this study.[3] I have tried to limit the impact of this judgment, against the overarching criticism of Hesselink, to the case before the ECJ; in this case the ECJ only authorised the German court to impose upon the consumer an obligation under the German rules of good faith which was not expressly included in the relevant Distance Contracts Directive, but which now has been put into Article 14(2) of the new Consumer Rights Directive 2011/83 (2.1). I am not aware of later references by the ECJ to a general principle of good faith in EU civil law. But of course this would not exclude its autonomous development once EU civil law becomes more coherent and comprehensive.

Another distinction draws on the ambiguity of the concept of "good faith" itself: it may be used in a more *objective sense* in modifying existing rigidities of contract law, for example by allowing a debtor who is unable to pay his debt because of circumstances external to him a defence of hardship, *rebus sic stantibus*, or even social *force majeure* as advocated by Wilhelmsson;[4] on the other hand "good faith" may refer to such rather subjective and individual concepts as abuse of rights or unjust enrichment, as was seen in the discussion on avoiding "over-protection" by mandatory rules of EU consumer or employment law (5.9–5.10). Still other authors like Hesselink[5] regard it as an authorisation for judicial law-making without being a norm as such, following the traditional English concept of equity.

In a similar sense, Zimmermann and Whittaker write:[6]

"The recognition of a principle of good faith does not require a particular result in the circumstances, it merely allows the possibility of a particular result, leaving the court to decide whether or not it should be brought about. From this perspective it could indeed be argued there would be no substantive legal change were English or Scots law to accept a general principle of good faith. [… A]ll legal systems included in

---

3   S. Weatherill, 'The "principles of civil law" as a basis for interpreting the legislative acquis', ERCL 2010, 74.

4   T. Wilhelmsson, 'Varieties of Welfarism in European Contract Law', ELJ 2004, 712 at 730.

5   M. Hesselink, in: A. Hartkamp et al. (eds.), *Towards a European Civil Code*, 4th ed. 2011, 687, 700.

6   R. Zimmermann/S. Whittaker, *Good Faith*, 2000, 653, referring to the cases studied (emphasis added).

our study moved away or are in the process of moving away from a paradigm of contract which focuses almost exclusively on the autonomy of parties. Instead, *we find a growing significance given to party loyalty, the protection of reliance, (occasional) duties of cooperation, the need to consider the other party's interest or the substantive fairness of the contract."*

This is of course an important statement suggesting a *rapprochement* of different jurisdictions in the EU with regard to the recognition of a general "good faith" principle that may emerge; and this will also be seen later in the many "soft law" initiatives of European contract law as part of an *acquis commun* (7.14). But is the "good faith" principle already part of an *acquis communautaire*?

7.2 The quotation from the study by Zimmermann and Whittaker, which was based on the different yet converging approaches and concepts of good faith in civil and common law jurisdictions, can serve as a good starting point for this study devoted exclusively to EU civil law, as defined in the introduction. In order to demonstrate this approach to an (objective) concept of good faith as a *duty of loyal cooperation* in recent EU civil law, I will try to use a "bottom-up" approach, looking at existing EU law provisions – mostly directives and their (still rather scant) interpretation by the ECJ – where the concept of good faith plays a prominent and distinctive role (7.3–7.8); the concept is nevertheless absent in an area where it seems particularly important, namely financial services (7.9–7.10). For a more *subjective* understanding of "good faith", it will be linked to some existing case law, in particular of the ECJ, to find out whether and how far case law can be used to make more nuanced the application of EU civil law in areas where there seems to be a shortfall because of legislation that is too rigid and formalised. It will also be shown that similar results – namely the establishment and enforcement of a duty of loyal cooperation in civil law relations under EU law – does not necessarily require a reference to the term "good faith", but can be attained using other concepts like "co-responsibility" of the consumer-creditor in adjusting the obligations of the debtor in an action for civil liability (7.11–7.14). Section 6 (7.15–7.17) will briefly mention the different "soft law" initiatives where the concept of "good faith" – usually reinforced by the requirement of "fair dealing" – has been used quite extensively in a sort of principled *acquis commun*, supplementing a somewhat unsatisfactory *acquis communautaire* (0.10). A conclusion brings the discussion to an end with a critical overview (7.21) of the present patchwork of the "good faith" principle in EU law.

2. GOOD FAITH IN COMMERCIAL LAW SETTINGS

7.3 The older Directive 86/653/EEC on Commercial Agents[7] contains an explicit "good faith" duty of loyal cooperation between the agent and the principal, expressed in Articles 3 and 4. Article 3 reads:

> "1. In performing his activities a commercial agent must look after his principal's interests and act dutifully and in good faith.
> 2. In particular, a commercial agent must:
>   (a) make proper efforts to negotiate and, where appropriate, conclude the transactions he is instructed to take care of;
>   (b) communicate to his principal all the necessary information available to him;
>   (c) comply with reasonable instructions given by his principal."

A similar duty of good faith is put upon the principal in Article 4.

This duty is particularly important in determining whether the agent has a right to payment of an indemnity or compensation according to Article 17 under certain circumstances, a provision which cannot be excluded even in international agency contracts according to the controversial *Ingmar* case of the ECJ,[8] and which has been subject to some litigation before the ECJ that will not be discussed here. Article 18 allows an exclusion of the liability of the principal under certain restrictive conditions including a violation of the agent's good faith obligation, which the Court had to decide on in the *Volvo* case.[9] Unfortunately the Court did not provide a more detailed analysis of this mutual good faith obligation of the parties to an agency contract, neither in the *Volvo* case nor in the earlier *Honeyvem* case.[10] In *Poseidon*,[11] the Court reiterated the mutual good faith obligation of the parties:

> "It should be noted in this connection that, as is clear from Article 1 (2) of the Directive, a commercial agency contract is characterized in particular by the fact that the agent, defined as a self-employed intermediary, is invested by the principal with continuing authority to negotiate. That is clear from several provisions of the Directive especially Articles 3 and 4 on the obligation of the parties to act dutifully and in good faith towards each other."

---

7   [1986] OJ L 382/17.
8   C-381/98 *Ingmar GB Ltd v Eaton Leonard Technologies Inc.* [2000] ECR I-9305.
9   C-203/09 *Volvo* [2010] ECR-10721.
10 Case C-465/04 *Honeyvem Informazioni Commerciali v Mariealla de Zoti* [2006] ECR I-2879; see S. Grundmann, in: S. Grundmann/D. Mazeaud (eds.), *General Clauses and Standards in European Contract Law*, 2006, 148; and the comment from a common law perspective in F. Randolph/J. Davey, *The European Law of Commercial Agency*, 3rd ed. 2010, 56, leaving this to Member State law.
11 Case C-3/04 *Poseidon Chartering NV v Marianne Zeeship et al* [2006] ECR I-2505, para 24.

A more explicit statement on the duties of the agent under the good faith clause can be found in the opinion of AG Bot of 3 July 2010 in *Volvo*. He wrote:[12]

> "[A] commercial agent is required by Article 3 of the Directive to fulfil certain obligations. Thus, the commercial agent must carry out his mission and must report on that performance. The commercial agent's obligation to carry out his mission has three aspects, namely, that the agent must comply with his principal's instructions, act with diligence and conduct himself loyally. With regard to compliance with the instructions given to him by his principal, it must be observed that, although the commercial agent generally enjoys considerable freedom in carrying out his mission since, by definition, he is a self-employed professional, he is bound to comply with mandatory instructions concerning certain aspects of his mission which he may receive from his principal concerning, for example, the conditions governing contracts to be concluded with customers. Moreover, a commercial agent must show diligence in the accomplishment of his mission, that is to say, he must carry out his contract as a 'good professional'. He would fail to fulfil that obligation, for example, were he to fail to visit customers, be insufficiently active, make patchy efforts at promotion, whether in space or in time, or maintain an unsatisfactory organisational policy. Lastly, a commercial agent is bound by an *obligation of loyalty towards his principal*. In that regard, he must ensure that information concerning the principal's commercial strategy remains confidential and he cannot agree to represent an undertaking which competes with that of his principal without the latter's agreement. In addition to the obligation to carry out his mission, a commercial agent is required to report on his performance to his principal. That obligation consists in keeping the principal informed of the results of his mission and communicating to his principal all the necessary information available to him. For example, the agent must provide all useful information concerning the market situation, including competitors present on that market."

Since the Court reached nearly the same conclusion in the *Volvo* case as the AG did, it can be presumed that his opinion also expresses that of the Court. Quite obviously, this strict interpretation of the loyalty obligation is a result of the particularly close relationship between the principal and the agent which does not exist in "ordinary" commercial transactions, which according both to the common and continental law of commercial agents has a fiduciary character[13] and therefore cannot be made more generally applicable beyond its narrow scope of application to develop a general principle of "good faith" in contracting.

It is also an open question whether the good faith obligation can be extended by analogy to similar fiduciary relationships like franchising contracts and other distribution agreements. There is no ECJ case law available yet. EU competition law plays a certain role in the regulation of these types of "vertical cooperation agreements" but is more concerned with efficiency arguments than with

---

12   C-203/09 *Volvo* [2010] ECR-10721, paras 39–45 (emphasis added).
13   F. Randolph/J. Davey, *supra* note 10, at 55.

determining any good faith obligation of the parties (1.16). Since Directive 86/653 is a minimum directive, Member States may extend it to cover services or to supplement the (seemingly alternative) remedies of Article 17, thereby creating "overriding mandatory provisions" in the sense of Article 7 of the Brussels Convention (now Article 9(1) and (2) of the Brussels Regulations 44/2001) to be applied by the *lex fori*, according to a recent opinion of AG Wahl.[14]

7.4   Another rather unusual application of the good faith principle to commercial relations has been the recently recast Directive 2011/7/EU on late payments in commercial transactions (6.22), as a successor to the earlier Directive 2000/35/EC.[15] In contrast to the latter, it contains a clause on "grossly unfair terms" which are contrary to "good faith and fair dealing". This clause is supposed to protect the creditor in a B2B situation, not the debtor, against "grossly unfair" exemption clauses, unilateral cancellation or increase-of-prices clauses and the like. It has been suggested that this concept of good faith should be extended to other commercial contracts, but this must be done by specific EU legislation. A first recognition of this need has been the introduction of such a provision into the Draft Regulation of a Common European Sales Law (CESL) which however has not yet been enacted and where the parties must particularly agree to its application, if one of them is an SMU (6.13). There seems to be no possibility at the moment to extend this concept to a "general principle of EU civil law".

3.   DIRECTIVE 93/13 ON UNFAIR TERMS

3.1. THE UNCLEAR UNFAIRNESS TEST

7.5   Article 3(1) of the Unfair Terms Directive refers expressly to the concept of "good faith" as a criterion for determining the unfairness of a contractual term in a B2C contract which has not been individually negotiated.[16] It reads:

> "A contractual term which has not been individually negotiated shall be regarded as unfair if, contrary to the requirement of good faith, it causes a significant imbalance in the parties' rights and obligations arising under the contract, to the detriment of the consumer."

---

[14]   Case C-184/12 *UNAMAR v Navigation Maritime Bulgare*, opinion of AG Wahl of 15 May 2013, para 57.

[15]   [2000] OJ L 2000/35.

[16]   For details see H.-W. Micklitz/N. Reich/P. Rott, *Understanding EU Consumer Law*, 2009, para 3.20.

Can this be regarded as a recognition of a general principle of good faith, at least in consumer contracting, because of the wide scope of application of the Directive, including contract terms on goods and services contracts, even those under public law within the limits of Article 1(2)?[17] Does this principle have an autonomous meaning in EU civil law, like the other principles discussed in this book? This is a highly debated question in EU law, made more difficult by the rather confusing case law of the ECJ which is to some extent the result of the ambiguities of Directive 93/13 itself and which only lately seems to have become more clear.[18] On the one hand, recital 16 refers to just such an autonomous concept:

> "Whereas [...] the requirement of good faith may be satisfied by the seller or supplier where he deals fairly and equitably with the other party whose legitimate interests he has to take into account."

Somewhat contradicting this recital, in its highly publicised *Freiburger Kommunalbauten* judgment,[19] the Court seemed to suggest that this is a concept to be determined exclusively by national law, based on the strong opinion in this vein of AG Geelhoed of 25 September 2005, who argued:[20]

> "The jurisdiction of the Court to interpret Community law does not, however, extend to the interpretation of contractual terms at issue in a specific case before a national court. After all, [...] this does not involve a question of Community law."

This statement was more or less repeated by the Court in its judgment of 1 April 2004:[21]

> "It should be noted in that regard that in referring to concepts of good faith and significant imbalance between the rights and obligations of the parties, Article 3 of the Directive merely defines in a general way the factors that render unfair a contractual term that has not been individually negotiated [...] The Annex to which Article 3(3) of the Directive refers only contains an indicative and non-exhaustive list of terms which may be regarded as unfair. A term appearing in the list need not necessarily be considered unfair and, conversely, a term that does not appear in the list may none the less be regarded as unfair [...] As to the question whether a particular term in a contract is, or is not, unfair, Article 4 of the Directive provides that the answer should be reached taking into account the nature of the goods or services for which the contract was concluded and by referring, at the time of

---

[17]   See H.-W. Micklitz/N. Reich/P. Rott, *supra* note 16, at 3.15, and now ECJ case C-92/11 *RWE Vertrieb v Verbraucherzentrale NRW* [2013] ECR I-(21.03.2013) para 31: a mere reference clause to mandatory provisions applying to other even though related types of contracts does not qualify for the exemption under Article 1(2) of Directive 93/13.

[18]   H.-W. Micklitz/N. Reich/P. Rott, *supra* note 16, at 3.1–3.6.

[19]   Case C-237/02 *Freiburger Kommunalbauten v Hofstetter* [2004] ECR I-3403.

[20]   Ibid., para 26.

[21]   Ibid., paras 19–22.

conclusion of the contract, to all the circumstances attending the conclusion of the contract. It should be pointed out in that respect that the consequences of the term under the law applicable to the contract must also be taken into account. This requires that consideration be given to the national law. It follows, as the Advocate General has observed at point 25 of his Opinion, that in the context of its jurisdiction under Article 234 EC to interpret Community law, the Court may interpret general criteria used by the Community legislature in order to define the concept of unfair terms. However, it should not rule on the application of these general criteria to a particular term, which must be considered in the light of the particular circumstances of the case in question."

In the case referred to it by the German BGH concerning the unfairness of a prepayment clause in a construction contract secured by a bank guarantee, the ECJ left it to the national court to determine its unfairness, a result which seems to be correct as far as the division of competences under the preliminary reference procedure is concerned. On the other hand, the Court could and should have given interpretation guidelines to the national court concerning the concept of unfairness itself in relation to the two criteria of "good faith" and "imbalance", in particular whether the EU legislator used an *autonomous* concept of unfairness independent of Member state law. The autonomy of EU civil law concepts like "contract" and "tort" had been underlined by the Court in other civil law cases, in particular those interpreting the Brussels Convention of 1980.[22]

The Court could also have insisted on the importance of whether the prepayment clause does not pose a risk to the consumer of losing his payment in the event of the supplier's bankruptcy because of the additional bank guarantee. The Court did not do so, thus rejecting any harmonising effect of the directive. As a result, the concept of "good faith" continues to differ between Member State jurisdictions: a more procedural concept seems to have prevailed in English law,[23] while continental law seems to prefer a more substantive test based on a balancing of interests between the parties of a B2C contract (5.4–5.8).

7.6 On the other hand, concerning jurisdiction clauses, the Court has been rather critical and seems to regard them as unfair *per se*, a view first developed in the *Océano* case[24] cited with approval in *Freiburger Kommunalbauten*:

"It is true that in [...] *Océano Grupo Editorial* [...] the Court held that a term, drafted in advance by the seller, the purpose of which is to confer jurisdiction in respect of all disputes arising under the contract on the court in the territorial jurisdiction of

---

22   For an overview see N. Reich et al., *Understanding EU Internal Market Law*, 3rd ed. forthcoming, para 2.17.

23   H.-W. Micklitz, *The Politics of Judicial Cooperation*, 2005, 401, referring the *First National Bank* case and the judgment of (what was then) the House of Lords ([2001] UKHL 52, 481, *per* Lord Bingham); a similar "pre-conception" (*Vorverständnis*) can be found in the more recent *Abbey National* case, discussed *supra* 5.5.

24   Case C-240–244/99 *Océano Groupo ed. et al v Quintero et al* [2001] ECR I-4941, para 23.

which the seller has his principal place of business, satisfies all the criteria necessary for it to be judged unfair for the purposes of the Directive. Nevertheless, that assessment was reached in relation to a term which was solely to the benefit of the seller and contained no benefit in return for the consumer. Whatever the nature of the contract, it thereby undermined the effectiveness of the legal protection of the rights which the Directive affords to the consumer. It was thus possible to hold that the term was unfair without having to consider all the circumstances in which the contract was concluded and without having to assess the advantages and disadvantages that that term would have under the national law applicable to the contract."

Quite contrary to what it had said before, the Court here seems to accept an autonomous concept of unfairness based on good faith, which is followed, as suggested in this study, by a duty to loyal cooperation of the parties in B2C contracts; it is also related to the EU civil law principle of effective judicial protection (4.15). This principle has been confirmed in many later cases and most clearly in *Penzügyi Lizing*[25] as follows:

"It must be observed that the term which the national court is examining in the main proceedings, like a term whose purpose is to confer jurisdiction in respect of all disputes arising under the contract on the court in the territorial jurisdiction of which the seller or supplier has his principal place of business, obliges the consumer to submit to the exclusive jurisdiction of a court which may be a long way from his domicile. This may make it difficult for him to enter an appearance. In the case of disputes concerning limited amounts of money, the costs relating to the consumer's entering an appearance could be a deterrent and cause him to forgo any legal remedy or defence. Such a term thus falls within the category of terms which have the object or effect of excluding or hindering the consumer's right to take legal action, a category referred to in subparagraph (q) of paragraph 1 of the Annex to the Directive [...] In addition, such a term enables the seller or supplier to deal with all the litigation relating to his trade, business or profession in one court, which is not the one within whose jurisdiction the consumer lives, which makes it easier for the seller or supplier to arrange to enter an appearance and makes it less onerous for him to do so."

Later cases are for instance concerned with unilateral price increases:[26]

"[T]he jurisdiction of the Court of Justice extends to the interpretation of the concept of 'unfair term' used in Article 3(1) of the Directive and in the annex thereto, and to the criteria which the national court may or must apply when examining a contractual term in the light of the provisions of the Directive, bearing in mind that it is for that court to determine, in the light of those criteria, whether a particular contractual term is actually unfair in the circumstances of the case [...] It is thus

---

25   Case C-137/08 *Penzügyi Lizing v F. Schneider* [2010] ECR I-10847, paras 54–55.
26   Case C-472/10 *Nemzeti F.H. v Invitel* [2012] ECR I-(27.04.2012), paras 22–28; see also the *RWE* case, *supra* 4.8.

clear that the Court of Justice must limit itself, in its response, to providing the referring court with the indications which the latter must take into account in order to assess whether the term at issue is unfair [...] If the content of the annex does not suffice in itself to establish automatically the unfair nature of a contested term, it is nevertheless an essential element on which the competent court may base its assessment as to the unfair nature of that term. [...] Consequently, in the assessment of the 'unfair' nature of a term, within the meaning of Article 3 of the Directive, the possibility for the consumer to foresee, on the basis of clear, intelligible criteria, the amendments, by a seller or supplier, of the GBC [general business terms of the supplier] with regard to the fees connected to the service to be provided is of fundamental importance."

It seems that the Court is recognising, against the somewhat dismissive rejection in *Freiburger Kommunalbauten*, that the terms "unfairness" and "good faith" emerge as general principle of EU civil law of contracting at least in B2C relations, and that the restrictive approach of UK courts can no longer be upheld, at least insofar as their merely procedural interpretation of Directive 93/13 is concerned.

This has been confirmed in the recent *Aziz* judgment of 14 March 2013 (4.5):[27]

"With regard to the question of the circumstances in which such an imbalance arises 'contrary to the requirement of good faith', having regard to the sixteenth recital in the preamble to the directive [...] the national court must assess for those purposes whether the seller or supplier, dealing fairly and equitably with the consumer, could reasonably assume that the consumer would have agreed to such a term in individual contract negotiations."

This confirms the development of an *emerging autonomous concept of "good faith" of EU law*, depending on a case-by-case assessment – which must be done by the national court according to a "reasonable supplier standard" – of whether the consumer would have agreed to the term. That means that, as already formulated in recital 16, the supplier, in a contract situation where there has been no "individual negotiation" in the sense of Article 3(2) of Directive 93/13, must take reasonable account of the consumer's ability to bargain. He cannot simply pursue his own business interests of contractual efficiency against the legitimate expectations of the consumer. In this sense and against the critique of Teubner,[28] "good faith" is not an "irritant" but can become an integral principle of EU civil law – although in the narrow sense as defined above as *acquis communautaire*, not as *acquis commun* (0.10).

---

[27]   Case C-415/11 *Mohamed Aziz v Catalunyacaixa* [2013] ECR I-(14.04.2013), para 69.

[28]   G. Teubner, 'Legal Irritants: Good Faith in British Law or How Unifying Law Ends Up in New Divergencies', ModLR 1998, 1.

Whether this emerging principle in consumer contracting can be extended to commercial relations is still an open question, but first signs seem to be appearing on the legal horizon, as we will see later (7.9).

3.2. CONSEQUENCES OF UNFAIRNESS

7.7   Another important element for an autonomous EU civil law principle on good faith has been the considerations of how to determine the consequences of an unfair term in a B2C contract. Can the consumer, based on his subjective preferences, reject the contract as a whole if it contains an unfair term, or must he accept a continuation of the contract without the unfair terms, if this is still commercially viable for the supplier? A subjective approach seems to be, from the point of view of the consumer, more consumer friendly, whereas an objective approach is more in line with a duty of loyal cooperation as part of the general good faith obligation, creating obligations not only for businesses but also (to a limited extent) for the consumer. The Court in *Pereničová*,[29] following the opinion of AG Trstenjak of 29 November 2011, clearly preferred the second reading, which seems to confirm the approach developed in this book of taking "good faith" to contain an overall duty to loyal cooperation of contract partners in B2C situations:

> "As regards the criteria for assessing whether a contract can indeed continue to exist without the unfair terms, it must be noted that both the wording of Article 6(1) of Directive 93/13 and the requirements concerning the legal certainty of economic activities plead in favour of an objective approach in interpreting that provision, so that, as the Advocate General observes in points 66 to 68 of her Opinion, the situation of one of the parties to the contract, in this case the consumer, cannot be regarded as the decisive criterion determining the fate of the contract Consequently, Article 6(1) of Directive 93/13 cannot be interpreted as meaning that, when assessing whether a contract containing one or more unfair terms can continue to exist without those terms, the court hearing the case can base its decision solely on a possible advantage for the consumer of the annulment of the contract as a whole."

AG Trstenjak wrote:[30]

> "The arguments advanced in connection with the need to uphold the principle of the freedom of the parties to arrange their own affairs and to guarantee that contractual relations between sellers or suppliers and consumers are balanced must, finally, be assessed in the light of a further objective of the directive. It should be remembered that, as its first recital shows, Directive 93/13 was adopted with the aim of progressively establishing the internal market. As can be seen from its second and

---

29   Case C-453/10 *Pereničová and Pereni v SOS financ* [2012] ECR I-(15.03.2012), paras 32–33.
30   Ibid., para 67.

third recitals, it seeks to remove the marked divergences in national legislation on unfair terms in contracts with consumers. Besides affording the consumer better protection, the legislature intended, according to the seventh recital, to promote commercial activity in the area of application of the directive ('sellers of goods and suppliers of services will thereby be helped in their task of selling goods and supplying services, both at home and throughout the internal market'). However, a commercial activity is capable of developing only where economic operators are guaranteed legal certainty. That includes the protection of their confidence in the endurance of contractual relations. An arrangement in which the validity of a contract as a whole depends on the interests of only one party is not only incapable of promoting that confidence, but may even unsettle it in the long term. Just as the willingness of sellers or suppliers to make contracts with consumers would be likely to decline as a consequence, so might the goal of establishing the internal market be frustrated. Article 6 of Directive 93/13 takes that into account by confining itself to ensuring a balance in contractual relations."

3.3. AN EU-SPECIFIC BLACK OR GREY LIST OF UNFAIR TERMS

7.8   Within this emerging autonomous concept of "unfairness", the Court seems to be developing a black or grey list of terms specific to EU civil law which (with the facts to be determined by the national court) will be regarded as unfair. The list so far provides a reference point without having binding force as foreseen in the recent Articles 84 and 85 CESL (6.13). To some extent this EU-specific concept of unfairness implements the above mentioned general principles of EU civil law, to name just a few:

– the principle of "framed autonomy" to protect the weaker party against unilateral renunciation of civil rights (2.8);
– the principle of non-discrimination requiring unisex tariffs in insurance (3.17);
– the principle of effectiveness by blacklisting "jurisdiction clauses" (4.15) and grey-listing a limitation of defences available to the defaulting debtor in mortgage contracts (4.17);
– the need to balance opposing interests in clauses relating to price elements in a pre-formulated contract term (5.8); and
– strict limits of unilateral price increases (7.5).

4. ABSENCE OF GOOD FAITH OBLIGATIONS FOR THE BANK IN B2C FINANCIAL SERVICES

7.9   EU civil law has so far only influenced the margins of the contracting of financial services. Article 22(3) of the Consumer Credit Directive 2008/48[31] contains a rather general rule forbidding any circumvention:

> "Member States shall [...] ensure that the provisions they adopt in implementation of this Directive cannot be circumvented as a result of the way in which agreements are formulated, in particular by integrating draw downs or credit agreements falling within the scope of this Directive into credit agreements the character or purpose of which would make it possible to avoid its application."

However, the creditor does not have any good faith obligations vis-à-vis the consumer, for instance concerning assessing his creditworthiness. Article 8(1) limits this to information obtained "where appropriate" from the consumer or "where necessary" by consulting a database. The Directive does not set out any consequences in the event of the bank's failure to comply with Article 8; nor does it contain any precise and unconditional obligation on the bank which could serve as a basis for its direct effect because of its imprecise formulation that the obligation exists only "where appropriate" or "where necessary". Recital 26 stresses the importance of the creditor not engaging in irresponsible lending or giving out credit without prior assessment of creditworthiness, but rather leaves sanctions to the Member States and does not contain any civil law remedies in case of a violation of this (imprecise) obligation. At the same time, consumers are reminded "to act with prudence and to respect their contractual obligations". The original proposals in the draft on responsible lending have been completely watered down and replaced by requirements simply to inform the consumer.[32]

7.10   Concerning the marketing of investment services in the EU, Article 19(1) of the Markets for Financial Instruments Directive 2004/39/EC (MIFID)[33] contains a general clause on "Conduct of Business Obligations", which could be interpreted as containing a good faith obligation on the provider (the investment firm, normally a bank, in the vocabulary of the directive) vis-à-vis the (non-professional, namely private) retail client:

> "Member States shall require that, when providing investment services [...] an investment firm act honestly, fairly, and professionally in the best interest of its clients."

---

31   [2008] OJ L 133/67.
32   For a critique see H.-W. Micklitz/N. Reich/P. Rott, *supra* note 16, at para 5.16.
33   [2004] OJ L 145/1; see S. Grundmann, *supra* note 10, at 142 and 149; O. Cherednyshenko, 'The Regulation of Retail Investment Services in the EU: Towards the Improvement of Investor Rights?', JCP 2010, 355 at 406.

This was specified by secondary legislation in Article 26/27 of Commission Directive 2006/73/EC[34] with regard to so-called inducements and information to be given to clients. These provisions can be regarded as an *ex lege* good faith and fair dealing obligation on the investment firm vis-à-vis its clients. Unfortunately, this standard is not meant to be an EU-contractual one, but rather one to be implemented by supervisory authorities. Whether it becomes part of the bank's obligations in its contractual or pre-contractual relations with retail clients in the sense of Article 4(12) MIFID has to be determined by Member State law; the MIFID does not give any suggestions in this respect, even though it might be argued that contract law has to be interpreted in this sense.[35] In its recent *Genil*[36] judgment, the Court however ruled that:

> "It is for the internal legal order of each Member State to determine the contractual consequences where an investment firm offering an investment service fails to comply with the assessment requirements laid down in Article 19(4) and (5) of Directive 2004/39, subject to observance of the principles of equivalence and effectiveness."

5. "CO-RESPONSIBILITY" AS AN INDIRECT GOOD FAITH-OBLIGATION: SOME EXAMPLES

7.11   The case law of the ECJ has to some extent indirectly recognised a good faith obligation on the creditor–consumer in a B2C contract. The ECJ has referred to (general) principles of civil law in order to avoid a perceived "over-protection" of the consumer (5.9) and to curb any eventual misuse of the right to free movement by the worker through an "abuse of rights" (5.10). According to the *Weber-Putz* judgment of the ECJ (4.18),[37] in consumer sales law under Article 3 of Directive 99/44 the consumer-purchaser of a product that does not comply with its specifications has a right to have that product replaced with one that is compliant at the seller's expense, but only "to an amount proportionate to

---

34   [2006] OJ 241/26.

35   O. Cherednychenko, 'The legal matrix for retail investment services in the EUI: where is the individual investor', in: J. Devenny/M. Kenny (eds.), *Consumer Credit, Debt, and Investment in Europe*, 2012, 253; O. Cherednychenko, JCP 2010, 409 (indirect effect with examples from the Netherlands, Germany and the UK); N. Reich, 'The interrelation between rights and duties in EU Law: Reflections on the state of liability law in the multilevel governance system of the Union – Is there a need for a more coherent approach in European private law?', YEL 2010, 112 at 150–160; S. Grundmann, *European Company Law*, 2nd ed. 2012, 525.

36   C-604/11 *Genil et al v Bankinter et al* [2013] ECR I-(30.05.2013).

37   Joined Cases C-65/09 + C-87/09, *Gebr. Weber et al v J. Wittmer et al* [2011] ECR I-5257, critical comment A. Johnson/H. Unberath, CMLRev 2012, 793 at 804; despite methodological problems, the German Federal Court (Bundesgerichtshof – BGH) followed suit, BGH, VIII ZR 70/08 NJW 2012, 1073; the BGH however did not extend this principle to B2B transactions, VIII ZR 226/11 of 17.10.2012, EuZW 2013, 157.

the value the goods would have if there were no lack of conformity and the significance of the lack of conformity" (para 74).

It may be possible to extrapolate from this rather haphazard and to some extent inconsistent case law a general "good faith" obligation applicable not only to businesses, but also to the consumer, the worker party to a contract. It is however not clear whether this is a genuine EU civil law concept, or whether the ECJ merely wants to give Member State courts the possibility to apply their specific good faith and abuse of rights concepts to a situation which they regard as violating the principles of their own civil law. The tendency of this study is to widen the application of the "good faith" concept to be more general and EU-wide, at least in the case of a contract or a question of civil liability within the scope of EU law, whether primary or secondary.

7.12   Another example of an implicit recognition of the good faith principle has been the rule on "co-responsibility" as a limitation to an EU-granted right, for instance as a defence against a claim of damages against a Member State that has breached EU law. In *Brasserie*,[38] the Court insisted on the principle of full compensation including "pure" economic loss. It has also made clear that interest must be paid.[39] Member States may however require that the injured party be reasonably diligent in limiting the extent of the loss or damage, otherwise that party may risk a loss or reduction of its claim.[40] The more recent *Danske-Slagter* case[41] justified the requirement of national law that an individual cannot obtain reparation for loss or damage which he has wilfully or negligently failed to avert by utilising a legal remedy, "provided that utilisation of that remedy can reasonably be required of the injured party, a matter which is for the referring court to determine in light of all the circumstances of the main proceedings" (para 69).

7.13   In *Courage*,[42] as I have already noted (4.11), the Court held that the British rule of *nemo auditur propriam turpitudinem allegans*, forbidding a partner to an anti-competitive agreement from claiming damages, was inapplicable against a claim of compensation for competition infringements. The Court set aside this rule because it prevented the full effectiveness of Community law. However, this consequence would not preclude an inherent "good faith" limitation on the right of a victim of an anti-competitive practice to claim damages:[43]

---

[38]   Joined Cases C-46 + 48/93 *Brasserie de Pêcheur et al v BRD* [1996] ECR I-1029, para 87.
[39]   See also case C-271/91 *Marshall II* [1993] ECR I-4367, para 32.
[40]   Joined Cases C-46 + 48/93 *Brasserie de Pêcheur et al v BRD* [1996] ECR I-1029, para 84; T. Tridimas, *The General Principles of EU Law*, 2nd ed. 2006, 458.
[41]   Case C-445/06 *Danske-Slagter* [2009] ECR I-2119.
[42]   Case C-453/99 *Courage v Crehan* [2001] ECR I-6297.
[43]   Ibid., paras 31–32.

"Similarly, provided that the principles of equivalence and effectiveness are respected
[...] Community law does not preclude national law from denying a party who is found
to bear significant responsibility for the distortion of competition the right to obtain
damages from the other contracting party. Under a principle which is recognised in
most of the legal systems of the Member States and which the Court has applied in the
past [...], a litigant should not profit from his own unlawful conduct, where this is
proven. In that regard, the matters to be taken into account by the competent national
court include the economic and legal context in which the parties find themselves and
[...] the respective bargaining power and conduct of the two parties to the contract."

Somewhat surprisingly, the Court refers here to a principle recognised in most
(but not all) legal systems of the EU. AG Mischo in his opinion of 22 March 2001
was somewhat more specific:[44]

"In order to assess the responsibility borne by the party seeking damages, account
must be taken of the economic and legal background against which the parties are
operating and, as the United Kingdom Government proposes, the respective
bargaining power and conduct of the two parties. In particular it should be
ascertained whether one party was in a markedly weaker position than the other.
That weaker position must be such that it seriously calls into question the freedom of
that party to choose the terms of the contract. Finally, it must be added that the fact
that a party bears negligible responsibility does not preclude its being required to
provide evidence of reasonable diligence to limit the extent of its loss."

7.14   Secondary law also contains elements of "co-responsibility" which can be
explained by a concept of "subjective good faith" incumbent on a person
claiming damages, for example in product liability cases under Article 8(2) of
the Product Liability Directive 85/374/EEC,[45] or in cases of compensation
against a package tour company under Article 5(4) of the Package Holiday
Directive 90/314/EEC[46] where the injured consumer has to give notice:

"The consumer must communicate any failure in the performance of a contract
which he perceives on the spot to the supplier of the services concerned and to the
organizer and/or retailer in writing or any other appropriate form at the earliest
opportunity. This obligation must be stated clearly and explicitly in the contract."

Member States have to determine the consequences of a failure to give notice. It is
not clear whether the failure to give notice may result in a rejection or reduction
of the compensation sought by the consumer, or whether the notice is merely
meant as an element of proof alleviating an eventual claim for compensation by
the consumer.[47] In my opinion, a complete loss or substantial reduction of the

---

[44]   Ibid., paras 73–75.
[45]   [1985] OJ L 210/29.
[46]   [1990] OJ L 158/59.
[47]   See H.-W. Micklitz, in: N. Reich/H.-W. Micklitz, *Europaisches Verbraucherrecht*, 4th ed.
2004, 692.

consumer's right to compensation seems to be at odds with the proportionality principle, which is a general principle of EU civil law, as has been argued in Chapter 6 (6.3–6.5). This corresponds with the insistence of the Court in *Leitner*[48] as to the importance of compensating the consumer for lost holidays, including non-material damage. Failure to give notice may make the enforcement of the consumer's claim more difficult as regards proof, but cannot exclude or substantially reduce it.

6. ELEMENTS OF GOOD FAITH IN RECENT SOFT LAW INITIATIVES

7.15   The Principles of European Contract Law (PECL: 0.10) expressly refer to the principles of good faith and fair dealing:
Article 1:201: Good Faith and Fair Dealing

> "(1) Each party must act in accordance with good faith and fair dealing.
> (2) The parties may not exclude or limit this duty."

Article 1:202: Duty to Co-operate

> "Each party owes to the other a duty to co-operate in order to give full effect to the contract."

Article 1.7 of the UNIDROIT Principles of International Commercial Law (PICL) has a similar formulation – a principle said to be unfamiliar to British lawyers.[49] Vogenauer is quite sceptical of its recognition as a "general principle" of (international) contract law:[50]

> "*Article 1.7 is certainly no 'international restatement'* of the common core of global contract law. The standard of good faith and fair dealing is far from settled even at the level of domestic laws […] different domestic approaches towards the notion of good faith do not only reflect concerns about purely technical matters. They rather go to the root of the understanding of the judicial function and the role of contract law that prevail in the respective jurisdictions."

Therefore Article 1.7 cannot be said to express a principle common to the law of Member States. Since the EU is not participating in either PECL or PICL, it cannot be considered to be a principle of EU civil law. It restates neither the *acquis commun* nor the *acquis communautaire*.

---

48   Case C-168/00 *Simone Leitner v TUI Deutschland* [2002] ECR I-2631, paras 19–23.
49   S. Vogenauer, 'Die UNIDROIT-Grundregeln 2010', ZEuP 2013, 7 at 11.
50   S. Vogenauer/J. Kleinheisterkamp (eds.), *PICL Commentary*, 2009, Article 1.7 at para 4 (emphasis added).

7.16 The Draft Common Frame of Reference (DCFR: 0.10 and 6.6) contains quite detailed references to the good faith principle. Article I. – 1:103 DCFR contains a definition of good faith which reads:

> "(1) The expression "good faith and fair dealing" refers to a standard of conduct characterized by honesty, openness and consideration of the interests of the other party to the transaction of relationship in question."

The commentary explains the importance of this general principle as follows:

> "What consideration is required for the interests of the other party will depend on the circumstances, including the nature of the contract. In many commercial contracts the rights and obligations of the parties will be so carefully regulated that in the normal course of events considerations of good faith and fair dealing will remain entirely in the background."[51]

Article II. – 1:102 establishes the principle of good faith as part of party autonomy:

> "(1) Parties are free to make a contract or other juridical act and to determine its contents, subject to the rules on good faith and fair dealing and any other applicable mandatory rules.
> (2) Parties may exclude the application of any of the following rules relating to contracts or other juridical acts, or the rights and obligations arising from them, or derogate from or vary their effects, except as otherwise provided.
> (3) A provision to the effect that parties may not exclude the application of a rule or derogate from or vary its effects does not prevent a party from waiving a right which has already arisen and of which that party is aware."

Article III. – 1:103 DCFR is a specific rule within the general law of obligations:

> "(1) A person has a duty to act in accordance with good faith and fair dealing in performing an obligation, in exercising a right to performance, in pursuing or defending a remedy for non-performance, or in exercising a right to terminate an obligation or a contractual relationship.
> (2) The duty may not be excluded or limited by contract or other juridical act."

The commentary explains this duty as follows:

> "The role of the duty […] is to serve as a direct and general guide for the parties. Its purpose is to give effect in legal transactions to community standards of decency and fairness. The law expects parties to act in accordance with the requirements of good faith and fair dealing."[52]

---

51   *DCFR*, full ed. 2009, Vol. I, 89.
52   Ibid., at 677.

7.17   The Draft Regulation on an optional Common European Sales Law (6.12) is quite explicit on the subject of the introduction of a general good faith obligation to all transactions covered by it, whether B2SMU or B2C. Its importance can be seen from its prominent position in the draft: it comes directly after the general principle of freedom of contract in Article 1. In this spirit, Article 2 on "Good Faith and fair dealing" reads:

> "(1) Each party has a duty to act in accordance with good faith and fair dealing [...]
> (2) Breach of this duty may preclude the party in breach from exercising or relying on a right, remedy or defense which a party would otherwise have, or may make the party liable for any loss thereby caused to the other party.
> (3) The parties may not exclude the application of this Article or derogate from or vary its effect."

Article 3 CESL contains a duty of cooperation on the parties in the performance of their contractual obligations.

However, as mentioned in the introduction, the recognition of the good faith principle as part of the *acquis commun* (0.10) does not necessarily make it part of the *acquis communautaire*, even if it is contained as a mandatory rule in the CESL. This should not exclude the possibility that Articles 2 and 3 may both become general principles of EU civil law one day, but they are still some way away at the time of writing.

7.   RELEVANCE OF ARTICLE 54 OF THE CHARTER TO AN EU CONCEPT OF ABUSE OF RIGHTS?

7.18   Can Article 54 on the prohibition of abuse of rights of the Charter be regarded as a (limited) "constitutionalisation" of the good faith principle in EU law? Is it supported by legislative enactments and judicial practice?

Article 54 reads as follows:

> "Nothing in this Charter shall be interpreted as implying any right to engage in any activity or to perform any act aimed at the destruction of any of the rights and freedoms recognized in this Charter or at their limitation to a greater extent than is provided therein."

The explanations of the Praesidium make clear that this provision has been literally taken over from Article 17 of the European Convention of Human Rights. This provision however has played only a very limited role in the case law of the European Court of Human Rights (ECtHR) because of its restrictive wording, which is understandable in a constitutional context.[53] In a civil law setting, a much more flexible formulation is needed by linking it to the good faith principle, but there are no precedents. The second part of Article 54 could be interpreted in this sense because it refers to a limitation of rights "to a greater extent than is provided therein" – a somewhat unclear formula which has not yet been given concrete consideration in judicial practice. The German author Kingreen[54] insists that Article 54 is addressed to private persons as subjects of fundamental rights, and that they may not limit civil law rights beyond their purpose set out in the Charter.

This could be applied both in B2C contracting and in employment relations where, in the first place, the protection of the weaker party is recognised as part of the general principle of "framed autonomy" in EU civil law (2.1), but where Court practice has imposed certain limits on "over-protection" (5.9–5.11).

7.19   Following this reasoning in an abuse of rights context, consumers would be covered by the principle of consumer protection in Article 38 of the Charter and the secondary legislation arising out of it. On the other hand it must be remembered that businesses enjoy freedom of contracting under Article 16 of the Charter (1.13). Neither businesses nor consumers should make use of their right to an effective remedy under Article 47 of the Charter beyond the scope of that right (4.10), in particular to deny or unnecessarily limit the opposing rights and freedoms of the other party. To give an example: if the consumer has entered into a distance contract for a product that he intends not only to examine, but also to use in full during the withdrawal period and then return (the famous example of the wedding dress to be used only once), this would amount to an "abuse" and a violation of the "good faith" principle, as the ECJ seemed to have stated in the *Messner* judgment (5.9).[55]

In a similar setting, workers enjoy a generous right of free movement including social benefits, while employers are also entitled to their freedom of contract under Article 16 of the Charter, which allows certain limitations of this right. The use of free movement rights in ways similar to the *Paletta* case may amount to an "abuse" because it unnecessarily extends the employer's contractual obligation to pay wages in case of (genuine) sickness abroad; the employer should not need to prove bad faith in the case of repeated illnesses during the Paletta family's vacation. The approach of the Court in referring to fraud as a limiting element to abuse of rights seems to be too narrow (5. 11).

---

53   See C. Grabenwarter/K. Pabel, *EMRK*, 5th ed. 2012, para 23.5; J.A. Frowein/W. Peukert, *Kommentar zur EMRK*, 3rd ed. 2009, Article 17 para 4, citing the case of hate speech which, as an abuse of the right to freedom of speech in Article 10 ECHR, is not protected.

54   T. Kingreen, in: C. Calliess/M. Ruffert, *Kommentar EUV/AEUV*, 4th ed. 2011, Article 54 Charta, Rdnr. 2.

55   Case C-489/07 *Messner v Firma Stefan Krüger* [2009] ECR I-7315.

Grundmann[56] has argued that:

"Abuse of rights has played a very prominent role in EC Law, more general than any other general clause or standard, and there are many interesting examples not directly related to the Unfair Contract Terms Directives."

In a somewhat different spirit, Metzger[57] has analysed the importance of the abuse concept in EU contract law, without however making reference to Article 54 of the Charter. His analysis is rather sceptical of the possibility of making an EU-specific principle of abuse of rights more generally applicable because

"it is neither supported by EU legislation nor is it recognised by the Court's case law. Although it is true that concept appears in some minor statements in specific directives and in single instances within the Court's case law, these fragments do not amount to the recognition of a general principle of law."

7.20   However, the previously mentioned rule in the Consumer Credit Directive 2008/48 on "circumvention" (7.4) can be regarded as a clear prohibition of an abuse of the bank and creditor's right to shape a credit agreement in such a way as to avoid the protective provisions of this directive as set out in the Member State law that implements it. This rule seems to be able to announce an emerging new principle of EU civil law, namely of abuse of rights by *contournement de la loi (Gesetzesumgehung)* – a principle now recognised in EU free movement, tax and financial law.[58] It is not so much based on the abusive intention of the person invoking his rights in a fraudulent manner, but on a disparity between the purpose of a legal entitlement given to the actor – whether a business, consumer or worker – and the way in which it is used contrary to the very purpose of this entitlement. *This can be seen as the implicit recognition of a general principle in EU civil law prohibiting an abuse of rights.* How it relates more specifically to the good faith principle still has to be elaborated, but it is suggested here that, as a general norm of behaviour of economic actors in (consumer and employment) markets, it also includes the prohibition of abuse of rights in horizontal relationships that come within the scope of EU civil law.

Vogenauer[59] concludes his analysis of the importance of the principle of the abuse of law and rights in EU law, after giving an exhaustive overview of the

---

[56]   S. Grundmann, *supra* note 10, at 147. However, Grundmann is referring mostly to company law, which is not part of this study.

[57]   A. Metzger, 'Abuse of Law in EU Private Law: A (Re-)Construction from Fragments', in: R. de la Feria/S. Vogenauer (eds.), *Prohibition of Abuse of Law – A New Principle of EU Law?*, 2011, 235 at 251.

[58]   See the many contributions in the book by R. de la Feria/S. Vogenauer, *supra* note 57, despite differences in the assessment of the scope and importance of this principle.

[59]   S. Vogenauer, *supra* note 57, at 571.

different cases, areas and doctrines where this concept has been used, in particular in free movement and tax law:

> "According to the judge made prohibition of abuse of EU law, a given rule of EU law will not be applied where (1) a particular set of facts is clearly and unambiguously covered by the wording of the rule but (2) the result of applying the rule would be contrary to the purpose of the rule and (3) the person's reliance on the rule is abusive [...] The doctrine exhibits all the necessary attributes in order for it to be recognised as a general principle of EU law [...] However, this general principle is still emerging. It still awaits universal recognition. Some of its doctrinal foundations are still shaky. The conceptual framework is not yet consistent."

The doctrine of abuse of rights must of course be used with care to avoid situations like those described by AG Trstenjak in her opinion in *Gybrechts* as being "*summum ius, summa iniuria*", criticising a Belgian regulation under which the seller was barred from taking the credit card number of the consumer as security before the lapse of right of withdrawal in distance contracts:[60]

> "A situation where the consumer is given absolute protection but the vendor has none, when it would be possible to give them both such protection at the same time, could be described as *summum ius summa iniuria* (excessive justice becomes injustice). The impossibility of providing protection for the consumer and the vendor simultaneously where other means of payment are used does not convince me that it is not possible to offer protection to both parties if a given form of payment so permits."

8. CONCLUSION: GOOD FAITH ON THE MOVE?

7.21 The examination of the good faith principle in EU civil law has shown a remarkable legal patchwork: it has clearly become part of B2C contracting and can no longer be regarded as (in Teubner's words) a "legal irritant", but so far it has been limited only to unfair terms practice under the firm grip of the ECJ in recent judgments. It has not however been extended to other areas, in particular consumer credit or investment services under the relevant directives, where such a good faith obligation of the bank in checking the consumer's creditworthiness or of the appropriateness of the investment for "retail clients" is absent despite the recent financial crisis. In B2B situations, good faith is almost unknown, with some rather inconsistent exceptions; the EU regulation in the "old" Commercial Agent Directive 86/653/EEC and the "new" Late Payment Directive 2011/7/EU appears to be limited to a rather piecemeal approach, without being in any way principle-oriented.

---

[60]   Case C-205/07 *Gysbrechts* [2008] ECR I-9947, opinion of 17 July 2008, para 87.

On the other hand, an indirect recognition of the good faith principle can be found in several instances where EU law imposes some sort of co-responsibility of the parties to a contract, including B2C, and allows the defendant the abuse-of-rights defence (which has in fact been constitutionally recognised in Article 54 of the Charter). However, all of these provisions lack legal clarity and oscillate between taking an objective or a subjective approach. Finally, and in some contrast to the *acquis communautaire*, several soft law and legislative initiatives in the EU place great emphasis on the good faith principle, which can be said to have found its general recognition in the *acquis commun*.

Whether the good faith principle is "on the move" to becoming a general principle of EU civil law depends on further legislation by the Union and on the case law of the ECJ. In my opinion such a trend can be observed, making it possible to talk of "half a general principle" – certainly one which will require more academic work beyond a comparative perspective to find out its specific place, role and function in EU civil law. The absenteeism of English law and the *lacunae* in financial services should not discourage us from such efforts.

From an economic analysis point of view, the recent monograph of Cooter and Schäfer[61] develops the "double trust dilemma of innovation" in B2B contracting: distrust – which implies absence of good faith and fair dealing – obstructs innovation. If in the words of Cooter and Schäfer the innovator fears that the investor "steals" his invention, and vice versa the investor that the innovator "steals" his money, no reliable contracting will be possible. An effective contract law should avoid this dilemma. Since EU policy is aimed at stimulating investment and innovation, a general recognition of the good faith principle in contracting in the internal market would be helpful in this respect.[62] Directive 2011/7 on late payments could be seen as a first recognition of the "double trust dilemma".

---

[61] *Solomon's Knot*, 2013, at 27.
[62] Ibid., at 93 illustrating the different attitudes of civil and common law judges.

SUMMARY: SEVEN THESES
AND A CONCLUSION

1. EU general civil law principles as understood in this study owe their origin both to the *acquis communautaire* and its link with the rights and principles contained in the Charter of Fundamental Rights, and to earlier documents of constitutional relevance of the EU. Their legitimacy can be found in Article 19(1) TEU, whereby the ECJ must "ensure that in the application the interpretation of the Treaties the law is observed" (Introduction).

2. Three of these general principles are substantive in nature ("framed autonomy", protection of the weaker party, and non-discrimination: Chapters 1 to 3), one remedial (effectiveness: Chapter 4), and two methodological (balancing and proportionality: Chapters 5 and 6). A "half" principle of "good faith" is just emerging but is so far rather narrow in scope (Chapter 7).

3. The first and foremost function of these general principles is one of interpreting the *acquis*. This task is conferred on the ECJ mostly within the framework of reference proceedings (Article 267 TFEU), as the many examples in Chapters 1 to 3 of this study have demonstrated. Member State courts at whatever level of the judicial hierarchy participate in this process. Conflicts between the substantive principles must be settled by a balancing approach (Chapter 5). An individualistic *Vorverständnis* (pre-understanding) of the ECJ can be seen to exist.

4. The second, more contested gap-filling function of general principles relates mostly to the three facets of the effectiveness principle, namely eliminatory, hermeneutical and remedial. This function must be coordinated with the so-called procedural autonomy of Member States which may result in a "hybridisation of remedies", for example in an *ex officio* control of unfair terms, or in creating a remedy of compensation for serious violations of Union-granted citizen rights.

5. Legality of EU action (as well as "implementing" Member State law in a broad sense) is monitored mainly by recourse to the proportionality principle (Chapter 6), as set out in the controversial *Test-Achats* judgment referring to the "coherence" criteria. This works against attempts to create some kind of comprehensive EU contract or sales law, even in the form of an optional instrument like the CESL. However, in its policy-oriented application it may

require positive action by the EU in specific contract law matters, both B2B and B2C.

6. The reference to "general principles of EU civil law" in no way extends the scope of application of EU competences (Article 5(1) TEU and Article 51(1) of the Charter).

7. General principles based on the Charter do not on their own have direct effect in "horizontal relations". They may however serve to "upgrade" secondary EU law in relations between private parties by interpreting "as far as possible" (according to Pfeiffer) and even eliminating Member State law that contradicts these principles (the *Kücükdevici* approach).

8. This book has demonstrated the specific nature of EU civil law which sharply differs from those of Member States. It is function-, not system- (codification) or commerce- (common law) oriented. It has developed principles of its own, based on the Charter, which guide interpretation, gap-filling, and legality analysis of EU law. It does not – and should not – replace Member State civil law, but supplements it in certain selected areas described in this book. It is founded on a strong judicial commitment by the ECJ and Member State courts in a European judicial network.

INDEX*

A

abus de droit 5.11, 6.11, **7.1, 7.18**
acquis commun 0.10, 6.8, 7.1
acquis communautaire 0.10, 6.8, 7.1
Acquis principles 1.3, 6.9
anti-competitive agreements 1.14
  block exemptions 1.16
  collective bargaining **1.18**
  cooperation agreements 1.16
  nullity 1.15
  price fixing 1.16
arbitration clauses 4.15

B

bank charges cases (UK/Germany) **5.4,
  5.7**
broadcasting services 3.21

C

CISG (Vienna Convention on
  International Sale of Goods) 6.15
commercial agents **7.3**
Common European Sales Law (CESL)
  0.11, 6.3, **6.12, 7.16**
competence (of the EU in civil law
  matters) 0.11, 6.3
consumer protection 2.1, **2.5**
  average consumer 2.11
  concept of vulnerable consumer
    2.11
  double purpose/mixed contracts
    2.9, 6.6, 6.13
  information 2.6
  paternalism 2.5
  withdrawal rights 2.7
co-responsibility **7.11**

core terms (in pre-formulated contract
  clauses) **5.4**
contract governance **6.20**
culpa in contrahendo 4.12, 4.20

D

digital content 6.12, 6.16, **6.23**
direct effect 0.6
  collective restrictions 4.28
  competition rules 1.15, **4.23**
  horizontal effect 0.2, 1.21, **3.3**
  negative effect 0.7, **4.14**
  vertical effect 0.9
discrimination (combating) **3.1**
  age **3.6,** 4.14
  access to goods and services 3.12,
    3.15
  citizenship **3.10**
  disability 3.9
  fundamental right/principle 3.2
  EU nationality **3.3**
  Honeywell judgment 3.7
  insurance (unisex tariffs) **3.15**
  indirect 3.3
  minority shareholders 3.22
  racial and ethnic 3.5, 4.36
  sex-based 3.4
  sexual orientation **3.8,** 4.36
Draft Common Frame of Reference
  (DCFR) 0.10, 5.9, **6.6,** 7.16

E

effectiveness **4.1**
  elimination rule 4.2, **4.3**
  hermeneutical principle 4.2, **4.7**
  hybridisation approach 4.11, 4.33
  remedial function 4.2, **4.10**

---

*   References in bold continue over several paragraphs.

equivalence 4.3, 4.30
ex officio control (of unfair terms) **4.15**

F
financial services 7.9
freedom of contract **1.12, 3.2**
freedom of establishment 1.11
free movement – general 1.4
    of capital 1.6
    of goods 1.4
    of persons 1.7
    of services 1.5

G
Gebhard test (of proportionality) 1.9, **6.1**

H
Heininger saga (mortgage credit
    negotiated at the doorstep) **4.20**

I
individualistic concept/*Vorverständnis* (of
    EU civil law) **1.8**, 2.2, 2.12, 5.3, 5.20

J
jurisdiction clauses **4.15**, 7.8

L
liability rules
    competition law 4.5, **4.25, 7.13**
    free movement 4.28
    state (*Francovich*) 7.12
    strict 4.18

M
mandatory provisions 0.9, 1.5, **2.8**
minimum harmonisation 1.9, **5.8**

N
network services 2.1, 2.12

O
optional instrument 6.7, 6.14
    blue button approach 6.7, 6.14
    conflict of law provisions 6.18
over-protection 5.9, 7.1

P
pacta sunt servanda 1.2
prescription periods 4.5
Principles of European Contract Law
    (PECL) 0.10, 6.8, 7.15
Principles of International Commercial
    Contracts (PICL) 0.10, 7.15
procedural autonomy **4.4**, 4.11, 4.15, 4.31
"purely internal matters/situations" **1.9**

R
regulatory civil law 0.9
res judicata 4.15
reverse discrimination 1.8
rule of law (*Rechtsstaatlichkeit/état de
    droit*) 0.2

S
sales law 2.8
services of general economic interest **3.19**
    solidarity 3.19
    universal service obligation 3.19,
        3.19a
social action (by trade unions) **5.12**
social justice/policy 1.20, 2.1, **2.8**
social market economy 1.1, 5.14
subjective rights under EU law 0.6, **4.31**
substantive justice (*Sachgerechtigkeit*) 0.2

T
transparency 5.2, 5.8, **7.5**

U
unfair terms
    in B2B 6.13, 6.22, 7.4
    in B2C (*see also ex officio* control)
        7.5
    black and grey lists 7.8
ubi ius ibi remedium 4.7, **4.10**, 4.27

W
working time **2.1**
    Directive (WTD) **2.2**
    on call duties 2.3
    paid annual leave 2.4